PSYCHOANALYSIS
and
EXISTENTIAL PHILOSOPHY

HENDRIK M. RUITENBEEK was born in Leyden, Holland, in 1928. He received his doctorate at the University of Leyden in 1955, and his doctoral thesis on the origins and rise of the Dutch Labor Party was published in book form in 1955. Dr. Ruitenbeek came to this country in 1955 and has taught at various colleges. He is now affiliated with Brooklyn College, where he teaches sociology, and he is also a practicing psychotherapist. In 1962 the New American Library of World Literature, Inc., will publish Dr. Ruitenbeek's book called *The Individual and the Crowd: A Study of Identity in America.*

PSYCHOANALYSIS and EXISTENTIAL PHILOSOPHY

Edited, and with an Introduction,
by
HENDRIK M. RUITENBEEK

NEW YORK
E. P. DUTTON & CO., INC.
1962

FIRST EDITION

Published simultaneously in Canada by
Clarke, Irwin & Co., Ltd., of Toronto.

ACKNOWLEDGMENTS

Grateful acknowledgment is made to the following for permission to quote copyright material:

Paul Tillich: *Existentialism and Psychotherapy*. Reprinted from *Review of Existential Psychology and Psychiatry*, Vol. 1, No. 1, Winter, by permission of the author and the editor. Ludwig Binswanger: *Existential Analysis and Psychotherapy*. Reprinted from *Progress in Psychotherapy*, Vol. I, edited by Frieda Fromm-Reichmann and J. L. Moreno, by permission of Grune & Stratton, New York. Copyright, 1956, by Grune & Stratton, Inc. W. Van Dusen: *The Theory and Practice of Existential Analysis*. Reprinted from the *American Journal of Psychotherapy*, Vol. XI, No. 2, April 1957, by permission of the author and the editor. R. D. Laing: *Ontological Insecurity*. Reprinted from *The Divided Self* by R. D. Laing, by permission of Tavistock Publications, London, and Quadrangle Books, Chicago. Copyright, ©, 1960, by Tavistock Publications, Ltd., and Quadrangle Books, Inc. Thomas Hora: *Psychotherapy, Existence, and Religion*. Reprinted from *Psychoanalysis and the Psychoanalytic Review*, Vol. 46, No. 2, Summer 1959, by permission of the author and the editor. Medard Boss: *"Daseinsanalysis" and Psychotherapy*. Reprinted from *Progress in Psychotherapy*, Vol. II, edited by Jules H. Masserman and J. L. Moreno, by permission of Grune & Stratton, New York. Copyright, ©, 1957, by Grune & Stratton, Inc. J. H. Van Den Berg: *The Human Body and the Significance of Human Movement*. Reprinted from *Philosophy and Phenomenological Research*, Vol. XIII, No. 2, December 1952, by permission of the author and the editor. Thomas Hora: *Existential Psychiatry and Group Psychotherapy*. Reprinted from *The American Journal of Psychoanalysis*, Vol. XXI, No. 1, 1961, by permission of the author and the editor. F. J. J. Buytendijk: *The Phenomenological Approach to the Problem of Feelings and Emotions*. Reprinted from *Feelings and Emotions*, edited by Martin L. Reymert, by permission of McGraw-Hill Book Company, New York. Copyright, 1950, by McGraw-Hill Book Company, Inc. Rollo May: *Dangers in the Relation of Existentialism to Psychotherapy*. Printed by permission of the author. Eugen Kahn: *An Appraisal of Existential Analysis*. Reprinted from *The Psychiatric Quarterly*, Vol. 31, Nos. 2 and 3, April and July 1957, by permission of the author and the editor.

For
Lee and Sheila

FOREWORD

Existential psychoanalysis has rapidly become a significant school of psychotherapy in the United States. Since Freud, many divergencies in psychoanalytic thought have occurred here. Few of the neo-Freudian schools, however, have been able to link their interpretation of psychoanalysis to such a significant philosophical movement as existentialism.

The literature on the school of existential analysis is limited (at least in English). The work of Binswanger, Minkowski, Kuhn and others is still largely untranslated; so we have to depend on occasional articles by those American psychoanalysts and psychologists who have made a serious effort to acquaint themselves with the aspects of existential psychoanalysis. Moreover, although most of the works of the major existentialist thinkers are available in English, there are almost no available translations of the phenomenological philosophers. This is especially true of the writings of Edmund Husserl.

One of the major contributions to the school of existential psychoanalysis in this country has been made by the publication of the book called *Existence,* which first presented major articles in English by Binswanger and Minkowski. The pioneering work done by the publication of *Existence* makes me believe that there is a real need for this book, which intends to present a selection of articles on the encounter of psychoanalysis and existential philosophy.

In this selection of essays, I have tried to present a widely varied picture of existential psychoanalysis today. The essays by Tillich, Binswanger, and Van Dusen should give the reader a good idea of the impact of existentialist thought on existential therapy and analysis. The paper by Tillich is particularly enlightening, for it was written by a man whose work in the field of existentialism, theology, and psychoanalysis is highly respected both here and abroad.

Laing's article on ontological insecurity has been included because of its sound clinical evidence and also because insecurity has become one of the major distresses of man in modern society. Medard Boss' essay on *Daseinanalysis* is a wonderfully lucid discussion of Heidegger's influence on existential analysis. Thomas Hora is represented by two essays, one of which particularly relates problems of religion to the emergence of existential psychotherapy. The other, on existential psychotherapy, becomes even more significant when one realizes the increasing importance of group psychotherapy in our society. The articles by Van Den Berg and Buytendijk are included because of their phenomenological aspects, for it seems to me that most of the credit for the emergence of existential psychoanalysis goes to phenomenology itself. Both of these writings are brilliant applications of the phenomenological approach in the field of psychology and psychiatry. The essay by Eugen Kahn is, in a sense, a summary, yet it is actually more, for the depth and learning of this essay surpass much of what has been written on the subject of existential analysis. I am happy also to have a contribution by Rollo May, who has himself been so instrumental in the development of existential analysis in this country. His paper reflects some of the criticisms and dangers in the encounter of existentialism and psychoanalysis and contributes greatly to possible reassessments of the relationship of both movements.

HENDRIK M. RUITENBEEK

CONTENTS

SOME ASPECTS OF THE ENCOUNTER OF PSYCHOANALYSIS AND EXISTENTIAL PHILOSOPHY

Existential philosophy is rooted in the basic, literal meaning of the word *existence,* which is *ex-sistere,* to emerge or stand out. Existence as emergence typifies the person in a state of becoming. Consequently, the emphasis is placed on the dynamic side of man coming *into being.* If a person has a strong sense of his identity, of the permanency of things, and of an integral selfhood, he will be secure. As soon as man experiences *non-being,* however, he is at once beset by the anxieties and insecurities which accompany the state of *non-being.* Thus if, by any chance, he cannot assert his identity, then he is likely to experience in his existential position what R. D. Laing has called *ontological insecurity.* What is the individual in such a state like? According to Laing:

> The individual in the ordinary circumstances of living may feel more unreal than real; in a literal sense, more dead than alive; precariously differentiated from the rest of the world, so that his *identity* and *autonomy* [my italics] are always in question. He may lack the experience of his own continuity. He may not possess an overriding sense of his own personal consistency or cohesiveness. He may feel more insubstantial than substantial, and unable to assume that the stuff he is made of is genuine, good, valuable.[1]

Laing might be painting a portrait of modern man in distress. And it is modern man in distress whom the existentialists have described not only in their philosophi-

[1] p. 43, R. D. Laing, *The Divided Self,* Chicago, Quadrangle Books, 1960.

cal works, but also in the *crisis* theology of Karl Barth and Emil Brunner. Even more poignant is the vision of the artist. One need only read Kafka's *The Castle* and Camus' *The Stranger* to experience the stark actuality of man's existence today. Was it not recently said: *Kafka ist wirklichkeit geworden?* Or, as one might translate: "Kafka's fiction has become current reality." The existentialist artists' portraits of twentieth-century man differ, and certainly the condition of man in our time is exceedingly complex and varied; nevertheless, Sartre, Camus, Eliot, Picasso, Klee—each in his own mode tells us the same story, for each illustrates the human condition, i.e., the jumbled, distraught existence of man in our time. As Paul Tillich puts it in *The Courage to Be:*

> The combination of the experience of meaninglessness and of the courage to be as oneself is the key to the development of visual art since the turn of the century. In expressionism and surrealism the surface structures of reality are disrupted. The categories which constitute ordinary experience have lost their power. The category of substance is lost: solid objects are twisted like ropes; the causal interdependence of things is disregarded: things appear in a complete contingency; temporal sequences are without significance; it does not matter whether an event has happened before or after another event; the spatial dimensions are reduced or dissolved into a horrifying infinity. The organic structures of life are cut to pieces which are arbitrarily (from the biological, not the artistic, point of view) recomposed: limbs are dispersed, colors are separated from their natural carriers. The psychological process (this refers to literature more than to art) is reversed; one lives in the future to the past, and this without rhythm or any kind of meaningful organization. The world of anxiety is a world in which the categories, the structures of reality, have lost their validity. Everybody would be dizzy if causality suddenly ceased to be valid. In Existentialist art (as I like to call it) causality has lost its validity.[2]

[2] pp. 146-147, *The Courage to Be,* New Haven, Yale Paperbound, 1959.

Every form of contemporary art—be it that of the poet, novelist, playwright, or painter—shows us the disintegration of identity. But this awareness is not wholly contemporary. A century ago, in his profound analysis of anxiety, Kierkegaard offered us a tremendously acute and prescient insight into the problem which philosophers, theologians, and many psychoanalysts see as characteristic of man's experience in our own time. Kierkegaard helps us understand the loss of selfhood, the problem of estrangement (self-alienation), utter loneliness, and the nature of anxiety. As Rollo May has remarked:

> Kierkegaard's penetrating analysis of anxiety . . . would alone assure him of a position among the psychological geniuses of all time. His insights into the significance of self-consciousness, his analysis of inner conflicts, loss of self, and even psychosomatic problems are the more surprising since they antedate Nietzsche by four decades and Freud by half a century. This indicated in Kierkegaard a remarkable sensitivity to what was going on under the surface of Western man's consciousness in his day, to erupt only a half-century later.[3]

Kierkegaard was clear both in foresight and in protest against the pressures which were changing the human condition; perhaps the very sensitivity which made him rebel also made him able to apprehend what were to be the basic problems of human existence of our own day. And protest continues to be an essential element in existentialist philosophy. In the poet's words, in the philosopher's works, in the case which the analyst seeks to treat, protest is evident as a basic element in *existence.* But it is the protest of *existing* man, man in estrangement, man aware of his guilt and meaninglessness.

[3] pp. 23-24, *Existence,* ed. Rollo May *et al.,* New York, Basic Books, 1958.

Yet protest is more than simply man's outcry against the human condition. It is also the protest of modern men against their depersonalized technological society, where people are so much in danger of merely becoming *things*—yes, perhaps even *no-things*—that Erich Fromm's "Man is not a thing" seems a peculiarly meaningful statement. Marx and Feuerbach, too, expressed the nineteenth-century protest against the dehumanization of man. Twentieth-century protest is heard in the philosophies of Karl Jaspers, Heidegger, Sartre, Marcel, and many others. Quite frequently, however, it is the poet who has given the most profound expression to the despairs of man's existence. Heidegger has said:

> Between the gods and the people stands the poet. He is the one who has been cast out—out into that *Between,* between gods and men. But only and for the first time in this Between is it decided who man is and where he is settling his existence.[4]

Holderlin's poems are a particularly vivid, early expression of the desperate venture of the existentialist poet who, in Heidegger's phrase, recognizes that "being must be opened up, so that the existent may appear." Thus in *Patmos,* one of Holderlin's most famous poems, we read:

> Nah ist
> Und schwer zu fassen der Gott.
> Wo aber Gefahr ist, wachst
> Das Rettende auch.
>
> Near is the God
> And difficult to grasp,
> But where danger is
> The Deliverer, too, springs up.
>
> *(Translation by E. Louise Mally)*

[4] p. 312, *Existence and Being,* London, Vision Press, 1949.

Along with its protest and its awareness of man's plight, existential philosophy is distinguished by its concern for the subjective experience of the individual. For this reason, perhaps, psychotherapists have found it a congenial frame of reference. Existential philosophy is especially concerned with the realization that man can feel himself as *nothing*. Here, existentialism turns to the concept of *Angst,* which means so much more than anxiety, its usual translation. *Angst* embodies that fear, total and indefinite, which encompasses alienation, isolation, despair, and death. Thus men know themselves as being thrown into the world, in Heidegger's phrase. To Heidegger, death and anxiety are related concepts. Thus, as Herman Feifel says, existentialism has "accented death as a constitutive part rather than the mere end of life, and highpointed the idea that only by integrating the concept into the self does an authentic and genuine existence become possible." [5]

In its recognition of the stark reality of man's situation, existential philosophy is both the outcome and the expression of a world in which peril is the norm of man's life. Psychotherapy, too, is concerned with man's problem of daily existence in such a world. Older therapies often ignored that total aspect of the patient's problem. Hence the encounter between existential philosophy and psychoanalysis.

Among existentialist thinkers, Edmund Husserl and Martin Heidegger have had the greatest impact upon the method and the language of existential analysis and psychiatry, although the contribution of Karl Jaspers (particularly in his early psychiatric papers) cannot be ignored. Unfortunately, very little of Husserl has been translated into English. Heidegger's principal work, *Sein und Zeit,* and his remarkable *Holzwege,* have not been

[5] p. 65, *Existential Psychology,* New York, Random House, 1961.

translated either, but a few of his other essays are available in English. The phenomenological existential approach to psychology and psychiatry has had an amazing impact in my native Holland, particularly as found in the works of F. J. J. Buytendijk, J. H. Van Den Berg, and J. Linschoten. In France, there is the work of Jean-Paul Sartre, which is readily available in English, and the more technical psychological publications of Merleau-Ponty.

Although Minkowski and Straus have done significant work, Ludwig Binswanger, whose essay "Existential Analysis and Psychotherapy" is reprinted in this book, may be taken as a representative and outstanding figure in existential psychiatry today. Binswanger's basic concepts are derived from Heidegger's most important book, *Sein und Zeit*. Heidegger emphasizes the concept of *Dasein* ("being-there" or "being-in-the-world"), and in search of an ontological analysis of "authentic" *Dasein,* he singles out three phenomena: "conscience," "guilt," and "resolve." Conscience is related to man's selfhood and redeems him from the sheer anonymity of *das Man*. This concept Reinhardt has labeled the "call of conscience." He observes, "This call itself issues from the innermost self of man and is generated by 'care.' " According to Heidegger, "Conscience reveals itself as the call of Care." Guilt points to an intrinsic and original deficiency or privation of *Dasein*. Only by accepting the possibility of his entering into the landscape of guilt can man open himself to his authentic potentiality for existence. And into this potentiality he projects himself by his "resolve," thus imparting to his *Dasein* a valid "lucidity." [6]

Heidegger holds further that authentic *Dasein* relates itself to past, present, and future, the three dimensions of "temporality." This concept has proved to be very useful in psychotherapy. The existential therapist sees

[6] p. 138, *The Existentialist Revolt,* New York, Frederick Ungar, 1959.

the past as the domain of the *Umwelt,* the biological world. The present is largely the domain of the *Mitwelt,* the social world. But the *Eigenwelt,* the world of the self and the person's relation to that self, is the domain of the future; there the future becomes manifest.

Rollo May says, "What an individual seeks *to become* determines what he remembers of his *has been.* In this sense, the future determines the past." [7] To the patient in therapy, the future is not a remote contingency. Rather, as soon as he can rid himself of neurotic anxieties and restrictions, he may begin to be himself and to realize himself in the present. True, neuroses generally operate as the block which prevents the patient from reaching that goal. Far too often he lacks self-awareness, what Heidegger calls *Seinverstandnis,* and thus cannot exert the ability to choose. This "ability to choose" is an assumption fundamental to existentialist thinking. The psychotherapist, however, must emphasize the *Eigenwelt;* a significant aspect of his work is demonstrating the range of relationships between the patient's self and the world, i.e., making the patient more familiar with the several modes of *being-in-the-world.* As Binswanger states the problem, existential analysis tries to understand the patient's life history, but it does "not explain this life history and its pathologic idiosyncrasies according to the teaching of any school of psychotherapy, or by means of its preferred categories. *Instead,* it understands this life history as modifications of the total structure of the patient's being-in-the-world . . ." [8] Since neurosis may operate to limit a patient to *Umwelt* and *Mitwelt,* past and present, the existential analyst's concern with the *Eigenwelt* be-

[7] p. 69, *Existence.*

[8] p. 145, Ludwig Binswanger, "Existential Analysis and Psychotherapy," in *Progress in Psychotherapy,* ed. F. Fromm-Reichmann and J. L. Moreno, New York, Grune & Stratton, 1956. This essay also appears in this volume.

comes even more crucial. For, as we have said, the *Eigenwelt* is the gate into the future, and it is in the future that cure may occur.

In noting further differences between the Freudian and the existential approach to psychoanalysis, it is significant that Freud never repudiated Binswanger. Although he did not accept Binswanger's point of view, the two continued a friendly relationship. Binswanger emphasized that Freud regarded their differences as "something to be surmounted by empirical investigation, not as something bearing upon the transcendental conceptions that underlie all empirical research." [9] Thus Binswanger's book *Sigmund Freud: Reminiscences of a Friendship* is entirely different in tone from the work of those who made a public break with "the master." On Freud's side, the relationship was equally amiable. In a paper read before the Viennese Medical Society on the occasion of Freud's eightieth birthday, Binswanger said that Freud's great contributions had been in the area of the *Umwelt;* he had not emphasized the *Mitwelt,* and he had ignored the *Eigenwelt* entirely. Freud wrote Binswanger in reply, saying:

> As I read it I was delighted with your beautiful language, your erudition, the vastness of your horizon, your tactfulness in contradicting me. As is well known, one can put up with vast quantities of praise . . . *Naturally, for all that, you have failed to convince me* [Binswanger's italics]. I have always confined myself to the ground floor and basement of the edifice. You maintain that by changing one's point of view, one can also see the upper story, in which dwell such distinguished guests as religion, art, etc. . . . I have already found a place for religion, by putting it under the category of the neurosis of mankind. But probably we are speaking at

[9] I am indebted to Rollo May's observations in "The Emergence of Existential Psychology," for the discussion of Binswanger's relation to Freud; see *Existential Psychology,* Random House, 1961.

cross purposes, and our differences will be ironed out only after centuries.[10]

It has been observed that nowadays patients rarely come to psychotherapy with the hysterias which were the most common neuroses in Freud's time. Instead, it is more usual for patients to complain of loneliness and isolation. David Riesman has put this aspect of the problem acutely:

Today . . . we are faced with a paradox: the United States and a few other rich countries have caught up with many Utopian ideals while at the same time literal belief in heaven has almost vanished. In this country people suffer less from nightmarish misery than from the more subtle disorders previously buried by the harsh struggle for existence. We can see an analogue to this development in the short career of psychoanalytic therapy, which is about 50 years old. When Freud began, patients came to him who were suffering from hysteria, from paralyzed arms, from inability to talk, from obvious symptoms. By helping them internalize what they had externalized, that is, what they had (so to speak) thrown into an arm, it was relatively easy and even speedy to cure them. Today, in contrast, one sees cases only, for instance in this country, among immigrant Poles in Pittsburgh or among rural southerners in West Virginia. Many therapists go through their entire lives without ever seeing such a case. People come to analysis today who do not suffer from an external subsistence problem, from a paralysis. Their limbs work and their sexual organs work, but somehow life does not live up to its billing for them [ed. note: they are experiencing Heidegger's non-being or Nothingness]; they carry on an unrepressed interior dialogue, but it bores them. Often, I might add, all they do is include the analyst in the dialogue and bore him. They need, usually without knowing it, a new vision and not merely a new way of talking about themselves; in fact, I was talking the other day with an analyst who said that patients talked today, as was no surprise, very freely

[10] p. 99, Ludwig Binswanger, *Sigmund Freud: Reminiscences of a Friendship,* New York, Grune & Stratton, 1957.

indeed about many of the things that in Freud's day they would have considered private and intimate.[11]

In contemporary mass society, the individual feels depersonalized, alienated, detached, and unrelated. Admittedly, existential analysts are not the only psychotherapists to be aware of the central role which such problems play in their patient's neuroses. Frieda Fromm-Reichmann, Erich Fromm, Harry Stack Sullivan, and Karen Horney all deal with the person who feels "lost" in his, and our, world. The existential analyst seems to have a more adequate frame of reference than they, however; and as A. H. Maslow observes, psychology and psychoanalysis require a firmer basis in philosophy than they now appear to have.

At this point, we may recapitulate some of the points of contact between existentialism as a philosophy and existential psychotherapy. Both are concerned with crisis; one with crisis as characteristic of the human condition, the other with the individual-in-crisis. Both reject the subject-object dichotomy and, with it, both the implicit estrangement of man from the world and "the endeavor to understand man by cutting below the cleavage between subject and object which has bedeviled Western thought and science since shortly after the Renaissance." [12]

Like existential philosophy, existential analysis is concerned for those human beings who have in one way or another deviated from the behavior called *normal*. Unlike Freudian analysis, which deals with the *Umwelt* and the *Mitwelt*, the biological and social worlds, but almost ignores the *Eigenwelt*, existential analysis stresses the self and the mode of the patient's relationship to that self.

[11] pp. 3-4, *New University Thought*, Spring 1960, David Riesman, "The Search for Challenge."
[12] p. 11, *Existence*.

The existential analyst does not stand aloof, but rather seeks to establish in what Arthur Burton has called the *here-now* situation of psychotherapy a new mode of existence for the patient.[13] In the relationship between the existential analyst and his patient, it is *essential* that all psychological phenomena shall be *experienced,* i.e., shared in the existential situation of the patient-therapist relationship. To cite Rollo May once more, the analyst must "catch what the patient is communicating on many levels." [14]

In existential analysis, as an orthodox Freudian practice, technique gives occasion for divergence of opinion and for dispute. Indeed in some instances, "the technical dogma protects the psychologist and psychiatrist from their own anxiety." [15] Rollo May emphasizes the need to put technique in its place, therefore, and to seek understanding of the patient's existence, his being-in-the-world, and the analyst's subsequent participation in it. Unlike the Freudian analyst, the existential analyst does not hold aloof from the patient, but rather he approaches the patient as an existential partner with whom he must share the totality of existence. He must be-in-the-world with his patient, i.e., be together with him in all phases of his total experience. Martin Buber has called this the "sharp edge of existence" which is experienced in the *encounter* with the patient.[16]

Binswanger has laid particular emphasis on the significance of existential philosophy for treating the mentally ill:

[13] See Ch. II, "The Quest for the Golden Mean: A Study in Schizophrenia," by Arthur Burton, in *Psychotherapy of the Psychoses,* ed. Arthur Burton, New York, Basic Books, 1961.

[14] p. 26, *Existential Psychology.*

[15] p. 28, ibid.

[16] Quoted by Ludwig Binswanger in "Existential Analysis and Psychotherapy."

The much-discussed *gap* that separates our world from the world of the mentally ill and makes communication between the two so difficult is not only scientifically explained but also scientifically bridged by existential analysis. We are now no longer stopped at the so-called borderline between that psychic life with which we can, and that with which we cannot empathize. Quite a number of case reports show that our method has succeeded beyond earlier hopes in communicating with patients, in penetrating their life-history, and in cases where all this seemed impossible before.[17]

Particularly in dealing with the insane, it is the therapist's interpretation of the *Eigenwelt* which enables the patient to look at his distorted *Mitwelt* and *Umwelt*. (See *The Divided Self* by the British existentialist psychologist, R. D. Laing.) Those who wish to see how existential psychiatry actually deals with the relation of the self to the self in the clinical situation should consult Binswanger's "The Case of Ellen West." [18] Here he shows that the patient

suffered from that sickness of the mind which Kierkegaard, with the keen insight of the genius, described and illuminated from all possible aspects under the name of "Sickness Unto Death." I know of no document which could more greatly advance the existential-analytic interpretation of schizophrenia. One might say that in this document Kierkegaard has recognized with intuitive genius the approach of schizophrenia; for at the root of so many "cases" of schizophrenia can be found the "desperate" wish—indeed, the unshakeable demand to one's *Eigenwelt, Mitwelt,* and "fate"—*not* to be oneself, as also can be found its counterpart, the desperate wish to *be* oneself.[19]

When treating schizophrenic patients, the existential analyst becomes involved with the philosophic concepts

[17] p. 213, *Existence.*

[18] Ellen West was one of the patients treated by Binswanger. Her case is discussed in the book *Existence.*

[19] p. 237, *Existence,* "The Case of Ellen West" by Ludwig Binswanger.

of nothingness and the absurd. *Nothingness* may be defined as a feeling of emptiness and loneliness "before which all else retreats." And the absurd is, in Camus' terms, the substance of nothingness, non-being.

Here, it is interesting to note the significance of the concept of death for the existential therapist. Reinhardt says: "Death may stand for *either all/or nought,* depending on whether the being of the individual is grounded in the plenitude of the *All* or in the emptiness of the *Nought.*" [20] Thus, for the existential analyst, suicide becomes a manifestation of Kierkegaard's "sickness unto death." When Ellen West killed herself, Binswanger observed:

> The positiveness of Nothingness has a very specific existential meaning: when the existence bases itself on or rests upon Nothingness (here again we are beyond guilt and fate) it stands not only in existential dread but, also—which is the same thing—in absolute isolation. The positiveness of Nothingness, and an existence in the sense of being a complete isolate, represent existential-analytically one and the same thing. Ellen West died her death not only as an individual "alone before God," as the religious individual dies it, that is, in religious We-ness, not only in the We-ness of earthly loving encounter, and not even in communication with "the others," but, after parting from the others, alone before Nothingness. From here a metaphysical shadow also falls on her gladness in the face of Nothingness. [21]

Existential philosophy thus provides the analyst with a set of principles which can serve as guidelines in a broad general interpretation of clinical material. For existentialism approaches man's life directly. By using its concepts, the analyst can press on to the bedrock of man's existence and so establish a more immediate and fruitful relation with his patients.

[20] p. 251, *The Existentialist Revolt.*
[21] p. 297, *Existence.*

In dealing with such concepts and problems as isolation, alienation, and loneliness, the existential analyst can profit by considering the findings of contemporary social psychologists. Here Riesman's analysis of the isolated other-directed man can be useful, as can Erich Fromm's portrait of the alienated marketer. Paul Tillich's theologically oriented observations on isolation can also be useful.

Existential philosophy may make a particularly valuable contribution to psychoanalysis and psychology as those must function in terms of the American scene. As I stress in my forthcoming book, *The Individual and the Crowd: A Study of Identity in America,* [22] the relationship between existence and identity is especially important in American social development. The concern of students like Erich Fromm, Allen Wheelis, Erik H. Erikson, Rollo May, Helen Merrill Lynd, and others, with the concept and problem of identity in terms of such existentialist issues as anxiety, despair, alienation, loneliness, and death points toward a reassessment of the concepts of creativity, autonomy, choice, and identity itself. By linking existentialist concepts and insights to parallel experiences of patients in psychotherapy, we can provide the comprehensive frame of reference which workers in social and clinical psychology have long required.

Because of its awareness of the philosophical meaning of anxiety, for example, existential analysis seems better adapted to meet the needs of the confused and disturbed person in our society than are the other post-Freudian schools of psychotherapy. Existential analysis can be more effective clinically if it makes use of such interpretations of contemporary problems of identity as those presented

[22] Hendrik M. Ruitenbeek, *The Individual and the Crowd: A Study of Identity in America* (forthcoming, New York, New American Library, 1962). See Ch. IV, "Existence and Identity."

by Wheelis and Erikson. For only through studies of this sort can the existential analyst fully understand the need for psychotherapy to change as the *Mitwelt* has changed from Freud's Victorian inner-directed, guilt-ridden society to the anxiety-ridden, other-directed society of our time.

If we turn to clinical material, however, what evidence have we that the existential analyst does try to give his patient a new vision of life? And just how successful are such analysts? In Europe, existential concepts are apparently most used in psychiatry (see "The Case of Ellen West" and other clinical material in *Existence*). They have proved especially useful in dealing with schizophrenics who, incidentally, have only lately been considered to be even potentially curable. In dealing with neurotics in psychotherapy, however, existential analysis appears to be still in an early stage of development.

Gordon W. Allport does consider several American schools of treatment as "movements of the quasi-existential order (client-oriented, growth, self-actualization, and ego-therapies)." [23] Nevertheless, he remarks that existential analysis holds out little hope "beyond acceptance of responsibility and the discovery of a meaning in suffering." [24]

The widespread acceptance of existential insights by practicing psychotherapists may actually operate as a serious deterrent to the further development of a separate school of existential analysis in the United States. The neo-Freudian schools of Horney, Sullivan (interpersonal psychiatry), Rogers (non-directive therapy), and the numerous group-psychotherapy approaches could well absorb existential analysis. Many of these therapies are sufficiently oriented toward society and the *Mitwelt* to be able to provide the man "in distress," the sort of patient

[23] p. 97, *Existential Psychology.*
[24] p. 97, ibid.

whom Riesman described earlier, with a new attitude toward existence.

Nevertheless, we should remember that the encounter of psychoanalysis and existential philosophy is still in an early stage of development. Many existential analysts still use the traditional Freudian techniques in therapy. It is difficult to escape from clinical practice in terms of free association and of interpretation in terms of the familiar concepts of sublimation, projection, reaction formation, displacement. The therapist is forced to encounter hazards when seeking to couple traditional psychoanalytic techniques with the implications of existential concepts. In his essay which concludes this volume, "Dangers in the Relation of Existentialism to Psychotherapy," Rollo May underlines his awareness of such hazards, and in that awareness he is certainly not alone.

Existential philosophy has made many contributions to an over-all interpretation of the crisis of our time. Few other philosophies have had such a direct impact on the content and the processes of modern thinking. Existentialism has enabled man to interpret his anxiety, loneliness, and despair at a time when such understanding was essential. Existential philosophy has given psychoanalysis a new dimension, a dimension which is desperately needed in order to meet the challenge of the individual's coping with the complexities of existing in a modern mass society. Whether existential analysis will become the definitive solution for the problems of psychoanalytic therapy in our time remains for the future to determine.

HENDRIK M. RUITENBEEK

PSYCHOANALYSIS
and
EXISTENTIAL PHILOSOPHY

EXISTENTIALISM AND PSYCHOTHERAPY

by PAUL TILLICH *

1. Existentialism and essentialism

The task given to me is a formidable one, provoking justifiable anxiety. In all schools of psychotherapy there are many concepts which have proved more or less useful for directing research as well as practical work, but which are devoid of a philosophical foundation and, consequently, without critical and uniting principles. As a non-expert in this vast realm of theory and practice, I can only pose the question of a possible philosophical foundation for psychotherapy on the basis of my own thought, in which the existentialist element has a definite place, although I would not call myself an existentialist.

It is an indication that one has misunderstood existentialism if one uses it without reference to its opposite. Philosophical ideas necessarily appear in pairs of contrasting concepts, like subject and object, ideal and real, rational and irrational. In the same way, existentialism refers to its opposite, essentialism, and I would be at a loss to say anything about the one without saying something about the other. The easiness with which the term existentialism and its derivatives have lately become the

* Paul Tillich has been University Professor at Harvard University since 1955. From 1933-1955 he was Professor of Philosophical Theology at the Union Theological Seminary, New York. He is the author of *The Protestant Era, Systematic Theology, The Courage to Be, Love, Power and Justice, Dynamics of Faith, The Shaking of Foundations, Theology of Culture,* and other books.

talk of the intellectual market is because from the very beginning in America, after the second World War, the term existentialism was used without reference to its opposite. Indicative for the general situation is the fact that the term essentialism did not even exist in the early discussions of existentialist philosophy. But it seems to me that in a group which seeks for an existentialist psychotherapy, the implicit reference to essentialism should be brought into the open.[1]

Instead of giving an abstract definition of essentialism and existentialism, I will point to an example par excellence, the nature of man. One can describe man's essential nature and one can describe man's existential predicament. Both tasks have always been performed but often the one has tried to eliminate the other. In religious thought, for instance, the view of man's predicament has frequently overshadowed the view of his essential nature. One can say this of ancient Gnosticism as well as of some forms of radical Protestantism. If man's estranged predicament is so much emphasized that his creative goodness appears completely destroyed, an impressive but untenable theological existentialism arises. Some theologians of the Reformation period, like the great church historian, Flacius, as well as some recent theologians like the early Karl Barth, have taken this position. None of them would have denied or even minimized the doctrine of creation and with it man's essential goodness, but they did not draw from it the consequences for the doctrine of man. The divine was cut off from the human without "point of contact." Man was seen as a mere object of divine action and man's

[1] Here the distinction between existential and existentialist should be brought out: "Existential" points to the universally human involvement in matters of genuine concern; "existentialist" points to a philosophical movement which fights the predominance of essentialism in modern thought, be it idealistic or naturalistic essentialism.

productive activities in culture and history were devaluated. This is the theological existentialism without the essentialist frame in which classical theology had stated it.

But the main stream of existentialist thought was running through philosophy, the arts and literature. In contrast to the situation in the last three years after the second World War, when most people identified existentialism with Sartre, it is now common knowledge in this country that existentialism in the western intellectual history starts with Pascal in the 17th century, has an underground history in the 18th century, a revolutionary history in the 19th century and an astonishing victory in the 20th century. Existentialism has become the style of our period in all realms of life. Even the analytic philosophers pay tribute to it by withdrawing into formal problems and leaving the field of material problems to the existentialists in art and literature.

There are, however, only rare moments in this monumental development in which an almost pure existentialism has been reached. An example is Sartre's doctrine of man. I refer to a sentence in which the whole problem of essentialism and existentialism comes into the open, his famous statement that man's essence is his existence. The meaning of this sentence is that man is a being of whom no essence can be affirmed, for such an essence would introduce a permanent element, contradictory to man's power of transforming himself indefinitely. According to Sartre, man is what he acts to be.

But if we ask whether his statement has not, against its intention, given an assertion about man's essential nature, we must say, certainly, it has. Man's particular nature is his power to create himself. And if the further question is raised of how such a power is possible and how it must be structured, we need a fully developed essentialist doctrine in order to answer; we must know about his body and his mind and, in short, about those questions which for millennia have been discussed in essentialist terms.

Only on the basis of an essentialist doctrine of freedom does Sartre's statement have any meaning. Neither in theology nor in philosophy can existentialism live by itself. It can only exist as a contrasting element within an essentialist framework. There is existentialist philosophizing but there is not, and cannot be, an existentialist system of philosophy. The answers given by existentialists to the questions they raise in their analyses are derived from essentialist traditions. Existentialism is an element within a larger frame of essentialism and it exists only as such an element, even in its most radical anti-essentialist statements. In order to describe the negative in being and life, one must see its impact on the positive. For only through this impact does the negative have reality. There is no existentialist description of the negativities of the human predicament without an underlying image of what man essentially is and therefore ought to be. The cutting power of existentialist novels, paintings, even philosophical analyses of man's predicament, is rooted in the implicit contrast between the negativities they show and the positives they silently presuppose.

But now we must ask the converse question: Is pure essentialism possible? It is possible only if man's searching mind is subjected to a strict censorship, prohibiting all those questions in which man asks about his existence within his world. Plato did not accept such censorship. He was aware of the conflict between the essential and the existential element in reality. And if he talked about "the destiny of the soul," namely, of man's predicament in space and time, he did not use dialectics, but myth.

He is the greatest example of a union of essentialism with existentialist elements. In the Middle Ages, existentialist descriptions of the human predicament were present in monastic self-scrutiny and in the penitential manuals for priest-confessors. These manuals contain materials which in many respects are an anticipation of the insights elaborated in the psychotherapeutic schools of the 20th century. In Protestantism, this concrete material disappeared, but certainly not the question of man's predicament. In philosophy the problem came to a dramatic height in the conflict between Descartes and Pascal in the 17th century. Both men stood in the Platonic-Augustinian tradition, both were creative mathematicians, and mathematics was always the pattern for essentialist thinking. But while Descartes reduced the elements to a minimum, Pascal put them against his own and Descartes' essentialist emphasis.

Ever since, this tension has remained alive, although in the modern period it has been under a definite predominance of the essentialist element. A change took place with the existentialist revolt against Hegel's essentialism in the middle of the last century and with the major victory of the existentialist attitude in the 20th century. But this victory does not mean that the tension has ceased between the two approaches to reality. And a slight recovery of essentialism seems to be noticeable, especially in the arts within the last decade.

2. THE PHILOSOPHICAL MATRIX OF PSYCHOANALYSIS

Seen in the background of this development, the question of the relation of existentialism and psychoanalysis can be asked in more definite terms. The term "psychoanalysis" has shared the fate of a large group of important concepts that have grown beyond the limits of their original meaning and in this way have received an increased significance and a growing indefiniteness. This makes it necessary to determine the sense in which psychoanalysis shall be used in its confrontation with existentialism.

Originally it meant a therapeutic technique, a refinement and transformation of earlier techniques. But this was possible only on the basis of a new understanding of the psychological processes which produce both the necessity and the possibility of psychotherapy. "Psychological processes" is a name for processes in the living *Gestalt* which we call "man." No understanding or even description of them is possible without an image of this *Gestalt,* without a doctrine of man in the several dimensions of his being. No therapeutic theory can be developed without an implicit or explicit image of man. But we must go beyond this step. No doctrine of man is possible without a general understanding of the general processes of life, their trends and their ambiguities. And finally, no understanding of life processes is possible without a doctrine of being and of the structure of being universally.

This consideration shows the basis of the question, how is psychoanalysis related to existentialism? The question is two-sided. The psychoanalytic practice is not only dependent on the doctrines of man and life and of being, but these doctrines are also dependent on the practice of psychoanalysis. Every practical dealing with reality provides experiences which have theoretical impact. This insight is as old as the gospel of John when it speaks of doing the truth and it is as new as Marx in his earlier writings when he fought against the separation of theory and practice. And it is as old and as new as the main emphasis of Nietzsche and the American pragmatists when they tried to reunite action and knowledge. Therefore, it is not astonishing that Freud's analytic practice became the source of ideas which changed the whole intellectual climate of the 20th century.

Unfortunately, the philosophical matrix in which the psychoanalytic techniques were conceived was rather inadequate to the implications and consequences of their conception. The naturalistic (and in some respect, idealistic) presuppositions of Freud do not fit the immense contribution he has made indirectly to the existentialist analysis of the human predicament. Therefore, it is a justifiable attempt by the different Neo-Freudian groups to overcome this inadequacy and, by doing so, to correct some shortcomings of the therapeutic method which follows from the inadequacy of Freud's philosophical presuppositions. This is what existentialist psychotherapy also tries to do. I believe that such a task is necessary, not only for psychotherapeutic practice but also for the contemporary intellectual situation.

If my philosophical assumptions are correct, an important consequence follows: It cannot only be existentialist, it must also be essentialist thought which provides the philosophical matrix for the psychoanalytic practice. Existential psychotherapy is almost a truism; for disease is one of the central existential concepts. Therefore, let us not talk of existentialist psychoanalysis as such, but of a possible philosophical matrix of psychoanalysis, being aware of the fact that every constructive philosophy and theology unites essentialist and existentialist elements. In order to understand sin, the theologian must understand creative goodness. In order to understand estrangement, the philosopher must understand that from which we are estranged, namely, our own essential nature. This means psychotherapy must remain aware of its dependence on the doctrine of man, on the doctrine of life, on the doctrine of being. As psychotherapy, it cannot create such a philosophy, though it can influence it.

This is a difficult relationship. The problem is the same as it is in all creative functions of the human spirit. Always and inescapably they have a philosophy in their background. We must bring this into the open and subject it to criticism and transformation. On the other hand, all creative functions of man's spirit must contribute to a philosophy which deals with all of them. This mutual dependence of philosophy and the other functions of the spirit produces a perpetual problem. For more than fifty years, I have been laboring under this problem in relation to the philosophy of religion; and I am consoled that now other groups are in the same predicament and will have to labor probably more than fifty years under the same problem. As a group of healers you cannot identify yourselves with a particular philosophy; but you cannot do without a philosophy. Instead of attempting a general answer, I want to give a description of some exemplary situations, thus leading to the next consideration: philosophical problems of psychoanalytic procedures:

3. PHILOSOPHICAL PROBLEMS OF PSYCHOANALYTIC PROCEDURES

Naturalism, the philosophy from which Freud came, is together with idealism the main expression of an essentialist philosophy. Freud's determinism was his naturalistic heritage, his moralism was his idealistic heritage. And in both he represented the basic attitude of the victorious and "Victorian" industrial society of the 19th century. But with the empirical rediscovery of the old philosophical concept of the unconscious, he broke through his own moralism, and with the concept of sublimation, he broke through his determinism. The first, the rediscovery of the unconscious was the confirmation of the inability of autonomous morals to lead man to his fulfillment. It was the destruction of the philosophy of the "men of good will," which is so rampant in American Protestantism. Freud showed the ambiguity of goodness as well as of evil, and in doing so, he helped to undercut Protestant moralism. This perhaps was the most important existentialist contribution of psychoanalysis to the doctrine of man. Man is not what he believes himself to be in his conscious decisions.

This is the point where Freud is a true existentialist in the sense of all existentialist descriptions of man's predicament. He is certainly not the moralistic idealist he sometimes gives the impression of being, especially in relation to sex. And he is not a determinist either, towards which his naturalistic heritage seemed to push him. I don't look for indeterministic utterances of Freud. They probably could not be found. And they should not, because the traditional fight between determinism and indeterminism is a dead issue. But I look at his concept of sublimation, which philosophically is completely unelaborated.

Sublimation is the act which transforms something not sublime into something sublime. And the sublime is a concept which deserves highest standing in formulating a philosophy of life. The structure of life shows that the sublime is the greatest potentiality of life. It is not a mere transformation of the not-sublime; then it would be only another form of it. But the sublime is something qualitatively new, it demands a creative act—and this means freedom, in a meaningful sense of the world. It belongs to the theories wherein Freud was "behind" himself—in that he tried to derive sublime things, like works of art, from non-sublime things like early psychological disturbances of the artists. But the very concept of the sublime requires that such disturbances be looked at as occasions and not causes of the creation of the sublime. This is not an existentialist but an essentialist question. It refers to man's essential nature and to the central concept in which converge all elements in man's essential nature, the concept of freedom. I do not mean the so-called "freedom of the will" (an obsolete concept), but the power of man to react centrally to a stimulus, by deliberation and decision.

This explains the fact to which Rollo May drew my attention, that in so many of his patients' dreams there appears the necessity of deciding. His patients have not yet lost the awareness that sublimation goes through decision, and that the power of deciding makes men human. This consideration is an essentialist one—although it shows the pre-condition for the possibility of man's existential self-loss. This should lead to the acknowledgment that biological and sociological methods of interpretation are by no means sufficient in order to explain the drive towards the sublime. The centered act of the centered self is the source of sublimation. This is a basic statement of an essentialist doctrine of man and is as necessary for psychoanalysis as the existentialist insight in the determining function of the unconscious is for morality and religion.

After these examples of existentialist as well as of essentialist elements in which psychoanalysis must find a solid philosophical ground, let me speak of a phenomenon in which elements of both sides are effective. I point to the difference and confusion of existential and neurotic anxiety, of existential and neurotic guilt, of existential and neurotic emptiness. I believe that Freud is partly responsible for the confusion because of his inadequate philosophical foundations which did not admit the distinction between essential goodness and existential distortion. The decisive question here is whether one believes that it is possible to remove by successful analysis not only neurotic forms of anxiety but also its genuine forms—the anxieties of finitude, of guilt, of emptiness. Of course, no one would deny that a completely successful analysis is highly improbable, but many analysts assert that in principle both forms of anxiety can be removed, because there is no qualitative difference between them. They all can be treated as neurosis, capable of being healed. This would include the anxiety of having to die, the anxiety of having become guilty, the anxiety of lacking a meaning of life. This however would imply, at least in principle, that the analyst is able to remove from human beings the awareness of their finitude, and consequently their basic anxiety; that he would be able to convince men who have become guilty that they are not really guilty; that he would be able to answer the question of the meaning of life to his patients. But all this is not realistic.

Actually the situation is quite different. Neurotic anxiety is misplaced compulsory anxiety, and not the basic anxiety about everything being finite. Basic anxiety is anxiety about being bound to the law of coming from nothing and going to nothing. Neurotic guilt is misplaced compulsory guilt feeling and not the existential experience of being guilty of a definite concrete act which expresses the general estrangement of our existence, an act for which responsibility cannot be denied, in spite of the element of destiny in it. Neurotic emptiness is a compulsory flight from meaning, even from that remnant of meaning which makes the experience of meaninglessness possible. It is the expression of an unreflective and unsophisticated understanding of men and life if these neurotic phenomena are confused with the universal structures of existence which make neurotic phenomena possible. No great physician has ever claimed that he can change the biological structures of life; and no psychotherapist from whatever school he comes should claim that he can change the structures of life in the dimension of self-awareness usually called the psychological dimension. But he can assert that he may heal disorders which follow from the relation of men's existential to his essential nature. Here are very obvious reasons why psychoanalysis needs a philosophical matrix.

There are other reasons, some existentialist, some essentialist. I can only point to them. What do norms of thought and action mean in relation to the therapeutic process? For Freud, the "superego" is the name for the consciousness of norms. But the material of the superego is taken from the "id." It has no standing in itself, no objective validity. It has only the power of psychological oppressiveness. The reason for this construction is that Freud did not distinguish the essential structure of man's being, from which forms and principles are derived, and their existential distortion in the images of the superego. Certainly, there are images of destructive power in most human beings; but they are not identical with man's essential nature.

Essential norms, if obeyed, fulfill and give the joy of fulfillment because they represent our own essential being against our existential distortion. Religious commandments, for instance, express a concrete understanding of man's essential nature. The superego gives arbitrary commands and produces unhappiness and revolt. Dr. Hanna Colm writes about the revolt of children, not only against oppressive education, but also against the lack of any direction. This is an interesting confirmation of the assertion that norms and principles are an expression of our essential being. In view of these facts, the distinction between essential and existential elements in human nature becomes empirically verifiable. In spite of this, the general acceptance of the id-ego-superego scheme has blinded many scholars against the distinction of the essential and the existential in human nature.

A further problem is that of the relation between the analyst and the patient in the therapeutic process. A person becomes a person in the encounter with other persons, and in no other way. All functions of our spirit are based on what I call the moral self-realization of the centered self. This is what morality is—not the subjection to laws. The only way in which this can happen is the limiting encounter with another ego. Nature is open to man's controlling and transforming activity indefinitely, but man resists such control. The other person cannot be controlled like a natural object. Every human being is an absolute limit, an unpierceable wall of resistance against any attempt to make him into an object. He who breaks this resistance by external force destroys his own humanity; he never can become a mature person.

This interdependence of man and man in the process of becoming human is a judgment against a psychotherapeutic method in which the patient is a mere object for the analyst as subject. The inevitable reaction then is that the patient tries in return to make the analyst into an object for himself as subject. This kind of acting and reacting has a depersonalizing effect on both the analyst and the patient. The transference phenomenon should be reconsidered in the light of a "philosophy of encounter," in which existentialist and essentialist elements are united.

My last example is the phrase "being in the world" (Heidegger), which plays a great role in existentialist literature. It points to the fact of "being-with" in spite of our aloneness in the world. But more important for the understanding of man is that he has the potentiality of having a world in contrast to other beings which have only environment. Man breaks through his environment in all directions, his language is his liberation from bondage to a limited situation. But this freedom is not easy to accept and many people turn back from the openness of their world to the prison of their environment. This is another description of the neurotic withdrawal from reality, and one which shows the neurotic character of many forms of seemingly normal behavior, as in conformism and submission to absolute authorities. Without a sharp essentialist distinction between world and environment, such approaches to the phenomenon of neurosis have no foundation.

Existentialism has discovered many characteristics of man's predicament which are able to provide a philosophical matrix for psychotherapy. But this does not mean that there should be a definitive marriage between existentialism and psychotherapy. It is an alliance which should not be exclusive. Without a powerful essentialist frame the alliance would not hold. It would fall into vagueness and irrelevance, both on the philosophical and the psychotherapeutic side. But it is the task of a philosophical matrix in all realms of man's intellectual life to help these realms towards definiteness, clarity, fundamental principles and universal validity.

EXISTENTIAL ANALYSIS AND PSYCHOTHERAPY

by LUDWIG BINSWANGER *

Zürich is the birthplace of existential analysis (*Daseinsanalyse*) as a psychiatric-phenomenologic research method. I emphasize the term *research method,* for if the psychoanalytic theory of Freud or the teaching of Jung arose out of a dissatisfaction with preceding psychotherapy, thus owing their origin and development predominantly to psychotherapeutic impulses and aims, the existential research orientation in psychiatry arose from dissatisfaction with the prevailing efforts to gain scientific understanding in psychiatry; so that existential analysis owes its origin and development to an attempt to gain a new scientific understanding of the concerns of psychiatry, psychopathology and psychotherapy, on the basis of the analysis of existence (*Daseinsanalytik*) as it was developed in the remarkable work of Martin Heidegger: "Being and Time" (*Sein und Zeit*), in the year 1927. Psychology and psychotherapy, as sciences, are admittedly concerned with "man," but not at all primarily with

* LUDWIG BINSWANGER served as Psychiatric Interne under Eugen Bleuler in Zürich and as Resident at the Psychiatric Clinic for Nervous Diseases of Jena University. In 1911 Binswanger succeeded his father Robert Binswanger as Chief Medical Director of the Sanatorium Bellevue at Kreuzlingen. He relinquished this directorship in 1956. Hardly any of his works have been translated into English. His personal memoirs of his friendship with Freud is available in English: *Sigmund Freud: Reminiscences of a Friendship* 1958).

mentally *ill* man, but with *man as such*. The new understanding of man, which we owe to Heidegger's analysis of existence, has its basis in the new conception that man is no longer understood in terms of some theory—be it a mechanistic, a biologic or a psychological one—but in terms of a purely phenomenologic elucidation of the total structure or total articulation of existence as BEING-IN-THE-WORLD (*In-der-Welt-sein*). What this expression, fundamental for existential analysis, means, I unfortunately cannot develop here; be it only emphasized that it encompasses alike the individual's own world and the simultaneous and coextensive relationships with and to other people and things. Nor can I go into the difference between an ontologic-phenomenologic analysis of existence, an empiric-phenomenologic existential analysis, and an empiric discursive description, classification and explanation.

Once, in his interpretation of dreams, Freud said that psychiatrists had "forsaken the stability of the psychic structure too early." Existential analysis could say the same thing, albeit with an altogether different meaning. Freud, as is well known, had in mind the stability of the articulation of the life-history with the psychic structure, in contrast to the psychiatrists of his day who, at the very first opportunity, considered the psychic structure to be disrupted, and who resorted instead to physiologic processes in the cerebral cortex. Existential analysis, on the other hand, does not have in mind the solidity of the structure of the inner life-history, but rather the solidity of the transcendental structure preceding or underlying, a priori, all psychic structures as the very condition of this possibility. I regret that I cannot explain in fuller detail these philosophic expressions, already employed by Kant but here used in a much wider sense; those among you conversant with philosophy will readily understand me. I want to emphasize only that philosophy is not here in any way being introduced into psychiatry or psychotherapy, but rather that the philosophic bases of these sciences are being laid bare. Obviously, this in turn has an effect upon one's understanding of what constitutes their scientific object or field. This effect reveals itself in the fact that we have learned to understand and to describe the various psychoses and neuroses as specific *deviations* of the a priori, or the transcendental, structure of man's humanity, of the *condition humaine,* as the French say.

Be it noted in passing that the existential-analytic research method in psychiatry had to investigate the structure of existence as being-in-the-world, as Heidegger had outlined and delineated it still further and along various new paths. Such, for instance, are its studies of various existential "dimensions," i.e., height, depth and width, thingness and resistance (*Materialität*), lighting and coloring of the world, fullness or emptiness of existence, etc. The investigation of psychotic or neurotic world-projects and existential structures such as, for example, those which we designate as manic, depressive, schizophrenic, or compulsive, have so occupied all of us who are engaged upon this work that only suggestions are at hand with regard to the significance of existential-analytic research for psychotherapy. I should like now very cursorily to indicate a few of the main trends of this relationship.

(1) A psychotherapy on existential-analytic bases investigates the life-history of the patient to be treated, just as any other psychotherapeutic method, albeit in its own fashion. It does not explain this life-history and its pathologic idiosyncrasies according to the teachings of any school of psychotherapy, or by means of its preferred categories. Instead, it *understands* this life-history

as modifications of the total structure of the patient's being-in-the-world, as I have shown in my studies "On Flight of Ideas" (*Über Ideenflucht*), in my studies of schizophrenia, and most recently in the case of "Suzanne Urban."

(2) A psychotherapy on existential-analytic bases thus proceeds *not* merely by showing the patient where, when and to what extent he has failed to realize the fullness of his humanity, but it tries to make him *experience* this as radically as possible—how, like Ibsen's master-builder, Solness, he has lost his way and footing in "airy heights" or "ethereal worlds of fantasy." In this case the psychotherapist could be compared to someone who is informed, e.g., a mountain guide, familiar with the particular terrain, who attempts the trip back to the valley with the unpracticed tourist who no longer dares either to proceed or to return. And inversely, the existential-analytically-oriented therapist seeks to enable the depressed patient to get out of his cavernous subterranean world, and to gain footing "upon the ground" once more, by revealing it to him as being the only mode of existence in which the fullness of human possibilities can be realized. And further, the existential-analytically-oriented therapist will lead the twisted schizophrenic out of the autistic world of distortion and askewness in which he lives and acts, into the shared worlds, the *koinos kosmos* of Heraclitus; or he will strive to help a patient who, in her own words, lives "in two speeds" to "synchronize" these (again using her own expression). Yet, another time the therapist will see (as happened in one of Roland Kuhn's cases of anorexia mentalis) that the goal may be reached much more rapidly if one explores not the temporal but the spatial structures of a particular patient's world. It came as a surprise to us to find how easily some otherwise not particularly intelligent or edu-

cated patients proved accessible to an existential-analytic kind of exploration, and how thoroughly they felt understood by it in their singularity. This is, after all, an altogether indispensable prerequisite for any kind of psychotherapeutic success.

(3) Regardless of whether the existential analyst is predominantly psychoanalytic or predominantly jungian in orientation, he will always stand on the same plane with his patients—the plane of common existence. He will therefore not degrade the patient to an object toward which he is subject, but he will see in him an existential partner. He will therefore not consider the bond between the two partners to be as that of two electric batteries—a "psychic contact"—but as an *encounter* on what Martin Buber calls the "sharp edge of existence," an existence which *essentially* "is in the world," not merely as a self but also as a being-together with one another—relatedness and love. Also what has, since *Freud,* been called transference is, in the existential-analytic sense, a kind of encounter. For encounter is a being-with-others in *genuine presence,* that is to say, in the present which is altogether continuous with the *past* and bears within it the possibilities of a *future.*

(4) Perhaps you will also be interested in hearing what is the position of existential analysis toward the *dream,* and this again particularly with regard to psychotherapy. Here again it is removed from any theoretic "explanation" of the dream, especially from the purely sexual exegesis of dream contents in psychoanalysis; rather, it understands the dream, as I emphasized a long time ago, as a specific way of being-in-the-world, in other words, as a specific world and a specific way of existing. This amounts to saying that in the dream we see the whole man, the *entirety* of his problems, in a different existential modality than in waking, but against the back-

ground and with the structure of the a priori articulation of existence, and therefore the dream is also of paramount therapeutic importance for the existential analyst. For precisely by means of the structure of dreams he is enabled first of all to show the patient the structure of his being-in-the-world in an over-all manner, and secondly, he can, on the basis of this, free him for the *totality* of existential possibilities of being, in other words, for open resoluteness (*Entschlossenheit*); he can, to use Heidegger's expression, "retrieve" (*zurückholen*) existence from a dream existence to a genuine capacity for being itself. For the time being, I will refer you to Roland Kuhn's paper, "On the Existential Structure of a Neurosis" in Gebsattel's *Jahrbuch für Psychologie und Psychotherapie*. I only ask of you not to imagine existential structure as something static, but as something undergoing constant change. Similarly, what we call neurosis represents a changed existential *process,* as compared with the healthy. Thus, existential analysis understands the task of psychotherapy to be the opening up of new structural possibilities to such altered existential processes.

As you see, existential analysis, instead of speaking in theoretic concepts, such as "pleasure principle" and "reality principle," investigates and treats the mentally-ill person with regard to the structures, structural articulations and structural alterations of his existence. Hence, it has not, by any means, consciousness as its sole object, as has been erroneously stated, but rather the whole man, prior to any distinction between conscious and unconscious, or even between body and soul; for the existential structures and their alterations permeate man's entire being. Obviously, the existential analyst, insofar as he is a therapist, will not, at least in the beginning of his treatment, be able to dispense with the distinction between conscious and unconscious, deriving from the psychology of consciousness and bound up with its merits and its drawbacks.

(5) Taking stock of the relationship between existential analysis and psychotherapy, it can be said that existential analysis cannot, over long stretches, dispense with the traditional psychotherapeutic methods; that, however, it can, as such, be therapeutically effective only insofar as it succeeds in opening up to the sick fellow man an understanding of the structure of human existence, and allows him to find his way back from his neurotic or psychotic, lost, erring, perforated or twisted mode of existence and world, into the freedom of being able to utilize his own capacities for existence. This presupposes that the existential analyst, insofar as he is a psychotherapist, not only is in possession of existential-analytic and psychotherapeutic competence, but that he must dare to risk committing his own existence in the struggle for the freedom of his partner's.

THE THEORY AND PRACTICE OF EXISTENTIAL ANALYSIS

by W. VAN DUSEN *

Existential analysis is a major movement in psychotherapy in Western and Central Europe, but it is relatively unknown in this country. One can count on the fingers of both hands the number of books and articles in English on the form of analysis that represent a major movement in Europe. These few books [1] (6, 17, 25, 29) and papers (5, 11, 28) leave a confused picture of what existential analysis might be. When one explores the larger field of existential philosophy, one finds apparently very different and conflicting works identified as part of the unclear whole. The only name commonly associated with it is that of the Parisian left-bank pessimist, Jean-Paul Sartre (24), whose existential analysis is a philosophy rather than a clinical practice in the ordinary sense.

Existential analysis, sometimes referred to as "dasein analysis" (*Daseinsanalyse* in German) is not simply a modification of old therapeutic techniques. It is a new program out of which several techniques are emerging. Moreover, it is part of a revolt which makes a powerful rebuttal to science and our general concept of Man. In many ways it is the direct opposite of "operationalism" and statistical exactitude of modern American science

* W. VAN DUSEN is with the Mendocino State Hospital in Talmage, California.

[1] The numbers in parentheses refer to the books listed as references at the end of this essay.

and psychology. Some, e.g., Ellenberger (11), who has had a broad experience in Europe and America, consider it to be *the* analysis of the future. Since almost all the major movements in American psychology and psychiatry (psychoanalysis, gestalt psychology, etc.) have been exported from the same general area of Europe, we should look closely at Europe's latest product, wrapped and ready for export.

Existential analysis is a clinical practice, outwardly similar to other forms of psychoanalysis. Inwardly, it is a relatively unique practice that arises from a specific philosophy. An understanding of the philosophy is essential to the clinical application of the method. For this reason, one's study has to cover not only the few books and articles on existential analysis, but also the whole field of existential philosophy. The analysis grows out and is part of a philosophy or a particular way of viewing the world. The history of existential philosophy has been treated adequately elsewhere (9) and will be omitted here in order to come directly to the theory of existential analysis.

Existentialism is distinguished by its frame of reference, that is, by its chosen mode of meeting the world. The term existential comes from the term existence. Existence in German is *dasein* or "being present" (*da sein*). The existential mode is to see the world from the vantage point of man's existence. If you will, this is subjectivity. The opposite mode is to attempt to eliminate man and see the world and all things in it as objects. Other people are also objects. Ontologically, Western science's approach is that of reaching for essences, for the nature of things, and explaining how they function (the objective processes in objects).

There are two fundamental approaches then: one, the hallmark of Western science, is to attempt to study objects and their functions directly while trying to eliminate man's subjectivity as far as possible. The other makes man's experience the center of the picture. The former, "objective" approach involves a deception; it implies that man, for all practical purposes, *can* be eliminated from the picture. Physics is the most objective, pointer-reading of all sciences. Yet modern physics has given up the possibility of eliminating the pointer-reader from the pointer-readings. It is all the more remarkable that psychology and psychiatry, the most subjective of sciences, are still trying to throw out the observer. Meanwhile, they are accumulating much evidence in perception psychology (4) and elsewhere to prove that it can't be done.

Existential philosophy is a modern name and a modern consciousness of a very ancient mode of encompassing the world. Its frame of reference is Man as he exists inside, in the full range of his fears, hopes, anxieties and terrors. It opposes the attempt to leave Man out of the picture and still to explore the world of objects and essences.

The second feature of existential philosophy and analysis is that it tends to search out and examine the most critical inner realities. In this way the overworked term "existential" often comes to mean "crucial." For instance, when Wolff (29, p. 214) speaks of "existential dreams" he means "critical dreams," dreams which reflect the total life orientation. Kierkegaard's works (15) are a searching examination of things critical. When Sartre writes a novel or a play, one has the impression that he is trying to get to the bedrock, the critical aspects of human experience. Existential works abound in studies of crisis, despair, anxiety, dread, the feeling of death, meaninglessness, etc. One might say that to know one's self existentially is to sense a crisis.

The third feature of existential philosophy and analysis arises from the first two. If one takes man's existing as a frame of reference and studies the essential or critical qualities in that frame, one tends to concentrate on the temporal Now. What is past is critical only in so far as it has representation in the Now and affects one's present adjustment. The future is critical to me here and now only in so far as it is involved in my judgments now. The temporality of the existentialists is the real present; but it is also the meeting ground of the past and future. This gives existentialism a unique outlook on the unconscious, which disappears as any other worldly thing in existential analysis, and reappears as the living potential of this moment.

If one concentrates on the more critical aspects of experiencing in the Now, one also tends to emphasize the importance of choice. Experience in the present moment is mere passivity and not too critical—until one sees the dreadful possibilities of Man's choice. Man is free to choose, even if he chooses to project this power onto someone else. Immersed in a sea of possibilities, with little knowledge of all consequences, he makes a choice which seals his fate. This is the tone of existential analysis.

Some writers (29, p. 3) commonly consider existential philosophy as a modern development deriving from Kierkegaard and Nietzsche. The narrow identification of existentialism with a few philosophers or even with one (Sartre) has led to its rejection before its scope was fully appreciated. Actually, the theologian Bultmann (8) showed that the *New Testament* is written from an existential point of view. Tillich (26) examines ancient philosophies such as Stoicism as well as many novels and plays, and shows them to be existential in character. If one adds that fairy tales, myths and most of the world's bibles are written from an existential point of view then the full sweep of the philosophy becomes clearer. The only thing modern about it is the new name and a conscious opposition to many tendencies of modern science and society.

Fairy tales use personifications of psychic life, as does Jung, but they are existential in that they take up critical human relationships. The witch is evil; she means death and destruction. The princess represents personified goodness, and so forth. Novels and plays which attempt to depict accurately the depths of human experience are existential—whether or not they are consciously identified with this philosophy.

Religion, of course, is intimately concerned with existentials. In each of the Western religions there are existentialist currents which are attempts to bring to light the present active sources of religion. In Judaism, Martin Buber and Saul Rosenzweig are prominent. In Protestantism, there are Sören Kierkegaard, Helmut R. Niebuhr, Karl Barth and Paul Tillich. In Catholicism, there are Gabriel Marcel and Miguel de Unamuno. Existentialism is consciously identified as a Western philosophy, but it has ancient protagonists in the Orient. In so far as Buddhism, Hinduism and Taoism are non-dogmatic and refer man to himself for discovery and advancement, they are also existentialist. In fact, the most advanced works in existentialism are to be found in the relatively ancient religious texts of the Orient.

If one divides the world's literature into the nonexistential (almost all of Western science) and the existential (psychological novels and plays, the world's major religious works, fairy tales, myths, etc.), much of the quality of existentialism emerges. On the one hand, we have factual analyses and reports of the objective world out there, and even of man as an object.

On the other, we have inside-personal accounts of man in his encounter with the world.

The basic features of existential philosophy and analysis are the frame of reference in Man's experiencing and examining the critical aspects as they are now, which leads to a knowledge of the importance of choice. Holding these in mind we can briefly examine the major findings of the existentialists. In a brief article we cannot re-create them out of our own experience as the philosophy demands, but will rather view them almost as objects on a sightseeing tour. These findings are so imbedded in experience that by an exploration of this type we are moving from philosophy to clinical practice. The reader should be warned that we are going to find not one body of findings to report but views that conflict somewhat with each other. These great differences among the experts are disconcerting and will leave those disappointed who want exactitude. They disconcerted me, until I realized that the different views in existentialism range themselves on a continuum, and the very opposition in these differences not only reflects the wide range of human experiences, but also reflects the livingness of the philosophy that can tolerate such conflicts. When existential philosophy has hardened into a consistent dogma, life will have gone out of it and existentialism will have lost its center in Man.

When the existential philosophers explore their experience they look beyond sensations, fleeting moods, and the shimmering surface of experience. Just as they concentrate on the critical Now-aspects, they tend to concentrate on the nearly stable ground underlying the transitory. One might represent this as the intersection between Eternity and the Now. If they kept to sensations and fleeting moods there would be nothing to hold the picture together. It is held together by something like an ego, sense of the self or, in existentialism, by Being. Being has its opposite of Non-being or nothingness, which is the epitome of all loss. The existentialists range themselves on a continuum stretching between the polar opposites of Non-being and Being. Others have spoken of atheistic and theistic existentialists. Speaking of these opposites they come to apparently conflicting results. Yet in the midst of the conflict is Man.

Both Being and Non-being, at first sight, appear to be metaphysical abstractions. To the existentialist both are discoverable in human experience, and it is always that experience to which they are referring. Being is the stable ground of experience—that which is. It lies just under anything transitory in our experience. Non-being is nothingness—the complete loss. There is a dynamism between the two, so that Being contains and interacts with Non-being.

If we arrange the existentialists along this continuum from Non-being to Being, Sartre is clearly on the Non-being end, Kierkegaard is on the darker side near him, Tillich, Wolff, Loehrich are nearer the center, reflecting both extremes. On the Being end are the Christian existentialists, especially Gabriel Marcel (19). It is easier, and psychologically more accurate, to describe these positions metaphorically. When Sartre plunges into critical experience he is throwing off all false pretences, all artificial dogmas, all that makes us feel safe, secure and conventional. To Sartre, if a man truly seeks what is real he throws off his clothes, disdains appetite and faces the cold of the night in fear and trembling. Whatever saving grace of positive religious feeling comes to him, he also throws it off as a mere comforting illusion. He reaches his greatness by this naked, deliberate facing of death (Non-being). He has chosen to explore the darkest part of the continuum and, in his plays and philosophy, he has done this ably. We have only to listen to his titles to realize this: *Nausea, The Flies, No Exit, The Chips Are Down,* etc.

Marcel stands at the Being end of the continuum where there is light and life. His findings are highly optimistic compared to Sartre's dark pessimism. Existentialism has been generally identified with Sartre; while Marcel's position is so different from Sartre's that the eminent critic Helmut Kuhn (16) was inclined to doubt whether Marcel was an existentialist at all. Excluding Marcel, he was left principally with a dark existentialism to criticize. Where Sartre's Man rejects any religious inspiration as a vain fancy, Marcel feels he is rejecting real truth (Being). In the delicate clinical studies of his own experience he finds the saving operation of Grace.

There is, of course, a dynamism between the extremes of Sartre and Marcel. Paul Tillich expresses this as "Being contains Non-being." To go all the way to Non-being and give up in despair is to open ourselves to the saving operation of Being. This play of opposites is well known in oriental philosophy. It is quite clear and prominent in jungian analysis. There are other attributes of this polarity which bring it closer to clinical practice. Non-being is the world of otherness, the purely material world of concrete objects. Moving in the direction of pure Being is to go inward through the realm of symbolic objects such as dream symbols. Each of these symbolic objects contain Non-being, in so far as they are projections from "out of myself." They also contain Being or "myselfness"—unknown to me. Moving into the realm of pure Being we are in a non-symbolic, non-objective realm which is so much pure experiencing that it has no representation, not even to itself. This continuum is also the continuum from the differentiated, objectified, completely projected into objects—to the undifferentiated, subjective. Human experience lies everywhere on the continuum. The differentiated or objectified extreme is spoken of as self-estrangement. This, in freudian terms, corresponds to the estrangement between ego and libido, an estrangement which leads to a projection of much of one's self into objects. Its extreme lies in schizophrenia. The undifferentiated extreme has been spoken of variously as "finding one's self," "finding the center," and the like.

Viewing it this way, one can begin to sense a unity in the apparent opposition between various existentialists. The objective end of the continuum is, of course, the clearer, the more easily represented and handled one. This is the reason why Sartre is readily understood even by his critics. The numinous, undifferentiated end of the continuum is further removed from science and Western mentality, and is in itself inaccessible to representation. One would expect it to be the more misunderstood and rejected of the two.

In a way, existentialism finds it almost impossible to be true to itself when its findings are to be communicated from one person to another. Inside himself a man can keep within the phenomenology of his subjective experience. But when he attempts to translate a living experience into dead signs (words) he has to go outside that experience. As Kierkegaard said, "Immediacy is reality, language is ideality, consciousness is contradiction. The moment I pronounce reality, contradiction is there, for what I say is ideality" (quoted 29, p. 34). Also there is a need to translate subjective experiences into categories in order to communicate them; thus the objects the existentialist revolted against reappear in their own work. Freud used biological objects close to the realm of physical experience in his concepts or oral, anal, and genital libido. Jung deliberately uses personifications of raw experience in his persona, shadow, anima, animus, wise man, etc., because he felt that personification was an ancient and adequate way of handling these dynamic areas. Heidegger (12) is a most systematic existentialist philosopher. He avoids the really objective categories, as do Freud and Jung, but feels forced into coining new terms, like his "Being-in-the-world." Much hostility has been directed against the existentialists for their coining of new terms. At first sight, Being-in-the-world seems abstract and may remind one of medieval metaphysics. Actually Heidegger and others have coined such terms because they need new words to convey experiential meaning. Being-in-the-world is man's feeling of being thrust into the vicissitudes of existence. As a category it is relatively non-restrictive. Marcel takes old terms, like *presence* and *recollection,* and gives them fresh experiential meaning.

There is a development in existentialism which tends to overcome the apparent solipsism of a philosophy centered in one's experiencing. Martin Buber's work has been aptly called co-existentialism (7) or existential communication. A vital part of human experience is how others are perceived, recognized, and become an intimate part of one's experience. Buber examines this relationship on three levels. On the shallowest, one attempts to educate the other but doesn't fully include the other. The second is friendship or true inclusion of one another. The third is mutual experience of spiritual inclusion; it has a numinous quality. Marcel speaks of the "presence" of the other or "intersubjectivity." Jaspers (13) moves in the same direction when he defines truth as communicability. But Buber is the leader of co-existentialism in which existential philosophy moves out of a possible solipsism into the interpersonal aspect of existentialism. In fact, one of the marks of theistic existentialism is the positive value given to the real meeting between man and man. This is very unlike American interpersonal psychology. In the American psychology two individuals are treated as interacting objects in the same field. In the European it is laden with the experience aspect of human relationships.

Historically, existentialism is consistent with the development of analysis in Europe, but very much at odds with American psychoanalysis. The development from Freud's biological representation of the unconscious through Jung's deliberate mythical personifications to existentialism's Being-in-the-world, etc., means both moving closer into human experiencing and, also, a movement toward maintaining the quality of the experience itself. Whatever the failure of individual authors, they strive to get into experiencing and to stay there; they also attempt to avoid, as much as possible, losing it in some kind of objectification and dogmatism. Were it really true to itself, existentialism would move in the direction of Eastern Taoism and Zen Buddhism, and would be inclined to answer the student's questions by pure silence (pure experiencing). The striving goes in the direction of imageless thought (a "more experiencing experiencing," as Heidegger might say).

The European development lies in the direction of penetrating deeper into experience and of keeping as close as possible to artistic modes of expression. The American trend is toward capturing the mind in its exact projection (data collection) and toward manipulating this objectification in as exact a mode as possible. This is shown in the American interest in statistics and in operationalism. To Americans, the European mode of approach appears to be outside of science. To Europeans, Americans, in their demand for exactitude and certainty, seem to squeeze the life out of things. True to their own program, existentialists like Sartre and Marcel feel that they are operating most intimately within their frame of reference—not when they are writing academic works on existentialism, but when they are writing plays and novels. Sartre's play *No Exit* (23) is a fine example of his own position and is far clearer than his *Être et le Néant* (22). In the play, three people meet for the duration of eternity in a windowless room in Hell and suspect that their salvation has something to do with understanding their relations to each other. To drive home a subtle point, Marcel will refer to lines from one of his plays (18, 20). Karl Jaspers has been very active in the sociologic field. In this way, one may in all fairness say that those existentialists who do only philosophic works are, to some extent, violating their own programs, since the programs center in actual experiences and give no pre-eminent value to philosophic speculation.

What does this philosophic mode of "entering the world" lead to, in analytic practice? First, the very philosophy of existentialism does not lead to a rigid, unchanging body of truths and practices as does, for instance, freudian analysis; when true to itself it leads to a variety of clinical practices. The variety is part of the essential humanness of its operation, and is proper to it. No one technique can be said to be the existential mode, even though Werner Wolff (29, p. 216) identifies it with non-directive technique. We can derive from the theory as it has been sketched here the basic tenor of analytic practices.

The technique must have certain general features to keep within the program. It must center upon the subjective experience. It will center upon the most existential or crucial of these experiences. It will center in the Now events and will emphasize the patient's own capacity to choose. To keep as close to the patient's experiences as they occur, i.e., to their phenomenology, it will tend to avoid categorizing, as is done for instance in introducing diagnoses or in structuring theories such as the psychodynamics of Freud. The critical aspects of that experiencing are those that cause symptom formation and hamper creative freedom. The emphasis on the Now will mean an avoidance of a practice which reduces the present to the historical past, as is common in freudian analysis. Both the past and the future play a role in the present experience; and in so far as they do so, they may be taken up. For instance, psychotics can be preoccupied with past events in which case these events still play a dynamic role in the present. Also the potentialities of the future are inherent in the present. The emphasis on the patient's own capacity to choose should remove existential analysis out of the realm of a directive therapy. In fact, to be existential, the patient has to relearn and use his own freedom of choice.

Many contemporary modes of therapy have these basic features, so that, in actual practice, existential analysis may not appear to be radically different. In these cases, the greatest difference will lie in the way the analyst understands the process. In the long run, the weltanschauung or understanding of the analyst will have subtle effects on therapy, especially on the sort of values the patient will adopt. Eventually, existential analysis may come to be identified with unique techniques; but for the present, in actual practice, it is not radically different from other techniques except in the understanding given to the events which are occurring, and to the points on which the analyst centers his attention in the practice.

However, subtle but important differences can be detected. For one thing, there is no "unconscious" in existential analysis. The idea of unconscious implies something different, foreign and distant. The concept rather removes it from human ken. Instead of the unconscious, the existential analyst works in a field of unlimited potentiality or freedom. This freedom exists here and now, but it is lacking the object-like clarity of consciousness. What to most analysts is unconscious and thus removed, to the existential analyst is present though as yet undifferentiated.

Also, the existential analyst has a stronger gestalt feeling for his case. He finds the existential pattern, which is the enduring, consistent mode of Being-in-the-world. Bits of behavior, dreams, fantasies, and even chance events in the patient's experience are seen as aspects of this pattern. There is then a much greater clarity in the therapeutic operation. Resistance, moods, transference phenomena are all aspects of the existential pattern. An individual aspect need not be explained in terms of historically remote family events. Knowing the existential pattern, minute advances in it from moment to moment can be detected. There is a coherent clarity coming from a grasp of the central person of which the various symptoms and symbolic expressions are merely signs. The unconscious—not a remote unknown—is rather an active amorphous potentiality in the present. The program of existentialism centers therapy in the present experiences and choices and tends to avoid being led away either into *symbolic* constructs, such as are seen in dream symbols, the symbolic use of biological zones (Freud) or as personifications of the unconscious (Jung) or into *social* constructs (effects of family, culture, etc.). It would seem to center in the very heart of the therapeutic situation itself. The goal of therapy is the releasing of the patient's dormant potentiality so that it can be communicated to the self and others as truth. In brief, as in other therapies, the goal is to know one's self.

Should Christian existentialism find its way into analysis, theologic concepts, such as grace and presence, will become part of the transference relationship. There are already hints of this among Rankians (10) and in Jung's work on transference (14).

The best case write-ups come from the leading European existentialist, Ludwig Binswanger (1, 2, 3). Looking beyond the complex and flowery German he uses, one can see the gestalt-like grasp of a case, the effort to keep phenomenology of the patient's experience and the emphasis on the patient's choosing. Rolf Loehrich has done an existential analysis of James Joyce's *Ulysses* (17) which includes, for instance, the existential interpretation of the Oedipus complex. The few other cases in English have been described by Wolff (29), Sonnemann (25), and Boss (6); the latter analyzed cases of sexual perversion. Even on the freudian homeground of sex perversions the interpretation and hence understanding of the case are very different.

Some may feel that existential analysis is an unwanted merging of philosophy and science and will decry the move away from exactitude and controlled experimentation. All of psychotherapy has grown up outside of exact experimentation; existential analysis is therefore not unusual in this respect. All therapies have a philosophy, but few are so explicit in their relation to a philosophic view of the world as is existential analysis. Experimentation is possible in this area, though experimentation as presently conceived in science can never become important to it. Unknown to most psychologists in the United States, Van Lennep's *Four Picture Test* (27) was conceived along existential lines.

It is early for this import to be generally accepted in the United States. The mode of scientific thinking here is different from that in Europe. One result may be that this form of analysis will be imported by ministers along with their present importation of existential philosophy. Other difficulties are that much of the critical literature is written in very difficult German, though enough is translated now. What little has been reported in the United States has often been inaccurate. So much so, that while *Time Magazine* (30) reports the death of existentialism in Europe, again identifying it only with Sartre, Joost Meerloo (21), reporting from Holland, decries its increase in Germany and the lowlands.

In conclusion, existential analysis is a form of clinical practice which arose in Europe from a philsophy with a new name and a new following—but it is as old as Man. While almost unknown in the United States, it is a leading movement in Europe today. It sheds new light on old processes. Perhaps its testing and developing in Europe are a prelude to its importation to the United States. The existentialists themselves would be the last to say that it can be a fixed body of truths. Rather, it is the rebirth (with greater awareness) of a lively way of seeing the world as it was known before the world of objects was mastered.

REFERENCES

1. Binswanger, L.: "Der Fall Ellen West." *Schweizer Archiv für Neurologie und Psychiatrie,* Vols. 53, 54, 55, 1945.
2. ———: "Der Fall Jurg Zund." *Schweizer Archiv für Neurologie und Psychiatrie,* Vols. 56, 57, 58, 1946–47.
3. ———: "Der Fall Lola Voss." *Schweizer Archiv für Neurologie und Psychiatrie,* 63, 1949.
4. Blake, R. R.: *Perception.* Ronald Press, New York, 1951.
5. Boss, M.: "Mechanistic and Holistic Thinking in Modern Medicine." *Amer. J. of Psychoanal.,* 14, 48–54, 1954.
6. ———: *Meaning and Content of Sexual Perversions.* Grune and Stratton, New York, 1949.
7. Buber, M.: *Between Man and Man.* Beacon, Boston, 1955.
8. Bultmann, R. K.: *Theology of the New Testament.* 2 vols., SCM Press, London, 1955.

9. Collins, J.: *The Existentialists.* Henry Regnery, Chicago, 1952.
10. Daim, W.: "Depth Psychology and Grace." *J. of Psychother. as a Relig. Process,* 1, 31–40, 1954.
11. Ellenberger, H. F.: "Current Trends in European Psychotherapy." *Amer. J. of Psychother.,* 7, 33–53, 1953.
12. Heidegger, M.: *Existence and Being.* Henry Regnery, Chicago, 1949.
13. Jaspers, K.: *Reason and Existenz.* Noonday, New York, 1955.
14. Jung, C.: "The Practice of Psychotherapy," in *Collected Works of C. G. Jung.* Vol. 16, Pantheon, New York, 1954.
15. Kierkegaard, S.: *Fear and Trembling and the Sickness unto Death.* Doubleday Anchor, New York, 1954.
16. Kuhn, H.: *Encounter with Nothingness.* Methuen, London, 1951.
17. Loehrich, R. R.: *The Secret of Ulysses.* Compass Press, McHenry, Ill., 1953.
18. Marcel, G.: *Homo Viator.* Henry Regnery, Chicago, 1951.
19. ———: *The Philosophy of Existence.* Harvill, London, 1948.
20. ———: *Three Plays.* Secker and Warburg, London, 1952.
21. Meerloo, J. A. M.: "Report from Holland." *Amer. J. of Psychother.,* 10, 208, 1956.
22. Sartre, J.-P.: *L'être et le néant.* Oxford, London, 1950.
23. ———: *No Exit and Three Other Plays.* Vantage Press, New York, 1955.
24. ———: *Existential Psychoanalysis.* Philosophical Library, New York, 1953.
25. Sonnemann, U.: *Existence and Therapy.* Grune and Stratton, New York, 1954.
26. Tillich, P.: *The Courage to Be.* Yale Univ. Press, New Haven, 1952.
27. Van Lennep, D. J.: *The Four Picture Test.* M. Nijhoff, The Hague, 1948.
28. Weigert, E.: "Existentialism and Its Relations to Psychotherapy." *Psychiat.* 12, 399–412, 1949.
29. Wolff, W.: *Values and Personality.* Grune and Stratton, New York, 1950.
30. *Time Magazine,* 77, No. 17, p. 76, 1956.

ONTOLOGICAL INSECURITY

by R. D. LAING *

A man may have a sense of his presence in the world as a real, alive, whole, and, in a temporal sense, continuous person. As such, he can live out into the world and meet others: a world and others experienced as equally real, alive, whole, and continuous.

Such a basically *ontologically* [1] secure person will encounter all the hazards of life, social, ethical, spiritual, biological, from a centrally firm sense of his own and other people's reality and identity. It is often difficult for a person with such a sense of his integral selfhood and personal identity, of the permanency of things, of the reliability of natural processes, of the substantiality of natural processes, of the substantiality of others, to transpose himself into the world of an individual whose experiences may be utterly lacking in any unquestionable self-validating certainties.

This study is concerned with the issues involved where there is the partial or almost complete absence of the assurances derived from an existential position of what

* R. D. LAING has been on the staff of the Tavistock Clinic, London, since 1956, and is now pursuing research in interaction within families with psychotic members. He is the author of *The Divided Self, An Existential Study in Sanity and Madness* and of numerous papers published in the *Lancet* and the *British Journal of Medical Psychology*.

[1] Despite the philosophical use of "ontology" (by Heidegger, Sartre, Tillich, especially), I have used the term in its present empirical sense because it appears to be the best adverbial or adjectival derivative of "being."

I shall call *primary ontological security*: with anxieties and dangers that I shall suggest arise *only* in terms of *primary ontological insecurity*; and with the consequent attempts to deal with such anxieties and dangers.

The literary critic, Lionel Trilling (1955), points up the contrast that I wish to make between a *basic existential position of ontological security* and one of *ontological insecurity* very clearly in comparing the worlds of Shakespeare and Keats on the one hand, and of Kafka on the other:

> . . . for Keats the awareness of evil exists side by side with a very strong sense of personal identity and is for that reason the less immediately apparent. To some contemporary readers, it will seem for the same reason the less intense. In the same way it may seem to a contemporary reader that, if we compare Shakespeare and Kafka, leaving aside the degree of genius each has, and considering both only as expositors of man's suffering and cosmic alienation, it is Kafka who makes the more intense and complete exposition. And, indeed, the judgment may be correct, exactly because for Kafka the sense of evil is not contradicted by the sense of personal identity. Shakespeare's world, quite as much as Kafka's, is that prison cell which Pascal says the world is, from which daily the inmates are led forth to die; Shakespeare no less than Kafka forces upon us the cruel irrationality of the conditions of human life, the tale told by an idiot, the puerile gods who torture us not for punishment but for sport; and no less than Kafka, Shakespeare is revolted by the fetor of the prison of this world, nothing is more characteristic of him than his imagery of disgust. But in Shakespeare's cell the company is so much better than in Kafka's, the captains and kings and lovers and clowns of Shakespeare are alive and complete before they die. In Kafka, long before the sentence is executed, even long before the malign legal process is even instituted, something terrible has been done to the accused. We all know what that is—he has been stripped of all that is becoming to a man except his abstract humanity, which, like his skeleton, never is

quite becoming to a man. He is without parents, home, wife, child, commitment, or appetite; he has no connection with power, beauty, love, wit, courage, loyalty, or fame, and the pride that may be taken in these. So that we may say that Kafka's knowledge of evil exists without the contradictory knowledge of the self in its health and validity, that Shakespeare's knowledge of evil exists with that contradiction in its fullest possible force (pp. 38–9).

We find, as Trilling points out, that Shakespeare does depict characters who evidently experience themselves as real and alive and complete however riddled by doubts or torn by conflicts they may be. With Kafka this is not so. Indeed, the effort to communicate what being alive is like in the absence of such assurances seems to characterize the work of a number of writers and artists of our time. Life, without feeling alive.

With Samuel Beckett, for instance, one enters a world in which there is no contradictory sense of the self in its "health and validity" to mitigate the despair, terror, and boredom of existence. In such a way, the two tramps who wait for Godot are condemned to live:

ESTRAGON: We always find something, eh, Didi, to give us the impression that we exist?

VLADIMIR (impatiently): Yes, yes, we're magicians. But let us persevere in what we have resolved, before we forget.

In painting, Francis Bacon, among others, seems to be dealing with similar issues. Generally, it is evident that what we shall discuss here clinically is but a small sample of something in which human nature is deeply implicated and to which we can contribute only a very partial understanding.

To begin at the beginning:

Biological birth is a definitive act whereby the infant

organism is precipitated into the world. There it is, a new baby, a new biological entity, already with its own ways, real and alive, from *our* point of view. But what of the baby's point of view? Under usual circumstances, the physical birth of a new living organism into the world inaugurates rapidly ongoing processes whereby within an amazingly short time the infant *feels* real and alive and has a *sense* of being an entity, with continuity in time and a location in space. In short, physical birth and biological aliveness are followed by the baby becoming existentially born as real and alive. Usually this development is taken for granted and affords the certainty upon which all other certainties depend. This is to say, not only do adults see children to be real biologically visible entities but they experience themselves as whole persons who are real and alive, and conjunctively experience other human beings as real and alive. These are self-validating data of experience.

The individual, then, may experience his own being as real, alive, whole; as differentiated from the rest of the world in ordinary circumstances so clearly that his identity and autonomy are never in question; as a continuum in time; as having an inner consistency, substantiality, genuineness, and worth; as spatially co-extensive with the body; and, usually, as having begun in or around birth and liable to extinction with death. He thus has a firm core of ontological security.

This, however, may not be the case. The individual in the ordinary circumstances of living may feel more unreal than real; in a literal sense, more dead than alive; precariously differentiated from the rest of the world, so that his identity and autonomy are always in question. He may lack the experience of his own temporal continuity. He may not possess an over-riding sense of personal consistency or cohesiveness. He may feel more insubstantial than substantial, and unable to assume that the stuff he is made of is genuine, good, valuable. And he may feel his self as partially divorced from his body.

It is, of course, inevitable that an individual whose experience of himself is of this order can no more live in a "secure" world than he can be secure "in himself." The whole "physiognomy" of his world will be correspondingly different from that of the individual whose sense of self is securely established in its health and validity. Relatedness to other persons will be seen to have a radically different significance and function. To anticipate, we can say that in the individual whose own being is secure in this primary experiential sense, relatedness with others is potentially gratifying; whereas the ontologically insecure person is preoccupied with preserving rather than gratifying himself: the ordinary circumstances of living threaten his *low threshold* of security.[2]

If a position of primary ontological security has been reached, the ordinary circumstances of life do not afford a perpetual threat to one's own existence. If such a basis for living has not been reached, the ordinary circumstances of everyday life constitute a continual and deadly threat.

Only if this is realized is it possible to understand how certain psychoses can develop.

If the individual cannot take the realness, aliveness, autonomy, and identity of himself and others for granted, then he has to become absorbed in contriving ways of trying to be real, of keeping himself or others alive, of preserving his identity, in efforts, as he will often put it,

[2] This formulation is very similar to those of H. S. Sullivan, Hill, F. Fromm-Reichmann, and Arieti in particular. Federn, although expressing himself very differently, seems to have advanced a closely allied view.

to prevent himself losing his self. What are to most people everyday happenings, which are hardly noticed because they have no special significance, may become deeply significant in so far as they either contribute to the sustenance of the individual's being or threaten him with non-being. Such an individual, for whom the elements of the world are coming to have, or have come to have, a different hierarchy of significance from that of the ordinary person, is beginning, as we say, to "live in a world of his own," or has already come to do so. It is not true to say, however, without careful qualification that he is losing "contact with" reality, and withdrawing into himself. External events no longer affect him in the same way as they do others: it is not that they affect him less; on the contrary, frequently they affect him more. It is frequently not the case that he is becoming "indifferent" and "withdrawn." It may, however, be that the world of his experience comes to be one he can no longer share with other people.

But before these developments are explored, it will be valuable to characterize under three headings three forms of anxiety encountered by the ontologically insecure person: engulfment, implosion, petrification.

1. ENGULFMENT

An argument occurred between two patients in the course of a session in an analytic group. Suddenly, one of the protagonists broke off the argument to say, "I can't go on. You are arguing in order to have the pleasure of triumphing over me. At best you win an argument. At worst you lose an argument. *I am arguing in order to preserve my existence.*"

This patient was a young man who I would say was sane, but, as he stated, his activity in the argument, as in the rest of his life, was not designed to gain gratification but to "preserve his existence." Now, one might say that if he did, in fact, really imagine that the loss of an argument would jeopardize his existence, then he was "grossly out of touch with reality" and was virtually psychotic. But this is simply to beg the question without making any contribution towards understanding the patient. It is, however, important to know that if you were to subject this patient to a type of psychiatric interrogation recommended in many psychiatric textbooks, within ten minutes his behaviour and speech would be revealing "signs" of psychosis. It is quite easy to evoke such "signs" from such a person whose threshold of basic security is so low that practically any relationship with another person, however tenuous or however apparently "harmless," threatens to overwhelm him.

A firm sense of one's own autonomous identity is required in order that one may be related as one human being to another. Otherwise, any and every relationship threatens the individual with loss of identity. One form this takes can be called engulfment. In this the individual dreads relatedness as such, with anyone or anything or, indeed, even with himself, because his uncertainty about the stability of his autonomy lays him open to the dread lest in any relationship he will lose his autonomy and identity. Engulfment is not simply envisaged as something that is liable to happen willy-nilly despite the individual's most active efforts to avoid it. The individual experiences himself as a man who is only saving himself from drowning by the most constant, strenuous, desperate activity. Engulfment is felt as a risk in being understood (thus grasped, comprehended), in being loved, or even simply in being seen. To be hated may be feared for other reasons, but to be hated as such is often less disturbing than to be destroyed, as it is felt, through being engulfed by love.

The main manœuvre used to preserve identity under pressure from the dread of engulfment is isolation. Thus, instead of the polarities of separateness and relatedness based on individual autonomy, there is the antithesis between complete loss of being by absorption into the other person (engulfment), and complete aloneness (isolation). There is no safe third possibility of a dialectical relationship between two persons, both sure of their own ground and, on this very basis, able to "lose themselves" in each other. Such merging of being can occur in an "authentic" way only when the individuals are sure of themselves. If a man hates himself, he may wish to lose himself in the other: then being engulfed by the other is an escape from himself. In the present case it is an ever-present possibility to be dreaded. It will be shown later, however, that what at one "moment" is most dreaded and strenuously avoided can change to what is most sought.

This anxiety accounts for one form of a so-called "negative therapeutic reaction" to apparently correct interpretation in psychotherapy. To be understood correctly is to be engulfed, to be enclosed, swallowed up, drowned, eaten up, smothered, stifled in or by another person's supposed all-embracing comprehension. It is lonely and painful to be always misunderstood, but there is at least from this point of view a measure of safety in isolation.

The other's love is, therefore, feared more than his hatred, or rather all love is sensed as a version of hatred. By being loved one is placed under an unsolicited obligation. In therapy with such a person, the last thing there is any point in is to pretend to more "love" or "concern" than one has. The more the therapist's own necessarily very complex motives for trying to "help" a person of this kind genuinely converge on a concern for him which is prepared to "let him be" and is not *in fact* engulfing or merely indifference, the more hope there will be in the horizon.

There are many images used to describe related ways in which identity is threatened which may be mentioned here, as closely related to the dread of engulfment, e.g., being buried, being drowned, being caught and dragged down into quicksand. The image of fire recurs repeatedly. Fire may be the uncertain flickering of the individual's own inner aliveness. It may be a destructive alien power which will devastate him. Some psychotics say in the acute phase that they are on fire, that their bodies are being burned up. A patient describes himself as cold and dry. Yet he dreads any warmth or wet. He will be engulfed by the fire or the water, and either way be destroyed.

2. IMPLOSION

This is the strongest word I can find for the extreme form of what Winnicott terms the *impingement* of reality. Impingement does not convey, however, the full terror of the experience of the world as liable at any moment to crash in and obliterate all identity, as a gas will rush in and obliterate a vacuum. The individual feels that, like the vacuum, he is empty. But this emptiness is him. Although in other ways he longs for the emptiness to be filled, he dreads the possibility of this happening because he has come to feel that all he can be is the awful nothingness of just this very vacuum. Any "contact" with reality is then in itself experienced as a dreadful threat because reality, as experienced from this position, is necessarily *implosive* and thus, as was relatedness in engulfment, *in itself* a threat to what identity the individual is able to suppose himself to have.

Reality, as such, threatening engulfment or implosion, is the persecutor.

In fact, we are all only two or three degrees Fahrenheit from experiences of this order. Even a slight fever, and the whole world can begin to take on a persecutory, impinging aspect.

3. PETRIFICATION AND DEPERSONALIZATION

In using the term "petrification," one can exploit a number of the meanings embedded in this word:

1. A particular form of terror, whereby one is petrified, i.e., turned to stone.
2. The dread of this happening: the dread, that is, of the possibility of turning, or being turned, from a live person into a dead thing, into a stone, into a robot, an automaton, without personal autonomy of action, an *it* without subjectivity.
3. The "magical" act whereby one may attempt to turn someone else into stone, by "petrifying" him; and, by extension, the act whereby one negates the other person's autonomy, ignores his feelings, regards him as a thing, kills the life in him. In this sense one may perhaps better say that one depersonalizes him, or reifies him. One treats him not as a person, as a free agent, but as an *it*.

Depersonalization is a technique that is universally used as a means of dealing with the other when he becomes too tiresome or disturbing. One no longer allows oneself to be responsive to his feelings and may be prepared to regard him and treat him as though he had no feelings. The people in focus here both tend to feel themselves as more or less depersonalized and tend to depersonalize others; they are constantly afraid of being depersonalized by others. The act of turning him into a thing is, *for him,* actually petrifying. In the face of being treated as an *it,* his own subjectivity drains away from him like blood from the face. Basically he requires constant confirmation from others of his own existence as a person.

A partial depersonalization of others is extensively practised in everyday life and is regarded as normal if not highly desirable. Most relationships are based on some partial depersonalizing tendency in so far as one treats the other not in terms of any awareness of who or what he might be in himself but as virtually an android robot playing a role or part in a large machine in which one too may be acting yet another part.

It is usual to cherish if not the reality, at least the illusion that there is a limited sphere of living free from this dehumanization. Yet it may be in just this sphere that the greater risk is felt, and the ontologically insecure person experiences this risk in highly potentiated form.

The risk consists in this: if one experiences the other as a free agent, one is open to the possibility of experiencing oneself as an *object* of his experience and thereby of feeling one's own subjectivity drained away. One is threatened with the possibility of becoming no more than a thing in the world of the other, without any life for oneself, without any being for oneself. In terms of such anxiety, the very act of experiencing the other as a person is felt as virtually suicidal. Sartre discusses this experience brilliantly in Part 3 of *Being and Nothingness*.

The issue is in principle straightforward. One may find oneself enlivened and the sense of one's own being enhanced by the other, or one may experience the other as deadening and impoverishing. A person may have come to anticipate that any possible relationship with another will have the latter consequences. Any other is then a threat to his "self" (his capacity to act autonomously) not by reason of anything he or she may do or not do specifically, but by reason of his or her very existence.

Some of the above points are illustrated in the life of James, a chemist, aged twenty-eight.

The complaint he made all along was that he could not become a "person." He had "no self." "I am only a response to other people, I have no identity of my own." He felt he was becoming more and more "a mythical person." He felt he had no weight, no substance of his own. "I am only a cork floating on the ocean."

This man was very concerned about not having become a person: he reproached his mother for this failure. "I was merely her emblem. She never recognized my identity." In contrast to his own belittlement of and uncertainty about himself, he was always on the brink of being overawed and crushed by the formidable reality that other people contained. In contrast to his own light weight, uncertainty, and insubstantiality, *they* were solid, decisive, emphatic, and substantial. He felt that in every way that mattered others were more "large scale" than he was.

At the same time, in practice he was not easily overawed. He used two chief manœuvres to preserve security. One was an outward compliance with the other. The second was an inner intellectual Medusa's head he turned on the other. Both manœuvres taken together safeguarded his own subjectivity which he had never to betray openly and which thus could never find direct and immediate expression for itself. Being secret, it was safe. Both techniques together were designed to avoid the dangers of being engulfed or depersonalized.

With his outer behaviour he forestalled the danger to which he was perpetually subject, namely that of becoming someone else's *thing*, by pretending to be no more than a cork. (After all, what safer thing to be in an ocean?) At the same time, however, he turned the other person into a thing in his own eyes, thus magically nullifying any danger to himself by secretly totally disarming the enemy. By destroying, in his own eyes, the other person as a person, he robbed the other of his power to crush him. By depleting him of his personal aliveness, that is, by seeing him as a piece of machinery rather than as a human being, he undercut the risk to himself of this aliveness either swamping him, imploding into his own emptiness, or turning him into a mere appendage.

This man was married to a very lively and vivacious woman, highly spirited, with a forceful personality and a mind of her own. He maintained a paradoxical relationship with her in which, in one sense, he was entirely alone and isolated and, in another sense, he was almost a parasite. He dreamt, for instance, that he was a clam stuck to his wife's body.

Just because he could dream thus, he had the more need to keep her at bay by contriving to see her as no more than a machine. He described her laughter, her anger, her sadness, with "clinical" precision, even going so far as to refer to her as "it," a practice that was rather chilling in its effect. "It then started to laugh." She was an "it" because everything she did was a predictable, determined response. He would, for instance, tell her (it) an ordinary funny joke and when she (it) laughed this indicated her (its) entirely "conditioned," robot-like nature, which he saw indeed in much the same terms as certain psychiatric theories would use to account for all human actions.

I was at first agreeably surprised by his apparent ability to reject and disagree with what I said as well as to agree with me. This seemed to indicate that he had more of a mind of his own than he perhaps realized and that he was not too frightened to display some measure of autonomy. However, it became evident that his apparent capacity to act as an autonomous person with me was due to his secret manœuvre of regarding me not as a live human being, a person in my own right with my own selfhood, but as a sort of robot interpreting device to which he fed input and which after a quick commutation came out with a verbal message to him. With this secret outlook on me as a thing he could appear to be a "person." What he could not sustain was a person-to-person relationship, experienced as such.

Dreams in which one or other of the above forms of dread is expressed are common in such persons. These dreams are not variations on the fears of being eaten which occur in ontologically secure persons. To be eaten does not necessarily mean to lose one's identity. Jonah was very much himself even within the belly of the whale. Few nightmares go so far as to call up anxieties about actual loss of identity, usually because most people, even in their dreams, still meet whatever dangers are to be encountered as persons who may perhaps be attacked or mutilated but whose basic existential core is not itself in jeopardy. In the classical nightmare the dreamer wakes up in terror. But this terror is not the dread of losing the "self." Thus a patient dreams of a fat pig which sits on his chest and threatens to suffocate him. He wakes in terror. At worst, in this nightmare, he is threatened with suffocation, but not with the dissolution of his very being.

The defensive method of turning the threatening mother- or breast-figure into a *thing* occurs in patients' dreams. One patient dreamt recurrently of a small black triangle which originated in a corner of his room and grew larger and larger until it seemed about to engulf him—whereupon he always awoke in great terror. This was a psychotic young man who stayed with my family for several months, and whom I was thus able to get to know rather well. There was only one situation as far as I could judge in which he could let himself "go" without anxiety at not recovering himself again, and that was in listening to jazz.

The fact that even in a dream the breast-figure has to be so depersonalized is a measure of its potential danger to the self, presumably on the basis of its frightening original personalizations and the failure of *a normal process of depersonalization.*

Medard Boss (1957a) gives examples of several dreams heralding psychosis. In one, the dreamer is engulfed by fire:

> A woman of hardly thirty years dreamt, at a time when she still felt completely healthy, that she was afire in the stables. Around her, the fire, an ever larger crust of lava was forming. Half from the outside and half from the inside her own body she could see how the fire was slowly becoming choked by this crust. Suddenly she was entirely outside this fire and, as if possessed, she beat the fire with a club to break the crust and to let some air in. But the dreamer soon got tired and slowly she (the fire) became extinguished. Four days after this dream she began to suffer from acute schizophrenia. In the details of the dream the dreamer had exactly predicted the special course of her psychosis. She became rigid at first and, in effect, encysted. Six weeks afterwards she defended herself once more with all her might against the choking of her life's fire, until finally she became completely extinguished both spiritually and mentally. Now, for some years, she has been like a burnt-out crater (p. 162).

In another example, petrification of others occurs, anticipating the dreamer's own petrification:

> . . . a girl of twenty-five years dreamt that she had cooked dinner for her family of five. She had just served it and she

now called her parents and her brothers and sisters to dinner. Nobody replied. Only her voice returned as if it were an echo from a deep cave. She found the sudden emptiness of the house uncanny. She rushed upstairs to look for her family. In the first bedroom, she could see her two sisters sitting on two beds. In spite of her impatient calls they remained in an unnaturally rigid position and did not even answer her. She went up to her sisters and wanted to shake them. Suddenly she noticed that they were stone statues. She escaped in horror and rushed into her mother's room. Her mother too had turned into stone and was sitting inertly in her armchair staring into the air with glazed eyes. The dreamer escaped into the room of her father. He stood in the middle of it. In her despair she rushed up to him and, desiring his protection, she threw her arms round his neck. But he too was made of stone and, to her utter horror, he turned into sand when she embraced him. She awoke in absolute terror, and was so stunned by the dream experience that she could not move for some minutes. This same horrible dream was dreamt by the patient on four successive occasions within a few days. At that time she was apparently the picture of mental and physical health. Her parents used to call her the sunshine of the whole family. Ten days after the fourth repetition of the dream, the patient was taken ill with an acute form of schizophrenia displaying severe catatonic symptoms. She fell into a state which was remarkably similar to the physical petrification of her family that she had dreamt about. She was now overpowered in waking life by behaviour patterns that in her dreams she had merely observed in other persons (pp. 162–3).

It seems to be a general law that at some point those very dangers most dreaded can themselves be encompassed to forestall their actual occurrence. Thus, to forgo one's autonomy becomes the means of secretly safeguarding it; to play possum, to feign death, becomes a means of preserving one's aliveness (see Oberndorf, 1950). To turn oneself into a stone becomes a way of not being turned into a stone by someone else. "Be thou hard," exhorts Nietzsche. In a sense that Nietzsche did not, I believe, himself intend, to be stony hard and thus far dead forestalls the danger of being turned into a dead thing by another person. Thoroughly to understand oneself (engulf oneself) is a defense against the risk involved in being sucked into the whirlpool of another person's way of comprehending oneself. To consume oneself by one's own love prevents the possibility of being consumed by another.

It seems also that the preferred method of attack on the other is based on the same principle as the attack felt to be implicit in the other's relationship to oneself. Thus, the man who is frightened of his own subjectivity being swamped, impinged upon, or congealed by the other is frequently to be found attempting to swamp, to impinge upon, or to kill the other person's subjectivity. The process involves a vicious circle. The more one attempts to preserve one's autonomy and identity by nullifying the specific human individuality of the other, the more it is felt to be necessary to continue to do so, because with each denial of the other person's ontological status, one's own ontological security is decreased, the threat to the self from the other is potentiated and hence has to be even more desperately negated.

In this lesion in the sense of personal autonomy there is both a failure to sustain the sense of oneself as a person with the other, and a failure to sustain it alone. There is a failure to sustain a sense of one's own being without the presence of other people. It is a failure *to be* by oneself, a failure to exist alone. As James put it, "Other people supply me with my existence." This appears to be in direct contradiction to the aforementioned dread that other people will deprive him of his existence. But contradictory or absurd as it may be, these two attitudes existed in him side by side, and are indeed entirely characteristic of this type of person.

The capacity to experience oneself as autonomous means that one has really come to realize that one is a separate person from everyone else. No matter how deeply I am committed in joy or suffering to someone else, he is not me, and I am not him. However lonely or sad one may be, one can exist alone. The fact that the other person in his own actuality is not me, is set against the equally real fact that my attachment to him is a part of me. If he dies or goes away, he has gone, but my attachment to him persists. But in the last resort I cannot die another person's death for him, nor can he die my death. For that matter, as Sartre comments on this thought of Heidegger's, he cannot love for me or make my decisions, and I likewise cannot do this for him. In short, he cannot be me, and I cannot be him.

If the individual does not feel himself to be autonomous this means that he can experience neither his separateness from, nor his relatedness to, the other in the usual way. A lack of sense of autonomy implies that one feels one's being to be bound up in the other, or that the other is bound up in oneself, in a sense that transgresses the actual possibilities within the structure of human relatedness. It means that a feeling that one is in a position of ontological dependency on the other (i.e., dependent on the other for one's very being), is substituted for a sense of relatedness and attachment to him based on genuine mutuality. Utter detachment and isolation are regarded as the only alternatives to a clam- or vampire-like attachment in which the other person's life-blood is necessary for one's own survival, and yet is a threat to one's survival. Therefore, the polarity is between complete isolation or complete merging of identity rather than between separateness and relatedness. The individual oscillates perpetually between the two extremes, each equally unfeasible. He comes to live rather like those mechanical toys which have a positive tropism that impels them towards a stimulus until they reach a specific point, whereupon a built-in negative tropism directs them away until the positive tropism takes over again, this oscillation being repeated *ad infinitum.*

Other people were necessary for his existence, said James. Another patient, in the same basic dilemma, behaved in the following way: he maintained himself in isolated detachment from the world for months, living alone in a single room, existing frugally on a few savings, day-dreaming. But in doing this, he began to feel he was dying inside; he was becoming more and more empty, and observed "a progressive impoverishment of my life mode." A great deal of his pride and self-esteem was implicated in thus existing on his own, but as his state of depersonalization progressed he would emerge into social life for a brief foray in order to get a "dose" of other people, but "not an overdose." He was like an alcoholic who goes on sudden drinking orgies between dry spells, except that in his case his addiction, of which he was as frightened and ashamed as any repentant alcoholic or drug-addict, was to other people. Within a short while, he would come to feel that he was in danger of being caught up or trapped in the circle he had entered and he would withdraw again into his own isolation in a confusion of frightened hopelessness, suspicion, and shame.

Some of the points discussed above are illustrated in the following two cases:

CASE 1. ANXIETY AT FEELING ALONE

Mrs. R.'s presenting difficulty was a dread of being in the street (agoraphobia). On closer inspection, it became clear that her anxiety arose when she began to feel on her own in the street or elsewhere. She could *be* on her own, as long as she did not feel that she was really alone.

Briefly, her story was as follows: she was an only and a lonely child. There was no open neglect or hostility in her family. She felt, however, that her parents were always too engrossed in each other for either of them ever to take notice of her. She grew up wanting to fill this hole in her life but never succeeded in becoming self-sufficient, or absorbed in her own world. Her longing was always to be important and significant *to someone else*. There always had to be someone else. Preferably she wanted to be loved and admired, but, if not, then to be hated was much to be preferred to being unnoticed. She wanted to be *significant* to someone else in whatever capacity, in contrast to her abiding memory of herself as a child that she did not really matter to her parents, that they neither loved nor hated, admired nor were ashamed of her very much.

In consequence, she tried looking at herself in her mirror but never managed to convince herself that she was *somebody*. She never got over being frightened if there was no one there.

She grew into a very attractive girl and was married at seventeen to the first man who really noticed this. Characteristically, it seemed to her, her parents had not noticed that any turmoil had been going on in their daughter until she announced that she was engaged. She was triumphant and self-confident under the warmth of her husband's attentions. But he was an army officer and was shortly posted abroad. She was not able to go with him. At this separation she experienced severe panic.

We should note that her reaction to her husband's absence was not depression or sadness in which she pined or yearned for him. It was panic (as I would suggest) because of the dissolution of something in her, which owed its existence to the presence of her husband and his continued attentions. She was a flower that withered in the absence of one day's rain. However, help came to her through a sudden illness of her mother. She received an urgent plea for help from her father, asking her to come to nurse her mother. For the next year, during her mother's illness, she had never been, as she put it, so much herself. She was the pivot of the household. There was not a trace of panic until after her mother's death when the prospect of leaving the place where she had at last come to mean so much, to join her husband, was very much in her mind. Her experience of the last year had made her feel for the first time that she was now her parents' child. Against this, being her husband's wife was now somehow superfluous.

Again, one notes the absence of grief at her mother's death. At this time she began to reckon up the chances of her being alone in the world. Her mother had died; then there would be her father; possibly her husband: "beyond that–nothing." This did not depress her, it frightened her.

She then joined her husband abroad and led a gay life for a few years. She craved for all the attention he could give her but this became less and less. She was restless and unsatisfied. Their marriage broke up and she returned to live in a flat in London with her father. While continuing to stay with her father she became the mistress and model of a sculptor. In this way she had lived for several years before I saw her when she was twenty-eight.

This is the way she talked of the street: "In the street people come and go about their business. You seldom meet anyone who recognizes you; even if they do, it is just a nod and they pass on or at most you have a few minutes' chat. Nobody knows who you are. Everyone's engrossed in themselves. No one cares about you." She gave examples of people fainting and everyone's casualness about it. "No one gives a damn." It was in this setting and with these considerations in mind that she felt anxiety.

This anxiety was at being in the street alone or rather at feeling on her own. If she went out with or met someone who really knew her, she felt no anxiety.

In her father's flat she was often alone but there it was different. There she never felt *really* on her own. She made his breakfast. Tidying up the beds, washing up, was protracted as long as possible. The middle of the day was a drag. But she didn't mind too much. "Everything was familiar." There was her father's chair and his pipe rack. There was a picture of her mother on the wall looking down on her. It was as though all these familiar objects somehow illumined the house with the presence of the people who possessed and used them or had done so as a part of their lives. Thus, although she was by herself at home, she was always able to have someone with her in a magical way. But this magic was dispelled in the noise and anonymity of the busy street.

An insensitive application of what is often supposed to be the classical psychoanalytic theory of hysteria to this patient might attempt to show this woman as unconsciously libidinally bound to her father; with, consequently, unconscious guilt and unconscious need and/or fear of punishment. Her failure to develop lasting libidinal relationships away from her father would seem to support the first view, along with her decision to live with him, to take her mother's place, as it were, and the fact that she spent most of her day, as a woman of twenty-eight, actually thinking about him. Her devotion to her mother in her last illness would be partly the consequences of unconscious guilt at her unconscious ambivalence to her mother; and her anxiety at her mother's death would be anxiety at her unconscious wish for her mother's death coming true. And so on.[3]

However, the central or pivotal issue in this patient's life is not to be discovered in her "unconscious"; it is lying quite open for her to see, as well as for us (although this is not to say that there are not many things about herself that this patient does not realize).

The pivotal point around which all her life is centred is her *lack of ontological autonomy*. If she is not in the actual presence of another person who knows her, or if she cannot succeed in evoking this person's presence in his absence, her sense of her own identity drains away from her. Her panic is at the fading away of her being. She is like Tinker Bell. In order to exist she needs someone else to believe in her existence. How necessary that her lover should be a sculptor and that she should be his model! How inevitable, given this basic premise of her existence, that when her existence was not recognized she should be suffused with anxiety. For her, *esse* is *percipi*; to be seen, that is, not as an anonymous passer-by or casual acquaintance. It was just that form of seeing which *petrified* her. If she was seen *as* an anonymity, *as* no one who especially mattered or as a *thing*, then she *was* no one in particular. She was as she was seen to be. If there was no one to see her, at the moment, she had to try to conjure up someone (father, mother, husband, lover, at different times in her life) to whom she felt she mattered, for whom she was a *person*, and to imagine herself in his or her presence. If this person on whom her being depended went away or died, it was not a matter for grief, it was a matter for panic.

One cannot transpose her central problem into "the

[3] For extremely valuable psychoanalytic contributions to apparently "hysterical" symptom-formation, see Segal (1954).

unconscious." If one discovers that she has an unconscious phantasy of being a prostitute, this does not explain her anxiety about street-walking, or her preoccupation with women who fall in the street and are not helped to get on their feet again. The conscious phantasy is, on the contrary, to be explained by and understood in terms of the central issue implicating her self-being, her being-for-herself. Her fear of being alone is not a "defense" against incestuous libidinal phantasies or masturbation. She had incestuous phantasies. *These phantasies were a defense against the dread of being alone,* as was her whole "fixation" on being a daughter. They were a means of overcoming her anxiety at being by herself. The unconscious phantasies of this patient would have an entirely different meaning if her basic existential position were such that she had a starting-point in herself that she could leave behind, as it were, in pursuit of gratification. As it was, *her sexual life and phantasies were efforts, not primarily to gain gratification, but to seek first ontological security.* In love-making an illusion of this security was achieved, and on the basis of this illusion gratification was possible.

It would be a profound mistake to call this woman narcissistic in any proper application of the term. She was unable to fall in love with her own reflection. It would be a mistake to translate her problem into phases of psychosexual development, oral, anal, genital. She grasped at sexuality as at a straw as soon as she was "of age." She was not frigid. Orgasm could be physically gratifying if she was temporarily secure in the prior ontological sense. In intercourse with someone who loved her (and she was capable of believing in being loved by another), she achieved perhaps her best moments. But they were short-lived. She could not be alone or let her lover be alone with her.

Her need to be taken notice of might facilitate the application of a further cliché to her, that she was an exhibitionist. Once more, such a term is only valid if it is understood existentially. Thus, and this will be discussed in greater detail subsequently, she "showed herself off" while never "giving herself away." That is, she exhibited herself while always holding herself in (inhibited). She was, therefore, always alone and lonely although superficially her difficulty was not in being together with other people; her difficulty was *least in evidence* when she was most together with another person. But it is clear that her realization of the autonomous existence of other people was really quite as tenuous as her belief in her own autonomy. If they were not there, they ceased to exist for her. Orgasm was a means of possessing herself, by holding in her arms the man who possessed her. But she could not be herself, by herself, and so could not really be herself at all.

CASE 2

A most curious phenomenon of the personality, one which has been observed for centuries, but which has not yet received its full explanation, is that in which the individual seems to be the vehicle of a personality that is not his own. Someone else's personality seems to "possess" him and to be finding expression through his words and actions, whereas the individual's own personality is temporarily "lost" or "gone." This happens with all degrees of malignancy. There seem to be all degrees of the same basic process from the simple, benign observation that so-and-so "takes after his father," or "That's her mother's temper coming out in her," to the extreme distress of the person who finds himself under a compulsion to take on the characteristics of a personality he may hate and/or feel to be entirely alien to his own.

This phenomenon is one of the most important in occasioning disruption in the sense of one's own identity when it occurs unwanted and compulsively. The dread of this occurring is one factor in the fear of engulfment and implosion. The individual may be afraid to like anyone, for he finds that he is under a compulsion to become like anyone he likes.

The way in which the individual's self and personality are profoundly modified even to the point of threatened loss of his or her own identity and sense of reality by engulfment by such an alien sub-identity, is illustrated in the following case:

Mrs. D., a woman of forty, presented the initial complaint of vague but intense fear. She said she was frightened of everything, "even of the sky." She complained of an abiding sense of dissatisfaction, of unaccountable accesses of anger towards her husband, in particular of a "lack of a sense of responsibility." Her fear was "as though somebody was trying to rise up inside and was trying to get out of me." She was very afraid that she was like her mother, whom she hated. What she called "unreliability" was a feeling of bafflement and bewilderment which she related to the fact that nothing she did had ever seemed to please her parents. If she did one thing and was told it was wrong, she would do another thing and would find that they still said that was wrong. She was unable to discover, as she put it, "what they wanted me to be." She reproached her parents for this above all, that they hadn't given her any way of knowing who or what she really was or had to become. She could be neither bad nor good with any "reliability" because her parents were, or she felt they were, completely unpredictable and unreliable in their expressions of love or hatred, approval or disapproval. In retrospect, she concluded that they hated her; but at the time, she said, she was too baffled by them and too anxious to discover what she was expected to be to have been able to hate them, let alone love them. She now said that she was looking for "comfort." She was looking for a line from me that would give her an indication of the path she was to follow. She found my non-directive attitude particularly hard to tolerate since it seemed to her to be so clearly a repetition of her father's attitude: "Ask no questions and you'll be told no lies." For a spell, she became subject to compulsive thinking, in which she was under a necessity to ask such questions as, "What is this for?" or "Why is this?" and to provide herself with the answers. She interpreted this to herself as her effort to get comfort from her own thoughts since she could derive comfort from no one. She began to be intensely depressed and to make numerous complaints about her feelings, saying how childish they were. She spoke a great deal about how sorry she was for herself.

Now it seemed to me "she" was not really sorry for her own true self. She sounded to me much more like a querulous mother complaining about a difficult child. Her mother, indeed, seemed to be "coming out of her" all the time, complaining about "her" childishness. Not only was this so as regards the complaints which "she" was making about herself, but in other respects as well. For instance, like her mother, she kept screaming at her husband and child; like her mother,[4] she hated everyone; and like her mother she was for ever crying. In fact, life was a misery to her by the fact that she could never be herself but was always being her mother. She knew, however, that when she felt lonely, lost, frightened, and bewildered she was more her true self. She knew also that

[4] That is, like her notion of what her mother was. I never met her mother and have no idea whether her phantasies of her mother bore any resemblance to her mother as a real person.

she gave her complicity to becoming angry, hating, screaming, crying, or querulous, for if she worked herself up into being like that (i.e., being her mother), she did not feel frightened any more (at the expense, it was true, of being no longer herself). However, the backwash of this manœuvre was that she was oppressed, when the storm had passed, by a sense of futility (at not having been herself) and a hatred of the person she had been (her mother) and of herself for her self-duplicity. To some extent this patient, once she had become aware of this false way of overcoming the anxiety she was exposed to when she was herself, had to decide whether avoiding experiencing such anxiety, by avoiding being herself, was a cure worse than her dis-ease. The frustration she experienced with me, which called out intense hatred of me, was not fully to be explained by the frustration of libidinal or aggressive drives in the transference, but rather it was what one could term the existential frustration that arose out of the fact that I, by withholding from her the "comfort" she sought to derive from me, in that *I did not tell her what she was to be,* was imposing upon her the necessity to make her own decision about the person she was to become. Her feeling that she had been denied her birthright because her parents had not discharged their responsibility towards her by giving her a definition of herself that could act as her starting-point in life was intensified by my refusal to offer this "comfort." But only by withholding it was it possible to provide a setting in which she could take this responsibility into herself.

In this sense, therefore, the task in psychotherapy was to make, using Jasper's expression, an appeal to the freedom of the patient. A good deal of the skill in psychotherapy lies in the ability to do this effectively.

REFERENCES

Boss, M., *Analysis of Dreams,* London, Rider & Co., 1957.

Oberndorf, C. P., "The Role of Anxiety in Depersonalization," *International Journal of Psychoanalysis,* 1950, Vol. 31.

Segal, H., "Schizoid Mechanisms Underlying Phobia Formation," *International Journal of Psychoanalysis,* 1954, Vol. 35.

Trilling, Lionel, *The Opposing Self,* London, 1955, Secker & Warburg.

PSYCHOTHERAPY, EXISTENCE, AND RELIGION

by THOMAS HORA *

I

The prevailing trend in present-day psychotherapy is to expand the psychodynamic and socio-dynamic perspectives into a broader existential viewpoint, based on the contributions of the schools of phenomenological anthropology and particularly ontology. These schools of thought illuminate the human being and his existence in an all-encompassing and deeply meaningful way and lead us to reconsider the objectives of psychotherapy in terms of broadening its scope beyond personality integration toward *ontic integration*.

In the psychotherapeutic situation as in all human encounters, patients appear not only as samples of various psychic mechanisms or disease entities, but above and beyond that, as people with specific ways of experiencing life, specific ways of responding to stimuli coming from the environment, and specific ways of responding to deep stirrings of inner potentialities which demand realization within a *limited and unknown time span*. According to Heidegger's ontological thesis, human beings have specific ways of "being-in-this-world."

These ontic characteristics apply to the total being of

* THOMAS HORA, M.D., is supervising psychiatrist and faculty member, Postgraduate Center for Psychotherapy; adjunct attending psychiatrist and Supervisor of Group Psychotherapy, Hillside Hospital. He was the recipient of the Karen Horney Award in 1959.

man as rated and described by Binswanger (1) as *being-able-to-be, being-allowed-to-be* and *having-to-be-in-this-world.*

Being-able-to-be relates to man's capacity to know that he exists. This consciousness implies certain ontic freedom and responsibility in relation to one's own existence.

Being-allowed-to-be refers to the phenomenon of love as being-beyond-the-world, which is one of the dual modes of existence. This is an extension of Buber's (2) depiction of the "I–Thou" relationship. *Being-beyond-the-world* refers to the experimental transcendence of space, time, object and subject in the act of love, or better, in the "happening" of love.

Having-to-be refers to the fact that man is "thrown" *(geworfen)* into this world with certain inherent but unknown potentialities which require realization. This is his fate.

These ontic characteristics apply to the total being of man as existent but can be observed and experienced in every function of the human organism as well.

The function of respiration can serve as an example. *Being-able-to-be* means here that man is able to know that he is breathing. He has a certain amount of freedom in relation to this function and he is responsible toward it, that is, he must live in such a way as not to lose his breath, or else he experiences discomfort; that is, a certain dispnoic tightness in the chest, *"angustia"* or anxiety. This could be considered a physiological equivalent of *existential guilt.* We could say that man is here guilty toward his own *"being-able-to-breathe."*

Being-allowed-to-be can be understood in reference to respiration as the blissful condition of *eupnea* when man is so comfortable that he is unaware of his breathing and feels *at one* with the air around him. Here, the subject-object split between man and air or man and respiration is transcended.

Having-to-be is clearly expressed in the respiratory function by the absolute necessity of man to accept his condition of existence as a breathing organism. Man is "thrown" into this world and there is nothing he can do about it.

It is possible to conceive of man's relationship to the air around him as a biologic and ontologic model of all his other relationships. The principle may be described as the unencumbered, effortless coming and going of air into his lungs in complete freedom and harmony with the fundamental nature of his being, as manifested in his very life.

It appears that man is placed in a reverent relationship to air. He loves it, he must love it; he needs it, he craves it and yet he must *let it* come and go freely. Any kind of grasping, holding, clinging, or controlling of it leads to disturbances experienced in the core of his existence. Just as air is immanent and transcendent to man, so man is intimately related to all things and beings of this world. His proprioceptive and extroceptive equipment makes it possible for him to perceive and experience the outside world within himself and project his inside world unto the outside in a creative fashion. Thus, giving form and expression to his *individuality* and *unity* with the world around him. Man is simultaneously *apart* and yet *part* of the total Scheme of Things.

It seems rather self-evident that the moment we assume an ontological perspective in relation to man, we stand on metaphysical ground, that is, we are confronted with the Mystery of Being (3). This means that psychotherapy is here on common territory with religion. It is understandable that existential psychotherapy would be meaningless and ineffectual if practiced on a purely conceptual basis. This appears to be equally true of religious guidance and pastoral counselling.

It is important to emphasize the difference between learning about, reading about, talking about ontic conditions and experiencing them. The former perspectives relate to a form of knowledge which is *discursive-inductive* (that is, intellectual, conceptual, or inferential-mediate, abstract-symbolic); the latter—direct experience—refers to a knowledge which is *phenomenological-empirical* (that is, direct-experiential, immediate-concrete). It is this possibility of phenomenological-empirical knowledge which forms the basis of Heidegger's concept of being-in-the-world as transcendence. The significance of this lies in the overcoming of the subject-object dichotomy of knowledge, and elimination of the gap between the self and the world. Furthermore, it leads us to the understanding of subjectivity as transcendence. Mental diseases and their somatic equivalents can thus be understood as resulting from modification or deviations from the fundamental or essential structure of being-in-the-world as transcendence. In other words, man suffers from being in disharmony with the fundamental Order of Things. (Parenthetically, we can say that when Adam and Eve partook of The Tree of Knowledge, they initiated an epistemological problem for all humanity which continues to give rise to an endless chain of tragic complications.)

II

The chief characteristic of the existential therapeutic process is a "being-together" of the therapist and patient in the spirit of "letting-be" (which must not be mistaken for "leaving alone"). The principle of "letting-be" is reminiscent of Albert Schweitzer's "Reverence for Life" (11). Heidegger speaks of "letting-be" as a mode of participating in a relationship in such a way that "all that is, could reveal itself in the essence of its being." The essence of a human being is his true self. Truth can reveal itself only under conditions of freedom. Freedom is letting-be; therefore, the essence of truth is freedom. Essence is the inner potentiality of something existing.

The concept of "letting-be" means the affirmation of the existence of another person. It connotes an attitude which favors the free emergence of the inherent creative potentialities of all. "Letting-be" expresses a therapeutic attitude of the highest ethical order, inasmuch as it refrains from treating the patient as an object of exploration and manipulation, but relates itself to the patient as *an existent* in an affirmative way. Affirmation of a person's freedom to be what he is is an act of love. Love is reverence. Being with a person in the spirit of "letting-be" makes it possible to comprehend this person in a *transjective,* that is, experiential way. The experience of being understood under such conditions is therapeutically beneficial in itself, for it is a transcendental experience (8).

The task of the therapist is not so much to cure the patient, as to perceive and comprehend the patient's specific mode of being-in-the-world, and by helping him become aware of the implications, enable him to alter it in accordance with his own existential choices and decisions. Changes in the psychodynamic picture are by-products of the changes which occur in the patient as a result of having altered his mode of being-in-this-world.

From an ontological point of view, psychopathology can be understood as a complex set of reactions elicited by *the silent voice of the existential conscience* reminding man of the fact that he has separated himself from the authentic ground of existence and that he has usurped for himself the right to live in opposition to the world; that he abuses his thinking capacity in the direction away from the world rather than fulfilling his existential task in using his gift of consciousness to come into harmony with the fundamental Order of Things. Suffering reminds man that his mind is not mindful of the "power which posited it" (9) and by the grace of which it exists.

This can be illustrated by considering the issue of *temporality*. Striving for security, success or attainment of a desired goal; expectation of an event; anticipation of a meeting, and in general, most life situations involve a certain experiential relationship to time. The discomfort of anxiety and of symptoms in general is connected with man's tendency to be in conflict with time. This conflict can be experienced as tension, restlessness, irritability, or depression. Striving to make time pass faster can give rise to agitation, anxiousness, and various somatic concomitant manifestations (such as heart palpitations, hunger, trembling). Striving to cling to the past and ward off the future can lead to melancholia, depression, as, for instance, in mourning which Heidegger so aptly calls "remaining with the dead" (7).

In the somatic sphere, a clinging to the past may take the form of constipation. Diarrhea may express a temporality which is ahead of itself. It may be a sign of inward hurry, running forward in thought. The digestive tract may be accelerated in its function in accordance with the acceleration of experienced time. The result can be poor digestion of food and loss of weight. Running forward in thought can be an attempt at warding off a threat which may be considered a form of defensive mobilization. It may be due to an unwillingness to accept insecurity concerning the future. It may express a striving to avoid the unfathomable.

It takes courage, commitment and faith to let the future come freely and to remain openly accepting toward it. Man is confronted with vital decisions, the outcomes of which are forever unknown. He calculates probabilities according to his own inner standards. Every step into the future confronts him with the necessity of decision, commitment and acceptance of existential dread.

Existential dread can be either repressed or fought against, or accepted in simple humility.

What is repressed is only hidden from consciousness, but not from existence. On the organismic level, the repressed has its free and unhampered sway. Fighting against existential dread makes it worse. It exaggerates suffering. Acceptance of existential dread as an ontic condition leads to tranquil humility and a realistic attitude toward what is.

Life flows like a river and man has the ontic freedom to swim with the current or struggle against it in either direction, upstream or downstream. He will only find peace if he will choose to swim in harmony with the current, that is, if he will be mindful of the ontically determined temporality of his existence.

It should be noted that the therapist's task is described as that of perceiving and comprehending, and that the doctor-patient relationship is conceived of as an *"inter-human encounter."* This broadly transcends the concepts of transference and counter-transference. The existential encounter implies a real meeting of real people in a mutual endeavor to understand each other through communing with one another. The therapeutic process is based on existential communication which is characterized by experiential perceptiveness and authenticity of response between doctor and patient.

Solowieff (12) expresses the essence of existential communication most beautifully in saying:

Friend, can't you see or gather
That Truth is only
What in silent whisper
One heart tells another?[1]

It is through existential communication that the patient is helped to develop a capacity for *dialogic* relation. Martin Buber's contribution to psychotherapy is as significant as his contributions to philosophy, religion, ethics, education, and other fields. His subtle and penetrating differentiation between monologic and dialogic existence reaches the very core of the human predicament and illumines the central issue of psychotherapy as well as religion and mental health. He points on the one hand to the nature of *sin as remaining with oneself* (4), on the other hand to the necessity of fulfilling the essential condition of human existence in the "dialogic meeting of the One with the Other."

The existential encounter between doctor and patient becomes the medium which enables the patient to be aware of his own existential process and learn to remain open to it by accepting the "holy insecurity" (Buber) which authentic existence requires. The self-alienated, isolated, striving and conflicted individual develops the capacity to transcend the boundaries of himself in an existential meeting with his fellow man, which Buber describes as "mutual spiritual inclusion" and Gabriel Marcel calls "intersubjectivity" (10). In a similar vein, Viktor von Weizsaecker (14) talks of "transjective" comprehending of the other, and the Zen doctrine teaches the transcendence of the subject-object split.

Martin Buber's "holy insecurity" or existential anxiety is the dynamic point where psychotherapy and religion meet on common ground. For here both, existential psy-

[1] Translation by T. H.

chotherapy and religion, are confronted with the task of helping man accept the "human condition" and through genuine acceptance transcend his despair and separation from the world, thus reaching an authentic existence which is ontically integrated.

Existential anxiety drives man to seek manifold modes of protection and avenues of escape. Such defensive strivings lead to inauthentic modes of existence and disorganization of the personality, that is, mental disorders of various kinds and degrees. Defensive strivings cripple man's existence by robbing him of his freedom and creative spontaneity. *Seeking to escape from the dread of losing his life, man lives in dread of losing his defenses.* He clings to them rigidly and becomes increasingly immobilized by them. Finally, that which he clings to, clings to him.

Such a tragically paradoxical dilemma was expressed by a successful businessman, suffering from coronary heart disease and high blood pressure, in the following way: "I know that my life is a 'rat race' and it is killing me, but I am afraid to stop because I might become a nobody and die." After a while he added: "It looks like fear of death is driving me to commit suicide."

It is understandable that the religious attitudes and practices of disorganized, fragmented human beings will of necessity be inauthentic and lacking in meaningfulness. Defensive strivings create barriers not only between man and his fellow man, but also between man and God as well.

In connection with this, Martin Buber (5) writes:

> If man tries to get rid of his insecurity by constructing a defensive armor to protect himself from the world, he has added to his exposedness. Conversely, if he accepts his exposed condition and remains open to those things which meet him, he has turned his exposedness into "Holy Insecurity."

The defensive man becomes literally rigid with fear. He sets between himself and the world a rigid religious dogma, a rigid system of philosophy, a rigid political belief and commitment to a group, and a rigid wall of personal values and habits. The open man, however, accepts his fear and relaxes into it.

Paul Tillich's (13) concept of "absolute faith" and of the "God beyond God" is very close and perhaps identical with Buber's position for he describes it as a state of being, or a way of relating to reality characterized by courage, acceptance and full commitment.

The fragmentation, disorganization, isolation, and unauthenticity of a defensive human being is often progressive in character. In such cases it may lead to existential crises of various degrees. It is at such critical points of anxiety and despair where man, having reached the limits of his endurance, becomes ready to surrender himself to God in the spirit of *Fiat voluntas Tua,* or seek psychotherapy in a serious and accepting way.

One patient who, prior to coming for treatment considered himself religiously indifferent, expressed his existential crisis in a dream the following way:

I dreamt that I left home and found myself in a strange city in a foreign country. I discovered to my dismay that I didn't know the language of the people, I couldn't remember where I came from, I didn't know where I was heading. I experienced a sense of isolation, helplessness and anxiety. I was walking the streets aimlessly hoping to remember where I came from. But to no avail. At the height of my despair, I cried out: "God help me." Then a single rain drop which impressed me as a tear drop fell from the sky and in the course of its falling, it reflected the sun in all the colors of the rainbow. I felt overwhelmed by this sight. The scene shifted and I found myself on my knees in a church. In the moment of awakening, the thought occurred to me that the meaning of life is to reflect in oneself the divine light, like the rain drop reflected the sun in the course of its falling from the sky.

In situations of existential crises, man often becomes open to meet his God and fellow man, and commit himself to dialogic existence. This is the point, where suddenly existence and religion become authentic and directly meaningful in an experiential sense. The reality of God is grasped in a direct phenomenological-empirical way with the "inward eye." As Meister Eckhardt said: "I see God with the same eye as God sees me." (6)

REFERENCES

1. Binswanger, L.: *Grundformen und Erkenntnis-menschlichen Daseins.* Zürich, 1942.
2. Buber, M.: *I and Thou.* New York: Charles Scribner's Sons, 1937.
3. ———: *Between Man and Man.* Boston: Beacon Press, 1955.
4. ———: As quoted by Maurice Friedman in *The Life of Dialogue.* Chicago: University of Chicago Press, 1956.
5. ———: *Ibid.*
6. Eckhardt: *Writings and Sermons in Meister Eckhardt.* Translated by R. B. Blakney. New York: Harper & Bros. (Torchbook), 1957.
7. Heidegger, M.: *Existence and Being.* Chicago: Henry Regnery Co., 1949.
8. Hora, T.: Existential Communication and Psychotherapy. *Psychoanalysis,* Vol. 5, No. 4, Winter 1957.
9. Kierkegaard, S.: *Fear and Trembling.* Translated by Walter Lowrie. New York: Doubleday & Co., 1954.
10. Marcel, G.: *The Philosophy of Existence.* London: Harvill, 1948.
11. Schweitzer, A.: *The Ethics of Reverence for Life: Christendom,* Vol. 1, No. 2, 1936.
12. Solowieff: As quoted by Binswanger in *Grundformen und Erkenntnis-menschlichen Daseins. Ibid.*
13. Tillich, P.: *The Courage to Be.* New Haven: Yale University Press, 1956.
14. Weizsaecker, V. von: *Zwischen Medizin und Philosophie.* Göttingen: Vandenhoeck & Ruprecht, 1957.

"DASEINSANALYSIS" AND PSYCHOTHERAPY

by MEDARD BOSS *

Modern Psychotherapy in Need of a Basis

All problems, answers and resulting actions are invariably guided by the prescientific notions about the general nature and goal of man which each investigator carries within himself. No matter whether he is explicitly aware of his "philosophical" assumptions or whether he rejects all "philosophy" and attempts to be a "pure empiricist," the fact remains that such more or less hidden philosophical presuppositions, which are at the root of all science, are of fundamental importance. Up to now modern psychologists believed that their therapeutic approaches had found a sound basis in terms of their various psychodynamic theories about the human psyche. Freud thought of the human being as a telescope-like psychic apparatus; Reich, Alexander and Horney on the other hand attempt to explain all instinctual reactions in terms of a Total I or a Total Personality; for Jung the "Psyche" is a self-regulating libidinal system controlled by the archetypes of the "Collective Unconscious"; Sul-

* Medard Boss studied under Freud and Jung and worked at the Psychiatric Clinic at Zürich under Professor Eugen Bleuler. He is at present professor of Psychoanalysis at the School of Medicine, University of Zürich. He is the author of a number of books in the field of psychotherapy and psychosomatics, some of which are available in English, such as *The Analysis of Dreams* and *Meaning and Content of Sexual Perversions: A daseinanalytic approach to the psychopathology of the phenomenon of love.*

livan conceives of man as the product of interactions between him and his fellowmen; Fromm and others speak of man as a Self molded by society. Yet all these modern anthropologic theories can't possibly warrant an adequate understanding of the psychotherapeutic processes. For none of them answers what ought to be the first and foremost questions: what would have to be the nature of such a "Psyche," such a psychic apparatus, such a human I or Self or total personality in order that something like a mere perception of an object and of a human being, or even something like object relations and interpersonal and social relations, be at all possible? How should a telescope-like psychic apparatus or a self-regulating libidinal system be able to perceive or understand the meaning of anything, or to love or to hate somebody? Even less can such anonymous psychic structures or forces develop a transference or a resistance in the course of psychotherapy. Yet all these phenomena are central factors for a true healing.

MARTIN HEIDEGGER'S "DASEINSANALYSIS" REVEALING MAN'S BASIC NATURE

The eminent importance of the "Daseinsanalysis" in the sense of Martin Heidegger's fundamental ontology for psychology and psychotherapy lies in the fact that it helps overcome just these shortcomings of the basic anthropologic concepts of our psychological thinking, shortcomings which until now actually kept us groping in the dark. The "Daseinsanalysis" is able to do so because its concept of man's basic nature is nothing more or less than an explicit articulation of that understanding of man which has always guided our therapeutic actions, independent of all secondary theories, although secretly only and without our awareness. Therefore, the daseinsanalytic understanding of man helps us comprehend directly and fundamentally why therapists *can* demand of their patients what they have in fact been asking all along, and why they even *must* demand it if they want to cure at all. In all their endeavors psychotherapists rely on the peculiar ability of man to exist in a variety of instinctual, feeling, thinking and acting relationships to the things and in social and interpersonal patterns of behavior towards the fellowmen of his world. The therapist tacitly counts on this human ability when he asks of his patient—and tries to help him achieve it by this or that psychotherapeutic method—that he knowingly and responsibly seize and adopt all his potentialities of relationships so that they no longer remain frozen in unconscious neurotic mental or physical symptoms because of early childhood inhibitions and repressions.

In order to gain real insight into these preconditions and this goal of all practical psychotherapeutic approaches, the daseinsanalytic thinking had to guard against approaching man dogmatically with preconceived notions about his reality, no matter how self-evident they might seem. It also had to avoid forcing man blindly, by means of such preconceived ideas, into categories whereby he would be nothing but a "Psyche," a "Person" or "Consciousness." On the contrary, the daseinsanalysis had to learn again to see man unbiased, in the manner in which he directly reveals himself, and, in so doing, it made a very simple but all the more significant discovery about the fundamental nature of man. It found that man exists only *in* his relations and *as* his relations to the objects and fellowmen of his world. In order to exist in such manner, however, man must intrinsically possess a fundamental understanding of the fact that something *is* and can *be* at all. Man's special manner of being-in-the-world can therefore only be compared to the shining of a light, in the brightness of which the presence of all that is can occur, in which all things can appear and reveal themselves in their own, proper nature. Man is fundamentally an essentially spiritual brightness and as such he genuinely exists in the world. As this world-revealing brightness he is claimed by the ultimate be-ness. If a primordial understanding of be-ness were not the very essence of man, where would he suddenly find the ability to acquire any special knowledge and insight? In fact, each single comprehension of the meaning of all the different encountering objects and all actual dealing with them is possible only because man is intrinsically "brightness" in the sense of being a primordial understanding of be-ness. This holds true in an all-embracing way: it is the prerequisite for the possibility to be concretely touched and affected by something as well as for all emotional experience and all conscious or unconscious instinctual behavior toward something: without it there can be no handling and grasping of mechanical tools, nor can there be conceptual grasping of scientific matters. This also refutes the widely heard objection that the daseinsanalysis is relevant only for the psychology of the conscious mind. The intrinsic ability of the human "dasein" to be open to the world in this way does not just discover things which can be located somewhere in space and time. It also opens up ways for the direct and immediate understanding of beings, who, as human beings, not only are altogether different from the things, but who, according to their manner of being as "dasein," are in this world in the same way as I am. These other human beings are likewise there and together with me. Humanity, as a whole, therefore, is best comparable to the full brightness of the day which also consists of the shining-together of all individual sun rays. Because of this being-together-in-the-world the world is always that which I share with others, the world of "dasein" is world-of-togetherness ("Mitwelt").[1]

Just as the objects cannot reveal themselves without such brightness of man, man cannot exist as that which he is without the presence of all he encounters. For if he did not find his proper place in the encounter with the objects, plants, animals and fellowmen, in his ability to be with them, in his relationship to them, how else could men be in this world as such brightening understanding of be-ness? Even physical light cannot appear as light unless it encounters an object and can make it shine.

THE DASEINSANALYTICALLY ORIENTED PSYCHOTHERAPIST

This then, is the anthropological essence of Martin Heidegger's Existential Analysis (Daseinsanalysis). Meanwhile, the term "existential analysis" has come to include a variety of philosophical, scientific, psychopathologic and psychotherapeutic schools of thought. Although they differ in their methods and goals, they are all derivatives of Heidegger's Daseinsanalysis. At least they received from it their initial impetus even if, as in the case of J.-P. Sartre's philosophy, they have turned the real substance of the "Daseinsanalysis" into its complete opposite, namely, an extreme, subjectivistic Cartesianism.

The psychotherapist who lets himself be thoroughly pervaded by Heidegger's ontologic insight will not be able to derive new words or phrases from the daseinsanalysis for his psychopathologic descriptions. But he will win by it a tacit, but all the more reliable and all-embracing attitude toward his patient and the therapeutic process. If the therapist really understands that man is intrinsically a world-unfolding and world-opening being

[1] M. Heidegger: *Sein und Zeit*. Halle, 1927. p. 118.

in the sense that in him, as the bright sphere of be-ness, comparable to a glade in a forest, all things, plants, animals and fellowmen can show and reveal themselves directly and immediately in all their significance and correlations, then he will have an unceasing reverence for the proper value of each phenomenon he encounters. At the same time he will have become aware that this way of being is the prerequisite that our destiny could claim man as a being who should care for the things and his fellowmen in the manner that all that is and may be can best unfold and develop. To exist in this sense is man's intrinsic task in life. How else could it be that his conscience tells him so relentlessly whenever he falls short of fulfilling it? This call from the conscience and this guilt feeling will not abate until man has taken over and responsibly accepted all those possibilities which constitute him, and has borne and carried them out in taking care of the things and fellowmen of his world. Thus, he has completed his full dasein and hence can consummate his individual, intrinsic temporality in a good death. The daseinsanalytic understanding of man makes the analyst gain so deep a respect for all phenomena he encounters that it bids him to abide even more fully and more firmly by the chief rule of psychoanalysis than Freud himself could, handicapped as he still was by theoretical prejudices. The therapist will now, according to Freud's technical prescriptions, really be able to accept as equally genuine all the new possibilities for communication which grow "on the playground of transference," without mutilating them through his own intellectual and theoretical prejudices and his personal affective censure. The daseinsanalytically oriented psychoanalyst will have a clear conscience if he remains unpartial to all unproved scientific theories and abstractions and therefore refrains from attributing sole and only reality to one kind of behavior—the instinctual reactions, for instance—and does not consider them more "real" than all other potentialities. Thus, the danger of a so-called unresolved transference can often be avoided. This therapeutic difficulty usually develops only because the analyst has attempted to interpret and thereby reduce a new possibility of communication which unfolded for the first time in the therapeutic situation to a mere repetition of a relationship which existed earlier in life, considering this one primary and causal. Therefore, this new possibility can never properly unfold and mature and thus must inevitably remain in its embryonic state, i.e., the "transference fixation." How different, though, if one respects for instance the divine, which also reveals itself during psychoanalysis, in its divineness, just as one is ready to concede to the earthly its earthliness, and does not degrade the divine to a mere product of sublimation of an infantile-libidinal fixation, nor to a mere subjectivistic "psychic reality" produced by some supposed archetypal structure in the psyche of a human subject.

Of equally decisive influence on the attitude of the analyst is a thorough daseinsanalytic understanding of the fact that man is intrinsically and essentially always together with others. Heidegger's fundamental ontology helps us understand this in terms of a primary participation of all men in being the same open sphere of the be-ness. This insight teaches us that there is a being-together which is of such intrinsic and essential nature that no man can in fact perceive another even in the distance, without being already—through the mere art of perceiving—involved in the other's particular world-relatedness in some specific way. Thus, from the very first encounter between the therapist and patient the therapist is already together with his patient in the patient's way of existing, just as the patient already partakes in the therapist's manner of living, no matter whether, either on the part of the therapist or the patient, their being-together manifests itself for some time only in aloof observation, indifference or even intense resistance.

Already the knowledge of just this one essential trait of man provides an enormous impetus and a firm basis even for psychotherapeutic endeavors which formerly were a venture requiring an almost blind courage. For, only in the primordial being-together as it was brought to light by Heidegger's "Daseinsanalysis" we are able now to recognize the very foundation of all psychotherapeutic possibilities. Owing to this basic structure of man's existence, the most seriously ill schizophrenic patient, for instance, partakes in some way or other as human being in the wholesome mode of living of his psychotherapist; hence, such a patient's fundamental possibility of being cured by the adequate being-together of a psychotherapeutic situation through which he may recollect his true self again.[2]

Apart from the confidence which we derive from the daseinsanalytic insights for our practical dealings with such difficult patients, the daseinsanalytic way of thinking affords us also some important "theoretical" gain. For example, it helps us understand such central phenomena as "psychic projection" and "transference." Until now modern psychology could conceive of them only in terms of a tossing-out and carrying-over of psychic contents from within a "psyche" into something in the external world. Those concepts, however, are entirely unexplainable and can only be maintained on the basis of abstract intellectual constructions. The daseinsanalytic thinking allows us to understand these phenomena sim-

[2] M. Boss:: *Psychonalyse und Daseinsanalytik*. Bern, Hans Huber, 1957.

ply and with full justice to reality out of the primary, intrinsic being-together of all men in the same world.[3]

REFERENCES

1. Binswanger, L.: Freud's Auffassung vom Menschen im Lichte der Anthropologie. Bern, A. Francke, 1947.
2. Boss, M.: The Dream and Its Interpretation. London, Rider, 1957.
3. ———: Einfuhrung in die psychosomatische Medizin. Bern, Huber, 1957.
4. ———: Psychoanalyse und Daseinsanalytik. Bern, Huber, 1957.
5. Heidegger, M.: Sein und Zeit. Tübingen, Niemeyer, 1927.
6. ———:Ueber den Humanismus. Frankfurt a.M, Klostermann, 1953.
7. ———: Einfuhrung in die Metaphysik, Tübingen, Niemeyer, 1933.
8. ———: Was heisst Denken? Tübingen, Niemeyer, 1947.

[3] M. Boss: *The Dream and Its Interpretation*. London, 1957.

THE HUMAN BODY AND THE SIGNIFICANCE OF HUMAN MOVEMENT

A Phenomenological Study

by J. H. VAN DEN BERG *

An attempt is made in this study to submit human movement to an analysis, so that an answer may be found to the question as to the place and the nature of the area from which human movement is directed or—in other words—from which it derives its *significance.*

The very putting of the question points to the fact that human movement is not considered here as a mechanical, blundering process, but as a significant performance, i.e., as a performance having its broad foundation in the whole of human existence.

This analysis will be of a phenomenological character. This does not mean that human movement will be submitted to a close and careful psychological examination (as aimed at by the phenomenology of Jaspers), but that we shall endeavor to find our way from the amazing harmony and discord of man and world to one of the ways demonstrating this harmony and discord: human movement. It will be clear to the reader that the technical term "Phenomenology" is here taken in the sense of Husserl, Heidegger, Sartre, and Merleau-Ponty.

* J. H. VAN DEN BERG is chief assistant of the Psychiatric Clinic at Utrecht, Holland, and also lectures on phenomenological psychiatry at the State University of Utrecht. He is the author of numerous books in the field of phenomenological psychiatry, most of them being in Dutch or French. His *The Phenomenological Approach to Psychiatry* was published in English.

Since until recently every consideration of the question of the significance of human movement was defeated by the supposedly bipartiteness in man of a material body and an immaterial subjectivity, it seemed necessary to me to demonstrate in a first chapter the recent development of the subject-conception and then, in a second chapter extensively to enter into modern phenomenological views about the human body.

It will then appear that the above-mentioned question can be answered without any considerable difficulty.

This study was appreciably promoted by the appearance of the latest, highly important book by Professor F. J. J. Buytendijk, at present professor of psychology at the University of Utrecht, on the *General Theory of Human Carriage and Movement,* which up till now has only been obtainable in the Dutch language.[1]

As in Professor Buytendijk's book the term movement is here too taken in its widest sense, also encompassing speech.

CHAPTER I. EMIGRATION OF THE SUBJECT

"I will close my eyes, my ears, and shut out all my senses, I will even wipe out from my thoughts all images of material things, or at least, since this can hardly be accomplished, I will consider them false and vain; and thus occupying myself exclusively with my inner self, I will try to make myself even better acquainted and more familiar with myself. I am a thing that thinks, that is to say that doubts, affirms, denies, that knows few things, is ignorant of many, loves, hates, who wills, who does not will, has also imagination and feeling." With these words Descartes[2] describes his *subject* in the opening lines of

[1] F. J. J. Buytendijk, *General Theory of Human Carriage and Movement* (Utrecht, Spectrum, 1948).

[2] *Méditations* (1641), In *Oeuvres de Descartes* (Paris, Gibert, 1940). Tome II, p. 117.

his third meditation. A thing, thinking, doubting, knowing, loving, hating, willing, imagining, and feeling. A *res cogitans,* within the body, separated from the world to which the senses are the misleading entrances, separates also, if possible, from the images presented by the imagination, products too of that same outside world, of whose truth I know nothing and of which I cannot say anything with certainty. An *extra-mundane subject,*[3] to which the world is but indirectly guaranteed through God's goodness alone.

Anyone reading closely the above famous quotation will notice that Descartes himself has had to state that the complete isolation of the subject in exclusive consciousness of self cannot be achieved. Of the wiping out of all images he is obliged to admit that "this can hardly be accomplished." Every rigorous effort to bring this about nevertheless confronts us with a void which has indeed little in common with the experiencing of one's own subjectivity. The isolated subject is, as Buytendijk rightly observes, "a metaphysical point, therefore without dimension, without contents and shape," and—we should be inclined to add—without psychological value: a theoretical abstraction of reality, of which neither psychology nor psychopathology can make anything.

It has surely been this last consideration which has induced Brentano to re-introduce the scholastic idea of the intention (*actus mentis quo tendit in objectum*) into psychology and even to attribute a major significance to it. He considers "every psychical phenomenon characterized by that which the scholastics of the Middle Ages have called the intentional (sometimes also mental) nonexistence ("Inexistenz") of an object and which we call the direction toward an object (by which we should not

[3] E. Straus, *Vom Sinn der Sinne* (Berlin, Springer, 1935), p. 8 seq.

understand reality), or the immanent objectivity."[4] It need not surprise us, as Brentano would say, when Descartes observes that the imagining cannot be separated from that which is imagined, no more than remembering from that which is remembered or observation from that which is observed, etc., and that for this simple reason that the imagining, remembering, etc., *suggest a direction,* in other words: because every state of consciousness must have an "object," if it is to exist, because every *cogito* implies a *cogitatum.*

Herewith the first step has been taken on the road toward the deliverance of the subject from its narrow unnatural bonds: every quality of the subject is directed and the arrow indicating the direction unquestionably points to the "outside world." The point at issue, however, is where the end is of the arrow-tip. Not in the outer world itself, as Brentano expressly warns us: by *cogitatum* we do not mean reality, but the immanent object abstracted from it, something like the image which the real object of the outer world represents within one. Hence the title of *non*-existence ("Inexistenz").

Husserl was not satisfied with the configuration. If we want to separate the object of the outer world from the immanent "subjective" object, he says, "We get into the difficulty of *two* realities facing one another, whereas only *one* is and can be there. I observe the thing, the natural object, that tree over there in the garden, that and that only is the real object of the observing intention.[5] Husserl therefore extends the arrow, which with Brentano came to a stop at something like the image, to the world itself. In this way every solipsistically in-

[4] F. Brentano, *Psychologie vom empirischen Standpunkt* (1874), (Ausg. O. Kraus, Meiner, Leipzig, 1924), pp. 124, 125.

[5] E. Husserl, *Ideen zu einer reinen Phänomenologie,* I (1913), (3e Abdr. Niemeyer, Halle, 1928), p. 186. This same observation already appears in his *Logische Untersuchungen,* B. II, Teil I, 4e Aufl., p. 425.

clined view of the subject is wiped out. This becomes quite clear when we see in what way Husserl corrects the intention idea. For Brentano intention was: direction, that is direction from a center (ego) to the outer world, stopping at the image. Husserl examines this road, this direction so to say with a magnifying glass and discovers that with commonplace unproblematic looking, remembering, imagining, etc., there is but very little to be found of the Brentano stages: "if we live so to say in the act in question, if for instance we are absorbed in observantly regarding an occurrence presenting itself or in the play of the imagination or in reading a fairy tale, then nothing is to be perceived any more of the ego as the relevant point in the act performed.[6] The same verdict holds good, according to Husserl—and we can but agree with him—with regard to the intention as an arrow between this absent ego and the object of the outer world: while reading, I usually know nothing of a "being directed toward the book"; what there *is*, is the book only. It was therefore bound to happen that a pupil of Husserl's, Specht, exclaimed relieved: "in immediate, unreflected experience nothing has remained of the fact that eyes are needed for seeing . . . there are just houses standing there." [7] We shall see further on that this statement is misleading.

On the whole Husserl agrees with Specht; for him "intentional relation to an object" and "intended object" are identical. And yet we should wholly misunderstand him, if, from all that has just been set forth, we concluded that his subject is to be found in the "outer world." Husserl shrinks from this dictum. When he states that the real object of the observing intention is

[6] *Logische Untersuchungen,* II, I, p. 76.

[7] W. Specht, Zur Phänomenologie und Morphologie der pathologischen Wahrnehmungstäuschungen (Z. f. Pathops., 1914), B. II.

"that tree over there in the garden" it seems as if he has burned his fingers and must at once redeem the committed error. He does so by emphatically stating that it is of no interest to him whatever whether this tree is really there, he wants to place this and other theses between brackets, he "counts himself out," and retires to a distance to subject the intentionality to a purely philosophical observation. The psychologist, however, cannot be satisfied with this. He will be grateful to Husserl for this second step on the road to the deliverance of the subject, but as far as he is concerned Husserl and his colleagues will be welcome to the subsequent *psychological* considerations. He wishes to attain a *philosophical* description of the subject.

The third and decisive step was taken by Heidegger. It presents such an entirely new character, however, that it will be necessary to start from another place in order to be able to repeat his step. This starting place is not the subject but the object, the thing in the outside world.

The object of the physical sciences and of the older psychology has been described by Sartre in a masterly fashion.[8] This object is the bare fact, saturated with being, compact and massive, absolutely independent, unrelated; it is identical with itself and "too much for eternity." This delightful, reliable objectivity is constantly being destroyed by man, more is the pity. His observation is faulty, he constantly makes mistakes. What he sees he confuses with what he saw before or with the figments of his fickle imagination. He turns a thing consisting of cardboard, linen, and pages covered with black marks into a book, a novel; a lock of hair, this bundle of horn threads, into a token of loving memory. A brightly lighted spot in a wood into a ghost and the glass of red liquid into a toast to the health of

[8] J.-P. Sartre, *L'être et le néant* (Paris, Gallimard, 1943), pp. 30 ff.

the guest of honor. He constantly attaches to the object things that are foreign to it and wrong it: "every day in the world we see interpretations applied to sensations without any essential affinity," says Leuret.[9] What is worse, he takes that which he has applied for the object, for be careful not to try, when love-making, to take the lock of hair for "what it is"; it will cost you dear. What we see, is not the object, but its signification; this holds equally good for the matter-of-fact, unemotional, practical attitude: we see, not a thing made of wood, but a hammer, not a piece of white material, but a handkerchief. What we see is exactly what we add to the object, if it is to become a *thing* to us. The object, a house, e.g., has no meaning for us in its simple state of being. We cannot give it a name, since with every name a special meaning stands out; it is frozen in meaninglessness. "There emanates a kind of stupor from it to me" [10] and even this is saying too much. What we see in a house is that it is a *house,* we see its inhabitableness. In historical terms: we see "the fringe" of James, the "Sphäre" of Schilder and Kretschmer, the "aurore d'image" of Spaier, the "Erlebnis" of Straus, terms which are intended to indicate that which is added to reality by ourselves. In short: man "projects" constantly what belongs to his sphere into the lucid, transparent, purely existing world of the objects (the word world is too much here) and turns it into an inextricable blend of what *is* and *appears.* "We have of the universe but formless visions, fragmentary, and which we complete with associations of arbitrary ideas, creating dangerous suggestions," Proust [11] splenetically exclaims in the chorus of the psy-

[9] F. Leuret, *Sur la folie* (Paris, Crochard, 1834), p. 75.
[10] M. Merleau-Ponty, *Phénoménologie de la perception,* p. 83.
[11] M. Proust, *A la recherche du temps perdu A l'hombre des jeunes filles en fleurs* (Paris, Gallimard).

chologists and philosophers. A spleen which is even surpassed, if possible, by Sartre. The views of the latter are so important that we must needs consider them for a moment.

If we define the purely objective as that to which the term *existing* can be applied, then all the rest not belonging to this is *nothing*. There is no word that can express what a cup *is*. We might describe it as a whole consisting of matter constructed in a special way (baked earth) covered with an outer layer of hard matter (glaze). This whole *is* to us, however, is a cup to drink from. What makes the cup a cup is, according to Sartre, a "nothing": for the way of handling it, its usefulness is nowhere to be discerned. The unfortunate creature who poisons what is with that "nothing" is man: man is the creature through whom this "nothing" comes into the world," he "secretes" the "non-being" and spoils the unproblematical of the objects. He does it thoroughly: "the nothing is at the very heart of the being, in its core like a worm." He renders the world worm-eaten with all his cogitations: with his observation ("to see the world as the world or to turn it into nothing, that is one and the same thing"), with his representation ("to give an image, that is to place an object *outside* the whole of reality, that is to keep reality at a distance, to get rid of it, in a word to deny it") and with his emotion. But after all the world can stand this, is proof against the poisonous flood that humanity pours out upon it: "the non-being is but on the surface of the being" says Sartre, by which he assures us once more that the object wins and must win owing to its sole possession of "being."

Sartre's speculations on "the nothing" do not just drop from the skies. He read Heidegger, although—be it said beforehand—inaccurately. It is important for the present-day psychologist to have made himself familiar with

Heidegger's views, since they preclude such misconceptions as Sartre's, misconceptions which—as Sartre convincingly shows us—have momentous psychological consequences.

Heidegger stops at what Sartre considers absolutely self-evident: that the object *is*. It *is* always something, however much I try to divest the cup, standing before me, of all the so-called accidental, man-imposed, which does not essentially belong to the cup; I find myself obliged to keep referring to the cup in words that express more than the cup may be in itself. It is "baked earth surrounded by glaze." I cannot go much farther indeed; but baked earth means only baked earth to man, to me, and should we want to drop the adjective "baked," because it implies too much the potter and his oven, even then "earth" is more than . . ., than what? "Earth" suggests already all that which, some years ago, Bachelard [12] put into words in such a masterly fashion. The same thing can be said of "the glaze," just as the same holds for all things surrounding us. Even the subtlety of presenting "the cup before me" as a whole of chemical formulas, cannot remove our conviction that the cup thus reduced to "objectivity" *is,* and that a particle of a human world, which, as a result of certain human activities, was turned into a new kind of reality (the chemical formula).

The object *is;* herein is contained the entire complex of problems of man and his world. The object *is;* this means that the object in its abstraction is immediately and continually transcended into a whole of (human) interpretations, a whole which, eventually, always encompasses the entire world. The cup is earthenware, this means: it implies in principle the potter's clay, the river,

[12] G. Bachelard, *La terre et les reveries de la volonté* (Paris, Corti, 1948); *La terre et les rêveries du repos* (Paris, Corti, 1948).

the mountains, the potter, the potter's wheel, and the oven; the oven in its turn implies the bricks, the metal, and the fuel. And so forth, the cup encompasses the entire so-called objective world, but at the same time the human world: the potter implies the house in which he lives, eats, and sleeps. The cup is a tea-cup, it suggests the cosiness of the time when it is used, it suggests possibly my loneliness in case the guests fail to appear; so it implies on occasion the intimacy of a whole existence, but at the same time the world of things: the chairs around the tables on which others sit or would have sat had they been there, etc. Who could draw the line here between the "objective" and the "human" world? The objective is human, because it *is,* the human is objective, because man interprets himself in the things around him.

The object therefore is never the anonymous, relationless, that is also: the invisible, inaudible, intangible being, with respect to this *being,* it is a non-being, a "nothing." The psychologist will no doubt always regret that Heidegger introduced the word *nothing* here as a terminus technicus. Philosophically speaking, he could to be sure point to a long and correlative history of this word. It remains a curious, and in the end to the psychologist unacceptable, contradiction to indicate the transferring of the abstract object to the fullness of human existence by the word *nothing*. In our opinion, therefore, it should be kept out of psychological terminology.

In Rilke's *Laurids Brigge* [13] we find an illustration of the above which should not remain unmentioned here. On the blank wall in the Rue St. Jaques, Brigge sees the "impression" of the adjacent house that has been pulled

[13] R. M. Rilke, *Die Aufzeichnungen des Malte Laurids Brigge* (Zürich, Niehans u. Rokitansky, 1948), pp. 52, 53.

down: the division into rooms, lavatory, staircase, peeled-off wallpaper, soot of a chimney, and similar records of an old dilapidated house. What he does see, however, is much more: "There stood the afternoons and the illnesses and the exhalations and the stale smoke of the years, and sweat breaking out below the shoulders and making one's clothes heavy, the flat smell coming out of mouths and the smell as of fusel oil exuded by perspiring feet. . . . The sweetish, long smell of neglected babies was there and the smell of fear of children going to school. . . . One would think I had stood a long time looking at it; but I can swear that I began to run away as soon as I recognized it. I recognize everything here and for this reason it just enters into me: *it is at home in me.*" And yet Rilke (Brigge) would have searched for it *within himself* in vain. In order to come to himself thus, he could not do without the wall, while on the other hand it is equally true that the wall "in itself," as object, could never have shown him what he saw, for "the thing ignores us, it rests in itself, hostile and foreign . . . an Other Thing, resolutely silent" (Merleau-Ponty, *op. cit.*, p. 372).

It might be said, not without justice, that the case cited above is too remote from what is ordinary and commonplace to be taken to demonstrate the way in which man realizes himself "at the objects." All the same it also holds good for our non-emotional human existence, that as a rule it interprets itself in a whole of meanings that stands out in the things of the world. We find a specially striking case in point with the biologist Von Uexkull,[14] who puts the question of the way different people see the same oak tree. For the hunter the oak is a shelter or a cover for game, for the timber merchant a calculable,

[14] A. o. in J. Von Uexkull and G. Kriszal, *Streifzüge durch die Umwelten von Tieren und Menschen* (Berlin, Springer, 1934), p. 91.

measurable, saleable object, the young girl sees in that same oak tree an aspect of the romantic landscape. Observing (and imagining, thinking, wishing, etc.: all cogitations mean world), these three persons explain themselves. Never, for instance, can we tell from the timber merchant that he is a timber merchant. He himself evaporates into a void, when we theoretically take his world away from him. Or rather, when we want to examine the timber merchant himself, e.g., in a psychological laboratory, then this examination will always prove to consist of an exploration of his world. On going to the "object" (in this case, the oak), we find a void there also if we reject every significance. The object in itself cannot be described, or rather, every description of an object proves to consist of an exposition of human world. "For man," says Sartre, "is not coiled up within himself, but is outside himself, always outside, from heaven to earth." [15] If we want to remember our youth, we cannot do without the things belonging to the child's world, bearing exclusively the marks of this youth. The psychology of a child's play, the psychology in general of the child is the psychology of his little room, the garden and the kitten, it is a psychology of the garret with its trunks, boxes, and dark corners, of the cellar with its significant smell and chilliness, of the cupboard without tangible boundaries, of the space under the table, where the legs of the parents and of the guests invited to the family feast have their lively play. Thus and in no other way is the psychology of the child a psychology that does not forget the child. And in the same way: solely by leaving the psychically sick child and by putting to one's self the question how the intimacy of his things have changed, a psychopathology becomes possible that does not leave out the child.

[15] *L'homme et les choses, Situations I* (1947), p. 291.

Exactly the same holds good for the psychology and the psychopathology of the adult. Whoever wants to get to know a man should leave him as quickly as possible. He is in the last place to be found there where he stands. All the time he silently moves away from himself by expressing himself in the world of things. So one can learn to know another best by traveling with him through a country or by looking at a town with him. One who often shows the same town to different people will be struck by the ever new way in which this town appears in the conversation that is held about the sights during such a walk. These different ways are identical with the people with whom one walks, they are forms of subjectivity. The subject shows itself in the things, if at least we dare take these things in their original form, i.e., as they appear, in this case as they appear in the conversation, or in Straus's words, if we take them at their *landscape* value. "Any landscape is a state of soul," says Amiel, who saw clearly the consequences of this observation for psychology: "Every soul has its climate, it is a climate; it has, so to say, its meteorology in the general meteorology of the soul; thus psychology cannot be achieved before the physiology of our planet, the science to which we give at present the inadequate name of physics of the globe." [16] Psychology is in the first place—or should be—meteorology, physiology of the elements: earth, air, water, and fire, as psychopathology is in the first place the dogma of catastrophes that afflict the human world. *Psychology* is *cosmology*.[17] This cosmology has found its Copernicus in Bachelard.[18]

Herewith we have arrived at a tentative reply to the

[16] H. F. Amiel, *Fragments d'un journal intime* (Genève, Georg, 1901).
[17] Cf. Minkowski's *Vers une cosmologie* (Paris, Aubier, 1906), a booklet that cannot be too highly praised.
[18] *Op. cit.*, and *La psychoanalyse du feu* (Paris, Gallimard, 1938); *L'eau et les rêves* (Paris, Corti, 1942).

question as to the place of the subject, of the "self" that moves. However, before formulating the answer it is advisable to give a recapitulation of the different phases of emigration of the subject in a few points.

1. Descartes: the subject is within the body of man, as in a "closed casket" (Sartre). The only psychological reality is *I think* (imagine, fancy, will, etc.). The inevitable results of this view consist of: the doctrine of the worldless subject, the doctrine of the fixed, stable object, the doctrine of the "sensations" which must be the anonymous building materials of the cognizance of a foreign world, and the doctrine of the projection which pours out over this world matter foreign to the things themselves. Another consequence is the representation of the body as a screen between subject and object, as the gateway to the "soul" and as the tool of the subject.

2. Brentano, who corrects Descartes's *I think* into *I think of,* or in order to make clear that this *of* is not used blindly but arrives at a representation: *I think of* (*this house*), so gaining the liberation of the subject from the paralyzing "commerce" with itself behind the sealed doors of the senses. With the brackets round "this house."

3. Husserl is not satisfied. He rightly contends that it is this house itself, that house there before me, to which the intention is directed. His correction runs as follows: *I think of this house,* which, however, on second thought he must correct into (*I think*) (*of*) *this house,* because during the being absorbed in thinking of the house there before me there is nothing to be found of an *I* that thinks, nor of an *of,* to which the thinking would be directed. Then, however, Husserl recoils and puts everything between brackets of the ἐποχή; we might show the final result by means of the formula [(*I think*) (*of*) *this house*].

4. Heidegger and Sartre object to the house "of bricks,

wood, and iron." Thinking of a house, I usually think of its habitableness, its intimacy. And should I happen to think of the house as bricks, wood, and iron, then I would be a builder, for instance, who at once passes on from these materials toward labor: bricks to be replaced, wood to be painted, etc. Formally I then do the same as the tenant who, returning home from his daily work, thinks of this house "to rest in" or "to pursue his hobbies." The house is, as everything is, always given "*in order to*," i.e., given in the form of a *gerundive* (Sartre [19]). Reduced to a formula: *I think of this house in order to . . .*, with which the *I think* as well as the *of* and *this house* have "passed," i.e., have not disappeared, but "have been passed over in silence," which we can express in the formula as follows: (*I think*) (*of*) (*this house*) in order to. . . . This *in order to . . .* comprises the house as well as myself. If we now ask where this *in order to . . .*, which implies the subject, is to be found, then the answer must be: by this house, for there I am, when thinking (observing or imagining), forgetting the house itself, I "am absorbed" in the operative signification of this house.

The answer to the question as to the place "the self that moves, that acts, expresses and represents" runs therefore as follows: this place is to be found in the world. For that is where "I am," when thinking, feeling, imagining or desiring. I am "with" the things of this world or as language puts it so literally "am absorbed in them."

And yet, we cannot possibly be satisfied with this view. If we fully endorse the final result of the above expositions, even then the phenomenon-in-itself, this man thinking of that house, proves that the definition of the

[19] *L'être et le néant,* p. 387: "Carthage est delenda pour les Romains, mais servanda pour les Carthaginois."

place of the subject cannot possibly be complete. Standing beside him engaged in a conversation with him about that house, then I, looking at him who is thinking, absorbed in that house, am obliged to recognize the other, standing there where he stands, concealed behind his eyes or behind his forehead, concealed in the heart of his tangible physical presence. If not, how would Descartes ever have arrived at his conception and with this conception have dominated theoretical psychology until quite recently?

Buytendijk describes a situation from which this relevant problem can be exceptionally well demonstrated. A pedestrian, thirsty and tired from his newly accomplished trip, reaches an inn, where he drops into one of the chairs standing outside. He taps on the table to advise the landlord of his arrival, or rather—for the landlord is only there "transcended" landlord—to obtain the cooling drink that is within the inn. Buytendijk's statement that "the interior of the inn is phenomenally something else than the interiority of the thirsty man" is only partly right. At the moment of the tap on the table, the pedestrian with his chair, his table, his tapping finger, and with everything else that ever was to be found in his inner self, has moved over to the cooling drink within the dark interior of the inn. Phenomenally the inner self of the man and the interior of the inn are *identical.* But the situation changes when we sit down by the side of the parched pedestrian and see him tap. We then see the *parched pedestrian,* we become convinced of an intention guiding his hand, an intention which for the pedestrian himself no doubt originates from the inn, but which for us, the spectators, can be observed in the pedestrian himself: "behind" and in his eager eyes, "behind" and in his testy tapping.

In the following chapter the significance of the phenomenologically unquestionable fact that the subject (or only the other subject, the fellowman?) is supposed to be *in* the body, that therefore the place of the subject is inseparably connected with the boundaries of the physical body, will be fully dealt with.

CHAPTER II. THE HUMAN BODY

"Our body," says Buytendijk, "is that which is most our *own* of all conceivable things, which is least opposed to us, least foreign and so least antagonistic." Any able-bodied person, endowed with animal spirits and full of resiliency, will be able to accept this view in its entirety. And yet it is in curious contrast to the discovery of Wolff [20] that out of ten persons, all in perfect health, only one on the average recognizes his hands out of a small series of photos of which they were told that it would contain the likeness of their own hands. No more does the view fit in with the fact conceivable to almost everyone that our own hand, foot, face, etc., may become curiously strange to us, when we begin to regard the parts of our body attentively, begin to "study" them. Whereas our body is unalienably ours, we do not "recognize" it, when we come to face it in some way or other. We must therefore assume that some fundamental change takes place in our body, which is so absolutely ours, when we *are* it no longer, but see it as a thing among others. This means: body and body make two at the very least; if we want to speak about "the" body, we shall first have to indicate exactly what we mean by it. "The idea 'body' is by no means one word for one thing," said Marcel,[21] who with this extremely important warn-

[20] W. Wolff, "Selbstbeurteilung und Fremdbeurteilung," *Psychologische Forschung,* B. VII (1932), pp. 251–328.

[21] G. Marcel, *Journal métaphysique* (1927); (5e Ed., Paris, Gallimard, 1935), p. 124.

ing put his finger on *the* weak spot in all pre-phenomenological views about the body. The distinction which Marcel described afterwards had been well known already for a long time: that between the body that we *are* and the body that ourselves and others have at our disposal, as we *have* it. It appeared that this division into two was insufficient to put into words the special problem of the human body, especially because too little attention was given to the role of the fellow-human in the constitution of the body.

Sartre [22] distinguishes three *dimensions* of the human body. We might describe them as follows.

1. The mountaineer who outlined his plans the day before and discussed his wish to reach a difficult top with his friends, destroys his intentions as soon as he takes his first step on the difficult ground. He no longer thinks of his shoes to which an hour ago he still gave such great attention, he "forgets" the stick that supports him while he climbs and with which he tests the reliability of a rock point, he "ignores his body" which he trained for days together beforehand with an eye to this trip, nor do his thoughts dwell on the closely calculated plan that occupied him so intensely the day before. For only by forgetting, in a certain sense, his plans and his body, will he be able to devote himself to the laborious task that has to be performed. What there still *is,* psychologically speaking, is only the mountain: he is absorbed in its structure, his thoughts are completely given to it. Just because he forgets his body, this body can realize itself as a living body. The body (just as the plan) is realized as *landscape*: the length of the body is demonstrated by the insurmountable steep bits necessitating a roundabout way, the measure of his stride by the nature of the gradient which it is just possible or just not pos-

[22] J.-P. Sartre, *L'être et le néant,* pp. 368–431.

sible for him to climb, the size of his foot is proved by the measurements of the projecting points which serve as footholds. The fatigue of his body shows itself in the first instance in the distance or the inaccessibility of the top and in the too steep parts of the way presaging the top. This fatigue shows itself in the first place as the changed aspect of the landscape, as the changed physiognomy of the objects (the rocks, stones, snowfields, the summit), it appears as an ever more obtruding "coefficient of the hostility of the objects" (Bachelard), but not—at least not yet—as a feeling in his muscles, a "sense of effort" (Maine de Biran). The vulnerability of his body becomes clear to him a long time before he falls, in the dangerous incline or as movable objects under his feet; and his pain is present, long before the knock, as pointed rock or sharp stone. Even when he knocks himself it may happen that the landscape takes up his attention so much that the pain is passed on to the *cave!* that concretes the terrain, his pain is projected: is the property of the stones, nature of the landscape.

The qualities of the body: its measurements, its ability, its efficiency and vulnerability can only become apparent when the body itself is forgotten, eliminated, passed over in silence for the occupation or for the landscape for whose sake the passing is necessary. *It is only the behavior that explains the body.*[23] However long I study my hand, I shall never discover its efficiency in this way. This essential quality is only revealed when I, forgetting my hand, become absorbed in the work the hand does. I may compare right and left hand as long and carefully as I please, I never see in this way the efficiency of the right hand and the inefficiency of the left; this difference is only revealed when I am going to carpenter or to

[23] H. Plessner, *Lachen und Weinen* (Arnhem, v. Loghum Slaterus, 1941), p. 6.

write, but then again this toll is paid, that I forget both hands.

The eye itself can never teach us that it is the axis of our world; what the eye is, is taught us by the world both visible and invisible; what the ear is: the world of that which produces sound and of that which is silence, etc., or rather—for in reality the senses cannot be put so simply side by side—that the body is a sense appears as accessibility and orientation of the objects of the world. "The senses are the contemporaries of the objects," Sartre [24] concisely formulates.

The same holds for *sexuality*. Psychologically this is not in the first place to be found "in the subject" or "on" his body, but shows itself as world. Nowhere do man and woman differ so fundamentally from one another as in the physiognomy of their world. Sexuality appears in the other, who is met, in the advertisement, the shop window, the reading matter, the landscape of the twilight, the aspect of the street. It appears amongst others clearly from the different value that what is hard, cold, dry possesses on the one side and what is soft, warm and moist on the other.[25] The child, here we must decidedly consider Kunz in the right, is much more primarily and deeply convinced of the difference of sex of his father and mother by "differences in tenderness of his parents' faces" (hard stubbly beard of the father and long soft hair of the mother), than by the results of his infantile sexual "explorations" (Freud). This observation of Kunz's appears to me of primary importance. It opens up a way to a phenomenology of child sexuality in which the

[24] *Op. cit.*, p. 382. Herewith Specht's view is criticized at the same time.

[25] Cf. for the meaning of the "hardness of man" and the "softness of woman," H. S. Schulz-Hencke's article "Über Homosexualität," Z. Neur., B. 140 (1932), p. 300. Cf. also Bachelard's "humidité chaude" (*L'eau et les rêves*, p. 136).

harsh handling of the analytical school might be avoided. Such a phenomenological sexology should find its first task in an exposition of the physiognomy of the world of the boy and the girl, for it is mainly in this physiognomy that the boy is boy and the girl, girl. Just as the grown-up is in the very first place man or woman as to his sexually different world.

Disease too shows itself primarily as a change of the "physiognomy of the world" (Straus). With compulsion neurosis we are accustomed to speak of a "compulsion," i.e., of a phenomenon that is said to be found with the obsessive compulsive character. Such a patient himself, however, knows nothing of this compulsion primarily; that which is constantly clear to him consists of a remarkable hostility of the objects around him: "For obsessive compulsive patients the whole world is filled with decay." [26] Thus the diabetes insipidus patient recognizes his pathological thirst by the predominant meaning that water has acquired. A patient of Von Weizsäcker expresses this almost infectiously: "There is for me a direct communication with water. . . . I bathe whenever and wherever I can. I often think that it is lovely to have a big jet of water running down one's neck. A brooklet suffices. That is why I want to go to the Black Forest. I am always looking for roads where a brook is flowing through a meadow. Water is purity. I should not at all like to symbolize that. But it must be cold. I do not only drink because I am thirsty; it is lovely in your mouth and throat." [27]

Every pathological change of the body reveals itself originally as a new order in the "external world." The

[26] E. Straus, "Ein Beitrag zur Pathologie der Zwangserscheinungen," *Monatschr. f. P. u. N.*, B. 98 (1939), p. 61. (Für die Zwangskranken ist die ganze Welt erfüllt vom Verwesenden.")

[27] Von Weizsäcker, *Studien über Pathogenese* (2e Aufl., Weisboden, Thieme, 1946), p. 45.

derangements of the cerebrally injured only become comprehensible when, as Goldstein convincingly demonstrated, we stop regarding the patient as an individual having at his disposal an injured body. At the ordinary neurological examination the integrated senile patient displays a set of symptoms which can never tell us in what the derangement of his life consisted which induced his relations to consult a doctor. We only see this when we enter his house and see the rigorous order of the utensils there. Just as we only receive an adequate impression of the senilely disintegrated man, when we see him creating nocturnal disorder in the collected relics of his life. The psychological center of his deranged behavior lies in the appeal emanating from these things in the night, just as the measuredly sedate and careful movements of the integrated senile man are controlled from the small strictly ordered world around him, which has only a limited number of possibilities, a world which he *is,* as has now sufficiently been determined. If this were not generally valid, if, as formerly, we should contend that a man's world was controlled from a center "within him," how could we then understand that his behavior, e.g., depends on the color of the light in which he moves? [28] How could we then ever understand that the knee jerk which occurs in accordance with the rules of the textbook, reverses, i.e., shows a relaxation of the quadriceps femoris instead of a contraction as when the foot is caught by the root of a tree? [29] The *psychological* center of this reflex lies in the world, which does not only furnish all the qualities of the body, but all the ways of behavior as well.

[28] K. Goldstein and O. Rosenthal, "Zum Problem der Wirking der Farben auf dem Organismus," *Schw. Arch. f. Neur. u. P.*, B. 26 (1930), p. 15.
[29] Example by Bethe, cf. Goldstein, *op. cit.*, pp. 111 ff.

If we do not in the very first place define our body as a *world of the gerundiva,* we cannot but consider it an incomprehensible coincidence that Förster's patient suffering from total asomatognosis says of the external world "I cannot recognize anything more" [30] or, like Lhermitte,[31] we shall get into difficulties, when he makes the statement that his patient with a serious disturbance in what is called the corporal scheme, "had at the same time lost the faculty of reacting to things, that his entire sense of space had been injured." These and similar observations must remain puzzling when we separate a man from his world.

2. The body that we defined above is the "passed-beyond-in-silence" ("le passé sous silence," Sartre), it shows itself as the world of the subject at the end of its emigration. The *second dimension* of the body comes into being under the eyes of his fellow-man. To describe this body we shall return to the mountaineer, who, absorbed in his task, forgets his body in order to be able to preserve it in all dangers. The only change that we shall introduce into this picture consists in the fact that we assume that the spectacle of the mountaineer in his situation is watched by another, who remains unperceived. Seeing him climb I concentrate on the very thing that the mountaineer himself must forget for the sake of the work he is doing. I see his boots that enable him to keep his footing on steep slopes. I can tell that his body is trained by the adroit movements of his body, legs, and arms. I see the scratches and the bruises that he sustains. *I see his body,* and the whole landscape with which this body contends is centered in this moving

[30] O. Förster, "Ein Fall von elementarer Somatopsychose," *Monatschr. f. P. u. N.,* B. 14 (1903).

[31] L. Lhermitte et E. Tchehrazi, "L'image du moi corporel et ses formations pathologiques," *L'encéphale,* 32e Année (1937).

living "object." This body is the pole from where the whole mountain and mountaineer are appreciated and understood. Just the thing that is farthest away to the climber is nearest to me, what must be left by him is for me the center from which comes the significance of all. If I could approach him more closely unnoticed, I could begin to observe and describe this center in detail. I could then see the tense muscles, the drawn eyebrows, the heaving chest, and the sweating face. My knowledge of anatomy and physiology allows me to see the man climbing before my eyes as a *functioning organism,* controlled by the nervous system, which from a center sends its impulses to the contracting muscles. Thus doing I am falling in with the imperative conviction that the body there before me is governed by a center *in* this body; that the muscles and glands are controlled by a principle which this body itself contains. This conviction is independent of my anatomical and physiological knowledge: the living, moving body urges me *originally* to assume an organism, parts of which are distinguishable, parts that are governed by a central principle, i.e., a principle contained within this organism. It is rather the reverse: this conviction makes anatomy and physiology possible: just because I can see the body of the other man as a moving thing is it possible for me to take up tweezers and scalpel and dissect this thing-body. This dissectable thing-body is a derivative of the second dimension of the body. It was especially with this body—not seldom solely with this body—that psychology occupied itself until recently.

Also the mountaineer himself can constitute his body in the second dimension. This happens, for instance, when he tends the wound in his leg. The wounded place is examined and touched *in order to* cure it, or: *in order to* be able to continue on his way. And it may even occur that he considers his body as thing-body, e.g., when he considers the blisters on his hands as "after all curious behavior" of his body, i.e., regards them as dermatological curiosities. He looks then, as it were, with the eyes of an extraneous "objective" spectator. It is also with the eyes of another that the girl inspects herself, after finishing attending to her appearance, though the objectivity is different here. Her smile, which she sees in the glass, is destined for other eyes. Through her eyes she allows the other to look at "that face" over there in the glass, which will have to be passed beyond to the meeting, at which the regard of another will play its important part.

3. The *third dimension* of the body comes into being when the mountaineer becomes aware that I am regarding him. Leaving out the improbable, or at any rate rare case that this is a matter of indifference to him, then there are two forms into which this dimension must be divided.

What is most probable and certainly also happens oftenest is that the mountaineer dislikes the regard of the other. He begins to feel hindered, because he knows that the other sees and criticizes just that which he himself must forget in order not to fail in his climbing. He feels vulnerable in an absolutely defenceless domain. It is inevitable that he should to a certain extent adopt the look of the other, now and then or continuously; he does not succeed any more in becoming entirely absorbed in the wall that is to be climbed. He has to a certain extent been deprived of this wall, his world has "flown over towards the other" (Sartre). He miscalculates, begins to make mistakes and will be ashamed of the faultiness of his attempts. There are but few people who can stand it that others look over their shoulder while they are writing a letter and certainly no one can stand it from everyone; regardless of the contents of the written page.

The girl that makes herself up carefully, attends to her eyes and lips, puts on her nylons and adopts an attitude that, as we know, shows nothing but hints at everything, has *"passed beyond"* all these things when she leaves the house and is convinced by the physiognomy of the town that she is well dressed and well groomed. When she passes a group of young men in a quiet street and hears (and "sees") by the shuffling of feet behind her, that everyone turns around to look at her, everything changes entirely. That which she should forget in order to be able to walk—and to flirt if necessary—is now regarded with an "objective" eye. The street before her disappears, the ground under her feet becomes less firm, her carriage becomes constrained, shows in this way even more what she wishes—and does not wish—to hide, she stumbles perhaps and blushes.

The third body appears when the look of the other destroys the "passing beyond."

In my opinion Sartre has no right to leave things at that. There exists—though it occurs less frequently—a look of another that influences the "passing beyond" for good: that makes the world bloom and renders the body straighter and suppler. Innumerable are the declarations of sportsmen that their achievements exceed their expectations owing to the eyes of thousands that are directed on them. There is a loving look that can bestow a *fiat* on my work and at the same time justifies the body that does this work. Just as the caressing hand can for the first time justify that my body is as it is, that the accidental configuration of the veins on the back of my hand appears to be such as it should apparently be (Sartre).

The third body is the body that is constituted while

being together with another, the body that falls or is justified in the glance of the other.

4. In the opinion of Van Lennep—which I am glad to adopt here—Sartre's construction is not sufficient for a phenomenology encompassing the body in all its significations. What there is no room for in his system, is the ubiquitous *primary appreciation* of the body and in particular of the parts of the body (e.g., the calf, legs, hair, hands, nose, eyes), an appreciation which is decidedly not constituted by the supposed or real glance of the other. Everyone lives in peace with the shape and nature of certain parts of his body and in a certain discord with other parts. In between lies the anonymous area which does not count in this primary appreciation. That the glance of the other can be of no importance in this respect may be proved from all those cases where a certain part of the body "primarily narcissistic" is positively appreciated, whereas under the glance of another it acquires an inescapably negative value. An invalid may cherish an immediate, unwarrantable sympathy for his maimed arm, which in the company of others appears a complete deprivation. On the other hand, a part of the body which does not meet with approval immediately may contribute to the justification of the whole body when making love. As a rule, however, the two evaluations are equally balanced, but not infrequently we find in that case a certain unconcern with regard to the appreciation of the other.

It is the body of this primary familiarity that is injured by illness, especially malignant disease. In Sartre's system the shock caused by the malignant disease (carcinoma!), the deception and the infidelity into which the primary familiarity is changed by the disease, cannot be placed anywhere. Also the regret at the lost, youthful soundness of the body can only refer to this fourth dimension. Rodin's woman mourning over her withered body ("She who was the beautiful Haulmière") does not in the first place appraise the glance of the other at her wasted beauty, but undergoes it specially as the irreparable loss of a primarily appreciated shape or form.

The signification of the attributes of the body coming under this fourth dimension, such as bath-water, soap, and certainly also clothes (these same attributes have a different signification for the first dimensions) require a study apart.

5. Just as there is a primary appreciation of one's own body, there is a primary affective appreciation of the body or of part of the body of the other. "There are 'unacceptable' hands, false, faithful, primitive hands, etc.," say Van Lennep and Strobl in their admirable study on the outward manner of the appearance of man. In all these cases it is possible that a primary appreciation of this part of the body has been expressed. This appreciation of depreciation is then of an entirely different—namely immediate and groundless—character than the constitution of the appreciation expressed in the adjectives, owing to the gesture that the part of the body executes before my eyes: the hands of the other may also *become* unacceptable, e.g., when I see how with this hand he extracts a tablet from a silly kind of medicine container and puts it in his mouth in a repellant way. His hand may become unacceptable through the way in which he rubs the two together (Uriah Heep in Dickens!). The gesture makes the hand that primarily may appear neutral and even acceptable, despicable.

CHAPTER III. THE SIGNIFICANCE OF HUMAN MOVEMENT

When Buytendijk at the beginning of his theory of movement distinguishes process from function, and considers every human movement as a function determined by a sphere of values which furnishes signification to this movement and makes it mean something, then an extremely valuable principle is indicated here, which can protect us against innumerable errors. The movements of the human body are, taken by themselves alone, as mere changes, shiftings, displacements of an organ or a system of organs, not movements any longer. They are only movements in the whole *man + situation*. We saw, however, that the plus mark represents the most central problematic of theoretical psychology. If it is taken as an algebraic addition, then the inevitable result is that we get caught in the determining of the place "containing" the significance of the movement: we are unavoidably compelled to the localization of this significance in the subject encompassed by the body, whereas everyday experience teaches us that the movement is determined by the situation in which man finds himself, that therefore the significance of the movement is supplied "from the outside." We shall now try to formulate an answer to the question regarding the locality of the field that furnishes significance, an answer that does not leave us in the uncertainty indicated here.

For this purpose we begin with the movements of the body described by Sartre as first dimension. This body of the "subject at the end of its emigration" is realized as "utensil," as "domain," in short as *landscape* in the sense of Straus; it defines itself through the chair on which it sits, the pavement on which it walks, and the threshold over which it stumbles. It is exclusivey present as the *world of the gerundiva*.

Just as perception, this movement of head and senses, can only occur at the same place where the object is perceived and *without distance*, is also the warning, beckoning, explanatory, pointing, or groping movement of my hand to be found exclusively there where the "intention meets its terminus": "When I make a sign to a friend to approach me . . . I make a sign there where my friend is," says Sartre, and when I perceive afterwards that my friend does not show any mind to accept my invitation, "my gesture of impatience proceeds from this situation without any intermediate thought." We can conclude from this: the field that furnishes significance to my movements, lies there where my friend is, where the indicated house stands, where the root of a tree nearly made me stumble. This is to say: there where phenomenally the movement is affected, is at the same time to be found the domain that causes my movements to be as they are, that determines these movements, gives them a meaning, or makes them significant. Since the mover must forget himself in order to move "over there," that is at the same time the place where the mover is. *Significance,* the *somewhere* where the movement is made and the *self* that moves, all coincide in the landscape, in the "things," but, be it understood, not in the things themselves (the objects), but in the things taken as *gerundivum.*

An essentially new constellation comes into being, when a second person observes the movement of another in a certain situation (body in the second dimension of Sartre: the body of the other as it appears to me, without the other being able to make my glance count in his movement). What I then see is a panorama, grouping itself round the similarly observed movements of the other. These movements are the center whence the landscape receives meaning: the body of the mountaineer exerts itself to the utmost through the long steep slope that it "takes" in its movements, it performs unbalanced antics because of the threshold, over which it stumbles, it shows certain movements of the hips through the physiognomy of the "Saturday night" street disclosing itself with these movements. That is to say: "the body forms itself in anticipation of the aim it serves, it assumes a 'shape,' . . . a shape for doing work, for fighting, for feeling," as well as a "shape for loving," which only awakes at the "similarly directed unfolding of a differently sexed body," as Von Gebsattel [32] so delicately expressed it. The flirting girl moves as I see her move, because her world is that of the game of love; the child moves as a child, because his world does not yet know the grown-up order and the use of things. Only in this way are the movements of the other-in-his-situation significant and comprehensible.

Buytendijk and Plessner have perfectly recognized this relationship which holds good for the animal as well: "Behaviour means replying, and we understand the answer, when we observe the animal from the situation that thrusts its question upon him." [33]

In this case therefore the *significance* of the movement lies in the situation in which the man who is observed performs his movements, for from this situation they receive their meaning. The *somewhere* where the moving takes place (the situation as gerundivum) is now, however, no longer identical with the *self* that moves. This *self* is now the mover himself, he there in front of me; it is true he *has* "to pass beyond" always, but for me, the spectator, he is the point of junction of the gerundiva; the center, which before my eyes replies to the appeal issuing from the landscape.

The incongruity which we meet here of the locality of "somewhere" and "self" makes possible a shifting of the field that furnishes significance. We will presently re-

[32] V. E. Von Gebsattel, *Süchtiges Verhalten im Gebiet sexueller Verirrungen,* Mschr. f. P. u. N., B. 82 (1932), p. 113.

[33] F. J. J. Buytendijk and H. Plessner, "Die physiologische Erklärung des Verhaltens," *Acta Biotheoretica,* Ser. A, Vol. I (1935), p. 169.

turn to this, when we have paused a moment at the consequences of what we have just observed.

The theory of movement which results from the above-described *first* dimension of moving, must consist in an exposition of the wealth of forms of the landscape (situations). Buytendijk has taken the first step in this field of scenic semantics when he compared the movements of herbivora on the one hand and of carnivora and monkeys on the other: the difference only becomes quite clear when we observe that carnivora and monkeys live in "a differentiated domain," which is diametrically different from that of the herbivora. Straus [34] made a similar observation in the field of psychiatry: "Feeling and movement have equally changed for the catatonic. Everything is already there for the catatonic." The only possibility for us to completely understand the behavior of the catatonic is if we understand the fact that his world has totally changed. Only when the world has been reduced to the rigidity of timelessness can man become motionless, his lack of movement receives its *significance* from the catatonic landscape.

We understand the *dance* only from space transformed by music or by silence. The "past- and futureless space" [35] of the dance, widely differing from our daily world of utility, creates the dance, inspires the dancer with new life that metamorphoses her body.

In the psychology of religion it was Guardini who made a first attempt at describing the liturgic gesture from the world of the faithful.

However valuable all these initiatives may be, psychology—just as psychopathology—is even now confronted with a gigantic task, rich in promise in my opinion, of

[34] E. Straus, *Vom Sinn der Sinne,* note on p. 153.

[35] Cf. Straus, "Die Formen des Räumlichen," *Nervenarzt,* V (1930), p. 633.

describing the variety of human landscapes. Only then a great gap in the theory of human movement will be filled.

The incongruity of the locality of the *somewhere* where movement takes place and the *self* that moves in the above-described *second dimension of movement,* makes it possible that the place from where movement receives significance is shifted from the landscape to the man who is moving there before my eyes. For, if I should wish to do so, I can see his movements as changes that are fed by a significant intention perceptible in the body itself. The mountaineer "has a plan," he "estimates all his possibilities," he "husbands his strength." In the same way I can tell from the pedestrian himself, i.e., from the movements of his body, whether it is his intention to walk 2 or 20 miles, just so—as was described above—it is possible for me to determine the length of the stage from the physiognomy of the landscape, which, as we know, is different with the short or the long distance march. In the first case the significance of the movement is *in the intention* of the pedestrian, i.e., *within* his physical body, within the *self* that moves; the second case, on the contrary, in the appeal issuing from the landscape, so: in the world, or: in the *somewhere* where the movements are performed.

De Balzac says: "All the women that have gone wrong are remarkable for the exquisite roundness of their movements. If I were the mother of a family, those sacred words of the dancing-master: *Round your elbows,* would make me tremble for my daughters." If we should ask what made De Balzac so apprehensive at the non-angular, rounded movement, then the answer must point to the pliant, accessible, immediate world, which rounded the movements of the fallible women. For he wishes to protect his future daughters against this *world*. The gracious rounded movement alone would never have made him uneasy—what he knows, however, is that this movement is exclusively constituted by a "dangerous landscape." The significance of this gracious movement is in this landscape. But in contradistinction to this we can without any trouble make an equally correct observation: the significance of the gracious movement is within the person who moves, in her "constitution," her "intention," at any rate *in her.* I deprive myself then it is true of a vision, which after all is alone able to show the movement to its utmost possibilities: the latter observation is therefore not only essentially different, but also poorer than the former.

We should wish to illustrate all this further from *the spoken word,* thus from a representative movement in the sense of Buytendijk.

If we ask about the locality of the domain that provides the spoken word with meaning, then the answer consists of different parts:

1. If I am with the other, speaking and listening, to the thing in question, just as the other, listening and speaking, is absorbed in the world that unites the two of us, then he and I go beyond the sounds produced by our organs of speech for the sake of the thing, visible or understood, to which our word refers. Speaking about "that dilapidated house over there," I am with the other at that house, word and answer originate from the house. Psychologically speaking there is only that house, which in its modus of gerundivum contains the subject of the other and of myself. In other words: the *somewhere* where the movement takes place and the *self* that moves, are there where the word—this representative movement —is furnished with significance. We have already paid attention to this construction, which lies within the first dimension of the body, defined by Sartre, as to the two

ways in which movement appears, when the body is taken in its second dimension. These two ways will be described once more under the following points—and now in connection with the spoken word.

2a. When I look at the other, while he speaks to me, I see him primarily as I watched the mountaineer in his field of activity. That is to say: I can let him, the speaker, be constantly announced by the meanings of his world, which, while he speaks, constantly provides him with words. In this case I understand his word from the plan of his world, from the nature of the landscape from which his words are born. The significance of the movements of his mouth, of the sound complexes that fill the room, of the movements of his hands, of his whole speaking body, are, just as described under point 1, provided by the landscape; it is also there that the word happens, i.e., where there is movement; but the *self* that moves is not identical with the place of the *somewhere* where the movement takes place.

2b. Looking at him, the speaker, I can shift the significance of the spoken word from the landscape to the speaker who is standing facing me. The problematic which is contained in every landscape—much could be said of it—then becomes dubiosity of the speaker. The partial or dubious elucidation of the common subject of conversation changes in the obscurity of the intention of the other toward me. The "cryptology of the psychical" which first consisted in the landscape illuminated from one point only—and consequently always partially hidden—becomes the hidden inner self of the other. His face, which was first (under 2a) the mirror of the landscape that called up his word, then becomes "a façade, a boundary—and a communication wall of his own self towards the other, of the inner self against the external world." [36] The face is then the mirror of his inner self, of the heart, this "place of his decisions." Then the *significance* of his movements is transplanted to the head and the heart of the other, to the centers of the *self* which moves there before me, while the *somewhere* where the movement takes place always remains his world, the "landscape" which he is speaking about. For there *he* dwells, transcending himself; *I*, however, do not take part in this transcending, but measure the intention of head and heart.

The view which wished to regard speech as the secretion of thought produced in cerebro is a derivative of this original perception. There is sense in this view in so far: it was born from a phenomenological datum, how for that matter could it ever have been formulated otherwise? The same holds for the different theoretical views on the dialogue. The association—the "analogy conclusion"—and the "Einfühlungs-theory," they all spring from this last way in which speech appears to our eyes. *They retain their validity.*

3. When the other perceives that I do not transcend with him to a common landscape, there arises in him Sartre's third dimension of the body and simultaneously the movement modus correlate to it. He perceives that my look does not aim at the subject (the house over there) via him, but knows that I scan his intention. My look hits him just there where he is unprotected: in his silently transcended body, which is now kept present by my look. Simultaneously he is entirely or partially deprived of the landscape. He becomes uncertain, stumbles over his words (for these are now no longer placed at his disposal by the landscape, but—also for him—flow out of his mouth), or masks his uncertainty by means of a hard, loud voice. The dialogue is wrecked.

[36] H. Plessner, *Lachen und Weinen,* p. 49.

The inquiry into the locality of the domain that provides the undermined words with *significance* is the inquiry into the origin of this undermining. The answer cannot be difficult: this domain is the *glance of the other*, for exclusively through and in that look originates the stumbling, stuttering, making mistakes, blushing, and converting. The *significance* of the movement lies in the look seeking unmasking, which is directed at this moving body itself. The somewhere where the movement takes place also lies in this look, for there the person who is regarded looks for a way of escape in vain. The self, which moves, is the person looked at compelled back within the bounds of his own body, looked at and requested to unmask.

We have already pointed out that Sartre's phenomenology of the look must be called one-sided. For to him the look of the other always effects an alienation; his eye robs me of my world, it makes me invariably "coagulate," as if I had been caught in the act. All the examples exposed in *L'être et le néant* to support this view are all equally misanthropic in character: a man peers through a keyhole at a scene not meant for his eyes and suddenly realizes that his reprehensible behavior is observed; another walks through a deserted street and hears behind him that an unknown person pulls aside the curtains to look silently after him. Sartre's look is the look from behind, the malicious look of an unknown person, the look that causes a shiver from neck to ankle. It would not be difficult to give a long list of examples showing a diametrically different meaning of the look of another. There is a look of understanding, of sympathy, of friendship, and of love. The mere wink may convince us of the reality of a being together not doomed to a Sartrian "échec."

Consequently the eye of a fellow-man may justify my

body and my movements. It may impart to me a happiness far exceeding in value any solipsistic satisfaction.

With this appreciation of the look of the other the structure of *significance, somewhere,* and *self* remains the same, however. The *significance* of the movements justified by the look lies, *in the look,* for it is the eye of the other that justifies my body, that makes my words sincere and my actions transparent. The *somewhere* where the movements take place lies in *this look.* The movements, it is true, take place in the landscape (the picture I make, while another lovingly looks on; the flag I hoist under the eyes of the eager spectators), but this landscape no longer concerns my own subjectivity, it has come into being through the instrumentality of the loving or friendly *glance of the other.* The *self* that moves, *I* am, in an entirely different fashion, myself, there in the spot where I stand. Under the encouraging stimulating look I know what I do and *that* I do it; every action that I perform is action of my hand, my arm, my body. The accepting look of the other gives me the almost exceptional right to be myself as a *moving body.*

Now that we have arrived at the end of this investigation, we can conclude that to the question as to the place of the domain furnishing significance to human carriage and movement, not one, but three answers must be formulated. Three domains can be indicated from where human movement receives significance, *viz.:* the *landscape* (in the sense of Straus), the *inner self,* and the *glance of another.* The theory of human carriage and movement ought therefore to be *divided into three chapters.*

The first chapter comprises the exposition of "the subject at the end of his emigration," i.e., therefore of the human landscape, of the physiognomy of the things in which man daily realizes, and reveals himself. This first chapter consists in the scientifically justified interpretation of the language of the "mute things," it indicates the manifold nature of the appeal that the world makes, makes in such a way, that the silently transcended body replies to it with a certain attitude or with a certain movement.

The second chapter treats of human movement as "visible expression of an invisibly organized unit, which —dwelling 'centrally' in head or heart—leads a life of its own, fed by a spate of impressions, which is conducted there by means of the receiving organs." [37] This chapter aims at the exposition of man's inner self; of the secrecy of head and heart, of the mystery that a fellowman remains and which is the cause that even in utter closeness he is the *other.* It shows in what way this hidden inner self becomes visible in the movements of the body. The chief word in the terminology of this chapter is *function,* and rightly too, for it is a question of reciprocity between two domains: the *functional reciprocity* of man's inner self and the world categorically separated from this inner self. In this chapter, but there only, the use of the words association, intention, projection, instinct, libido, etc., is justified, since these ideas are inseparably connected with the conception of the duality "inner self" and "external world." Within this chapter man *has* a soul and a body, a disclosure and a mystery, a conscious and an unconscious.

All the prephenomenological theories about human carriage and movement known up till now start from the just-mentioned dual conception. It is an additional, and in my opinion very important, task of this second chapter to rehabilitate these theories (also the Cartesian one) after a critical analysis of them.

[37] Buytendijk, *op. cit.,* p. 323

The third chapter shows the modification which human movement undergoes when it takes place under the regard of another. It does not only comprise all the forms of the alienation of the moving body, but at the same time all the ways in which this body is accepted in its movement by the friendly or loving look of the other. It goes without saying that in this chapter an important place is due to psychopathology of carriage and movement.

The first and the third chapter are still waiting for the author who can integrate the extensive material which has meanwhile accumulated.

EXISTENTIAL PSYCHIATRY AND GROUP PSYCHOTHERAPY

by THOMAS HORA

A therapy group is a structured life situation designed for the study and treatment of the diseased human being. The group situation illuminates the human personality in a multidimensional way and provides for a deeper understanding of the individual through the quality of his relationships to the other group members and the therapist.

The group-psychotherapeutic experience is a living, dynamic experience for all participants, including the therapist. In therapy groups the members function not as samples of various psychic mechanisms or disease entities, but as people with specific ways of experiencing life and specific ways of dealing and communicating with the environment, that is, as individually characteristic modes of "being there" (1, 2). Thus, in fact, the therapy group represents a microcosmos or a segment of the world, and as such it is a situation of an existential encounter for all participants. It is a crossroads at which eight or ten people meet and in this meeting reveal to each other and discover for themselves their particular modes of being-in-this-world (3). When they part, the course of their progression through life is for the most part altered to an appreciable degree.

As a personality, man is mostly a product of his family setting and his socio-cultural environment. As a human being, however, he is an existential phenomenon in terms of his unique characteristics among the living creatures of this world. Survival, growth, and fulfillment require man to adapt himself to his fellow man, his family, to social, cultural, and economic conditions. However, beyond all this he is inescapably faced with the necessity of adjusting to the fundamental order of things as well. Which means that in order to be healthy, man must live in harmony with the ontological conditions of existence.

The objectives of existential psychotherapy point beyond personality integration toward "ontic integration" (4). A fundamental aspect of this therapeutic process consists of liberating the patient's cognitive and creative potentialities, which are usually blocked by his defensive systems. The awakening of the capacity for *creative perception and response* enables the patient to commune with his fellow man in a meaningful (dialogic) way and, beyond that, opens the door to realization of the transcendental—that is, ontological—ground of existence. This realization appears to be necessary for man to come to terms with his finite reality and thus find relief from the omnipresent existential anxiety, or dread of nonbeing.

The aim of existential psychiatry, therefore, is to broaden the psychodynamic and sociodynamic viewpoints and arrive at an integrated image of man which includes the contributions of phenomenological anthropology and fundamental ontology. These schools of thought illuminate the human being and his existence in an encompassing and deeply meaningful way. Among the significant contributions of these schools, many have direct bearing on psychiatry in general and psychotherapy in particular. For instance: the problem of estrangement, temporality, intentionality, existential anxiety, human values, and various attitudes toward existence. The meaningful realization of these existential coordinates provides the participants of the therapy group with a broader and deeper consciousness of the structure of their existence.

Obstacles to Authentic Group Participation

Authentic group participation—that is, genuine being-in-the-group—is only possible under conditions of *openness, receptivity, and responsiveness* toward the world. These human capacities are more often than not thwarted, distorted, and blocked to various degrees. The removal of these obstacles to cognition, to authentic interhuman communication and communion, is an essential feature of the existential group psychotherapeutic endeavor. Man is to be liberated from the prison of his "idios cosmos" (private world of ideas) and enabled to live in the "coinos cosmos" (shared world of communing) (Heraclitus). Only here can his essential humanness come to fruition. The prison of his "idios cosmos" is built on various cognitive and conative disturbances acquired in the course of growing up under the combined influences of the environment and the inherent human inclinations. These result in the so-called "misguided modes of being-in-the-world."

Misguided modes of being-in-the-world reveal themselves as "contact disturbances" and "existential frustration." Man suffers from inadequate relationships with his fellow men and from inadequate realization of his inherent potentialities. While the various aspects of contact disturbances are well-known within the framework of traditional psychoanalytic schools of thought, Existentialism makes its contribution in illuminating the human being from the standpoint of his inherent ontic inclinations, which often cause him to be in disharmony with existence.

Considerations of space make it prohibitive to treat these existential phenomena exhaustively here. These may be found in the literature on existential philosophy and existential psychotherapy in general. The following paragraphs constitute but a small and short sampling of certain phenomena of existence which have immediate relevancy to group psychotherapy, inasmuch as they constitute some of the more frequently encountered obstacles to genuine being-in-the-group, that is, to free and authentic group participation.

ESTRANGEMENT

One of the predicaments of man is the peculiarity that his conceptual or abstract thinking tends to be dissociated from his experiential perceptiveness to such an extent that his reasoning power may actually hamper his capacities to experience, perceive, and cognize what is. A so-called "open mind" is difficult to attain because it entails the capacity for a temporary suspension of intentional (calculating) thinking in favor of heightened receptivity. Heidegger points up the difference between two modes of thinking which he terms *das Vorstellende Denken* and *das Andenkende Denken.*

This inclination often results in the phenomenon of estrangement or alienation, where the experiential aspects of cognition are dissociated and the individual may, for instance, seek to arrive at an understanding of his feelings through deductive reasoning. This is illustrated by a patient who, while sitting quietly in a group of rather heavy cigarette smokers, remarked in a casual way: "I must feel hostile toward smokers because I keep losing matches." Instead of experiencing the truth of his condition in the situation, he was deductively being "rational" about it.

C. G. Jung is known to have said that modern man

could be compared to someone who looks out of his apartment window on the twentieth floor and discovers that the house he lives in starts at the tenth floor. Below, there is nothing. The alienated individual is a stranger to himself and to his fellow man. The more he strives to bridge the gap between his thoughts and his experience, the greater it becomes because his efforts are primarily intellectual. (This, by the way, is one of the main pitfalls of introspection and self-analysis.) He is a stranger amidst his fellow men because he is unable to experience himself as authentically in contact with others. Minkowski speaks of the loss of vital contact (*La perte du contact vital*) which characterizes modern man who is dissociated from his existential core. Karen Horney's important contributions to the elucidation of this problem hardly needs to be emphasized in this Association which so faithfully continues to work in her spirit.

Estrangement makes it difficult for a person to be-in-a-group. Such a person tends to be a "nonparticipating pseudo-observer," not an actual member.

PRESENCE

Another obstacle to full and free group participation is the propensity to cling to the past and to be unduly preoccupied with the future. Consequently, the capacity to experience the present and respond to it is hampered. As one patient put it: "Before the group sessions I keep thinking, what I will say when I come here? And after the group sessions I keep ruminating over what I have said. While I am sitting here, inside I feel like I am running and cannot stop." Such is the dilemma of a person who finds it difficult to be in full perceptual contact with the lived moment. His mode of being-in-the-world is characterized by a disturbed temporality, that is, he lives in unceasing conflict with time.

Such a person may find it difficult to actually be-in-the-group. He may find himself repeatedly out of step with the context of the moment. He may repeatedly drift off into worrying about the future or may tend to divert the attention of the group from what is to what was. Conflict with time has its interhuman repercussions and is revealed in the group as an agitated mode of absent-mindedness and distractibility. The person whose mode of group participation reveals a disturbed temporality is often overly concerned with becoming. Such striving to become underlies a preoccupation with what was in order to change what will be in accordance with how it should be. The desire to become dislocates existence by interfering with the awareness of what is from moment to moment. Since existence is a process, man cannot really understand himself once and for all, only from moment to moment. Knowing oneself must not be confused with knowing about oneself. Transformation and healing can only occur through man's knowing himself. This entails a continuous awareness of what is from moment to moment. Living in harmony with the stream of time abolishes the problem of temporality. Man and time fuse. In this at-oneness the truth of oneself as process is revealed. Truth liberates and transforms man into that being which he really is.

INTENTIONALITY

Closely related to the problem of being present to the present is the problem of intentionality. This frequently occurring problem could be called "the dilemma of planned or intended experiencing." By living according to the Cartesian principle, "Cogito, ergo sum," man seeks to experience his thoughts. He plans in his mind the experiences which are to come to him. By putting thought before perception, man of necessity falsifies reality and blocks it from reaching him in its full scope. As a consequence, he finds himself in a state of inner emptiness and hunger for experiences which he tries to satisfy through ever-increasing efforts at feeling what he thinks he would like to feel or should be feeling. Patients sometimes ask: "What should I be feeling, doctor?"

The intention to experience something makes it impossible to experience the truth of what really is. The blunting of the capacity to experience can conceivably lead to such affective impoverishment and inward sense of emptiness that it may cause man to resort to violent attempts at providing himself with craved-for experiences. This may be an important aspect of sadism, masochism, manipulativeness, and even criminal acting-out.

One patient whom the group members called "the thinker" used to sit in her chair, looking seductively at the therapist and biting her fist in a fierce and rather disquieting way. Her standard complaint was that she could not "gratify her needs." Her intellectuality and intentionality were like a hard shell which stood in the way of tasting the flavor of life in free and reverent receptivity.

In another instance, a colleague one day confessed that he used to come to the session with the intention of taking home a "few pounds of psychotherapy." The intention to acquire knowledge, to learn, to remember, to accept or not-accept, to believe or disbelieve, to agree or disagree, are epistemological barriers to the open mind so essential for understanding to happen.

EXISTENTIAL ANXIETY

Man is the being who can be conscious of his existence. This consciousness presupposes the realization of the inescapable potentiality of nonexistence. Existential anxiety is a natural and omnipresent aspect of human life and is dealt with either by receptive awareness or by attempts at various and manifold escape mechanisms and defensive strivings.

One of the more frequent escape mechanisms is the avoidance of experiencing through flight into intellectuality. This in turn leads to estrangement and the cognitive disturbances mentioned above.

The striving for a sense of security of being drives man to reach out in a grasping and clinging fashion for countless possessions of objects, people, systems, concepts, ideas. He invests these with illusory importance and security value. He tends to objectify people and living creatures for the same end. That is, he wishes to cling to them as illusory protective devices against existential anxiety. As if saying: "I possess, therefore I am" (*Habeo, ergo sum*).

He hangs onto his thoughts and beliefs as onto straps in a subway train, and tends to view the straps to which others cling as inferior and unreal. Anyone who challenges the validity of his thinking or the value of his possessions tends to mobilize existential anxiety and may elicit hostile defensiveness.

The tendency to cling to one's thoughts and beliefs for security is certainly one of the main reasons of conflict between ideologies, schools of thought and frames of references, whether political, religious, scientific, social, economic, or psychoanalytic.

Needless to say, such defensive strivings cripple man's existence by robbing him of his freedom and creative spontaneity. Seeking to escape from the dread of losing his life, man lives in dread of losing his defenses. The more he clings to them, the more he becomes immobilized by them. Finally, that which he clings to, clings to him.

Such a tragically paradoxical dilemma was expressed by one successful businessman suffering from coronary heart disease and high blood pressure, in the following way: "I know that my life is a 'rat race' and it is killing me, but I am afraid to stop because I might become a nobody and die." Then he added: "It looks like fear of death is driving me to commit suicide."

ENCROACHMENT

The combination of so-called dependent and domineering, or passive and aggressive, tendencies in the same person can create severe interhuman contact disturbances, social anxiety, and psychosomatic conditions. What appears as a problem of domination and dependency is here understood as a problem of the tendency to encroach on existence. Domination is encroachment on the existence of others. Passivity and dependency may be viewed as encroachment on the existence of one's own. In either case, man suffers existential guilt which tends to become manifest in the form of embarrassment and social anxiety.

In group situations, the encroaching person tends to alternate between the supine (feet on the table) position and aggressive, intent leaning forward in his chair. In his manner of speech, he tends to alternate between hard, hammer-blow, staccato expressions and whining ("belly-aching") speech. He is alternately boastful and complaining—or even simultaneously. He is either overassertive or yielding and timid. His face may have hard, aggressive lines while in his eyes there may be softness. He may feel guilty if he is aggressive and ashamed of his timidity. He may fear asserting himself and be afraid not to assert himself. He may be afraid to be outspoken and afraid to be reticent. If he speaks, he may be afraid of being considered obtrusive and boastful. If he is silent, he may be afraid of being considered stupid, timid, shy, anxious, ignorant. He may feel himself caught in a "double bind." Whichever way he moves, he is liable to bring embarrassment or disaster upon himself. He may finally avoid meeting people: he may withdraw from his friends and limit his existence to a minimum.

The encroaching person has considerable difficulty in the group. His contact disturbances tend to be maximal and, therefore, he may require a great deal of preliminary elucidation, preferably in individual treatment.

HUMAN VALUES

As long as man is in the throes of existential anxiety, his ethics and morality are of necessity artificial and based on discipline, self-abnegation, or hypocrisy. Man's defensive preoccupation with security, status, power, and permanence will unavoidably drive him in the direction of egocentricity. Consequently, selfishness, greed, possessiveness, exploitativeness, coerciveness, dependency, domination, parasitism, ambition, vanity, hunger for power and influence, fame, and popularity remain problems regardless of moral codes, good intentions, or discipline.

The group situation invariably highlights the ethical conflict of the individual in his pathetic struggle to reconcile his sense of moral responsibility with his egocentric defensive needs. The problem of authenticity of being points to the significance of values in human existence in general and in psychopathology in particular. In general, it can be said that distorted human values are to be found in most psychopathological conditions. In a paper entitled "Group Psychotherapy, Human Values and Mental Health," (5) it was pointed out that sound human values are an inseparable aspect of mental health and that the process of personality integration through the medium of group psychotherapy provides ample evidence that positive principles of ethics and morality are integral to mental health.

The problem of human values is closely associated with the peculiarity of the human condition in general. The human condition as such is characterized by the fact that man is cast into this world and removed from it by forces beyond his control, therefore beyond his responsibility. Yet for the duration of his life he is charged with the task of making the best of his given potentialities. From an ontological standpoint, man has two freedoms: the freedom to fulfill his potentialities and the freedom to fail to fulfill them. If he fails to fulfill his given potentialities he may experience existential guilt.

As for human values, they too are mostly imposed upon man in his formative years by his environment. Man may not be responsible for having acquired wrong values, yet he is responsible and suffers the consequences if he keeps them. It is his responsibility to change his wrong values and adopt healthy ones. In addition to all this, there is a natural propensity for man to submit to group pressures, to deny his inner reality, and to conform to social mores. In Riesman's (6) words, man tends to become "other-directed," thus losing contact with himself and sinking into unauthenticity.

TRANSFERENCE AND NON-TRANSFERENCE

It is sometimes assumed that existential psychiatry neglects transference factors and pays more attention to non-transference factors. However, from the standpoint of existential psychotherapy, the concern with non-transference factors appears to be a mistake similar to the preoccupation with transference factors. For in either case we would fall prey to the self-defeating tendency of studying human beings in parts or in aspects only. A person who is taken apart becomes an object. An object is not a living creature. The sum total of parts of a human being does not add up to a whole human being. Scientific objectification is painful to the patient and defeats our endeavors to understand him.

If the issue of transference is considered, it can be said that transference is the misuse, avoidance, misunderstanding, misinterpretation, falsification, denial, or unawareness of the reality of a current situation. Furthermore, transference is personal history. To see transference in a person is to see primarily his historical conditioning, rather than the human being as he really is. The analyst or group psychotherapist whose attention is centered on transference factors or non-transference factors may tend to objectify his patient in accordance with a particular pseudoscientific bias. Instead of a forest, he may see only certain trees twisted in particular ways by some environmental or other influences in the distant past. Such partial and limited perspectives have their validity and usefulness in specialized areas of scientific research, especially in relation to the object world. But when it comes to the understanding of human beings, a holistic mode of perception, cognition, understanding, and response seems preferable.

The existential encounter is an event where the patient as a whole, that is, as a "being-in-the-world," is revealed to the therapist by way of the phenomenological mode of cognition.

What is the phenomenological mode of cognition? It may be described as the unbiased, "open-minded" understanding of another person as an existent from moment-to-moment. Why from moment-to-moment? Because man is an existential process. Therefore, he cannot really be known once and for all. Neither can man know himself once and for all. As mentioned before, knowing oneself must not be confused with knowing about oneself. The phenomenological mode of cognition opens up to human consciousness the loving mode of knowledge. It reveals to man the "realm of Love-Intelligence" (7).

If we carefully consider that which in traditional psychoanalysis is called "insight" we discover that it is actually "hindsight." Which means knowing oneself as one was in order to change oneself in accordance with how one "should be"—that is, in accordance with certain mentally projected standards. Now all this at times may lead to a form of psychopathology which could be called the "syndrome of the self-made man." Man who "makes" himself healthy may become sicker than he was. For health cannot be made. It comes into being when the truth of oneself as process is understood.

In the therapy groups, patients reveal themselves to each other and to the therapist in accordance with their particular modes of being-in-the-world. This revelation is a continuous process of elucidation of the ongoing stream of events without casual, genetic, historical, teleological, or other considerations. The continuous awareness and elucidation of what is happening contains all the above-mentioned aspects of being human—that is, it contains all transference, as well as non-transference, aspects of the participating individuals, but it transcends them all. Therefore, special interpretations are not required. That which is speaks for itself, provided it is understood phenomenologically rather than interpreted in accordance with certain theoretical presuppositions. That which is understood needs no interpretation. That which is interpreted is seldom understood.

THE GROUP PROCESS

In considering patients from an existential standpoint, it is found that, notwithstanding their diagnostic categories of psychopathology, they suffer from disturbed modes of being-in-the-world. In the group situation they are revealed as hampered in their capacities to communicate meaningfully with their fellow group members, and consequently they suffer both from a sense of isolation and from frequently recurring conflicts. They are further afflicted by a limited capacity for presence—that is, they are in conflict with time, with their own intentionalities, strivings, ethical codes, and defensive attitudes.

Whenever two or more people meet, they affect each other profoundly. Most of the impact which people have upon each other, however, remains below the surface of conscious awareness, or, as the neurophysiologist J. C. Lilly (8) puts it: "There is evidence that the greatest part of our experience comes into us through paths unbeknownst to consciousness."

When a group of people meets, every participant is exposed to the impact of the sum total of all stimuli present. This total of stimuli is the content of the group atmosphere. This atmosphere is charged with affective currents. The nature of man's ties to his fellow man is essentially affective (9). Emotional perceptivity and emotional communicativeness are essential features of human nature. Emotions are communicated through verbal, nonverbal, conscious, and nonconscious channels. We even speak of "emotional contagion" as a group phenomenon.

An undifferentiated state of affective stimulation creates a need to organize this affect into thoughts. This is experienced as group tension. The participants experience an inner urge to do something. This results in a need to talk. Language here is used as substitute action, serving the need to discharge inner tension. This (vicarious) use of language communicates little that is essential. It clarifies nothing. It is a verbal form of acting out and as such it serves the purpose of tension reduction. This, in turn, makes it possible for the participants to avoid becoming aware of what they are really experiencing.

Whenever a group meets, certain basic phenomena are observable from the start. These are: 1) The impact of the participants upon each other, 2) Unspecified affective cross currents, 3) A group atmosphere, 4) Group tension, and 5) A certain pervasive anxiety.

After the initial tension is discharged and the anxiety relieved, there follows a stage of curiosity about each other. This curiosity does not serve the purpose of really understanding one another, but rather to compare notes and see how one "stacks up" in comparison with the others. Language is used here in a superficial, exploratory, or concealing manner.

We see that right from the start the group members are primarily concerned with gratifying their own personal needs for tension reduction, even though they appear to be talking to each other and seemingly are interested in each other. This kind of duplicity or unauthenticity is so universal that few people give it a second thought. It is an accepted mode of social behavior. And yet this phenomenon is the first step in the direction of gradual self-estrangement. It is the first contact with the whirlpool of unauthenticity which threatens man throughout his life.

Patients find it very difficult to refrain from the usual ways of discharging their tensions. One patient remarked: "I feel like an overcharged soda bottle about to pop." This statement is an example of how a patient begins to become aware of what he is experiencing. This is the first step in the direction of broadening of his consciousness into the proprioceptive sphere of awareness. Having given expression to the truth of his inner experience, the patient finds relief from tension. One patient expressed it the following way: "The group is the only place where I feel truly alive because everywhere else I am mostly lying." By this she meant to say that in her social and professional life she is only aware of her thoughts and strivings and there is a disharmony between what she is usually saying and feeling. It appears that language is a "hidden door" which can lead either to alienation or to integrated authentic existence, depending on how it is used.

Essentially, group members act and talk in pursuit of their needs to escape existential anxiety. This leads unavoidably to conflict between divergent needs. The conflict is accompanied by neurotic anxiety which, phenomenologically, is an awareness of the inner disharmony between thought, feeling, experience, and striving. Thus, in therapy groups, man is revealed as being buffeted between his need to escape from existential anxiety and his need to avoid neurotic anxiety. What balance he strikes or how he goes about coping with his human predicament is quite specific to every individual and constitutes his special mode of being-in-the-world.

This mode of being-in-this-world includes all possible mechanisms of defense, diagnostic categories, or nosologic entities of psychopathology as part of a general adaptation to life. The group situation illuminates the significance of Martin Buber's dialogue. For the incapacity for genuine, reciprocal, nonmanipulative communication among the members of the group is indicative of their failure to come to terms with their human condition.

It was described above how inner tension drives the

group members to use language in an unauthentic, essentially noncommunicative way as a form of verbal acting out for the purpose of avoiding awareness of what is experienced. Existential anxiety drives the group members to become preoccupied with one another as objects. This leads to a use of language which again is essentially a form of acting out in a manipulative sense. That is, under the impact of existential anxiety, the members are driven to seek mastery over the object world and thus they attempt to master each other by a verbal form of manipulation and probing. For instance, one patient said to another in a group: "When you look at me, I feel like an automobile engine which needs to be repaired."

The human situation reveals itself in the therapy groups as a rather complex problem of adaptation requiring man to fit himself into a world into which he is "thrown" under rather difficult conditions. As one patient put it:

"Life is like being in jail, sentenced to die. Trying to escape makes things worse, you keep hurting yourself in the fruitless effort. There is no way out. I wish I could believe in God and trust Him that all this has some sense and purpose. Then perhaps I could accept my situation."

Another patient said:

"Here we are sitting in a circle, facing one another, yet we are keenly aware of our separateness. It is almost like being in solitary confinement. My eyes are windows through which I am peering at the world, wishing to get out of myself and fuse with everything that is outside of me to escape aloneness."

Every group session becomes an experience of looking into a multifaceted psychological mirror and discovering more and more details about one's own mode of being or failing to be-in-this-world due to a variety of defensive attitudes and strivings evolved in the course of a lifetime.

In the main, the group psychotherapeutic process could be vaguely considered as consisting of a phase of self-discovery, followed by a gradually increasing amount of self-understanding, which then yields to a phase of experimentation in learning to let-go of the defensive strivings. This phase is experienced as rather anxiety-laden. Success in learning to accept one's anxiousness is an important step in the direction of accepting one's "thrownness" (*Geworfenheit*), or ontic condition, and is rewarded by a new phase of discovering oneself as being-in-the-world in an authentic fashion. This may at times have phenomenological concomitants. For instance, one patient said:

"Willingness to be afraid has freed me of my fear and suddenly I realized that people are three-dimensional."

In other words, this patient discovered that her previous existence took place in a two-dimensional world. Spatiality is a phenomenological coordinate of human existence, as has been demonstrated by Binswanger.

In the therapy group, patients become increasingly aware of the difference between talking to people and communing with people (10). Furthermore, they discover the difference between knowing about oneself and understanding oneself.

Since the group is conceived of as a microcosmos and an arena for an existential encounter, all conceptualizations, historical references, and outside issues are considered as of secondary significance and interactions are viewed in the content of "here and now." The focus is on the creative understanding of "what is" (11) from moment to moment and from "heart to heart." By which is meant an increasing awareness of the unfolding of the existential process in each participant.

While the group setting is a structured one in terms of time, place, number of participants, circular arrangement of chairs, and so forth, the group process itself is unstructured except by the impact of the therapist's personality, which unavoidably and very meaningfully focuses on certain values reflected by his mode of being-in-the-world. These values are invariably and unavoidably communicated by the therapist's bearing, facial expressions, attitudes, and responses. The authenticity of the therapist as a being is obviously of utmost importance, since otherwise a great deal of confusion and conflict can arise from the disparity between his utterances and his attitudinal communications. For example, one patient said:

"You say that we are free and nothing is demanded of us, but when you sit there looking at us, we feel that you expect us to talk."

The road to authenticity of being leads through a rather painful phase of enduring periods of silence in the group. Since the habitual way of being for most group members is to treat one another as objects, and to attempt to probe, manipulate, influence, and use one another for the purpose of gratification of personal needs of selfish nature, the gradual renunciation of this habitual mode of relating with its acting-out use of verbal and nonverbal language leads eventually to a state which Heidegger calls "speechless silence."

According to Heidegger, "speechless silence" is the "Soundless voice of Being" which opens up the dread of Nothingness. "Nothingness in its otherness to all that is, is the Veil of Being." Which means that Nothingness, if confronted in personal experience, unveils "all that is" in a meaningful way.

One patient reported a dream to the group which immediately was recognized by the others as a turning point in his life. The patient spoke about it as a "dreadful encounter" with death which he miraculously survived. He dreamed that, while walking with a shadowy companion on a lonely road, he heard from a great distance the hum of an approaching plane. He had a vague premonition of disaster. This premonition grew gradually into panic when he noticed that the plane was actually in a nose dive and heading straight at him. In the last moment, while throwing himself to the ground, all fear left him and the thought passed through his mind that this was the end. He felt the wheel of the plane touch his shoulder as it crashed in flames a few feet away. He got up, and his first thought was: "I must try to save the pilot from the wreckage." Suddenly, life became for him a continuous miracle to be deeply appreciated. For this patient, reverence for life became a "tangible reality," rather than just a philosophical presupposition.

In the periods of speechless silence the group members experience existential anxiety and develop the capacity to endure it. These painful periods of silence reveal to them the phenomenon of boredom. Boredom is a state of meaninglessness of existence which emerges whenever one attempts to renounce the pursuit of false meanings or when the pursuit of such meanings is made impossible through psychotherapeutic illumination.

The periods of silent boredom prevail for a while until, one by one, the group participants arrive at the edge of the "wasteland" and begin to communicate in an increasingly authentic way. For example, a patient began his group session with an effusive expression of his gratitude to the group members and personal thanks to the therapist for his having succeeded in getting a job as a schoolteacher. He spoke with some insistence and tension in his demeanor. He gave the impression of someone who was trying to force a present on another person. After he had finished, there was a long uneasy period of silence. Some group members avoided responding; others congratulated him somewhat sheepishly, but there was one member who said the following:

"Your expressions of gratitude make me feel as though I were being bribed. It is an uncomfortable and embarrassing experience. You are forcing your thanks on us and trying to corrupt us to accept credit for something we do not deserve."

This authentic response had an immediate tension-relieving effect on all, including the patient. At this point, some of the other members reminded the patient that, while his gratitude was now so insistent, he tended at other times to blame people for his failures.

This is an illustration of the difference between the authentic and unauthentic ways of responding and communicating. We see that the unauthentic group members responded either with empty, superficial politeness or with evasive silence, while the authentic group member expressed the truth of his inner experience, thus relieving the group tension caused by the threatened breakdown in communication.

The participants learn to be aware of what they are experiencing and the interactions between patient and patient, or patient and therapist, are concerned primarily with the experiential aspects of the communications, while content is given secondary importance. For instance, a patient may break a prolonged silence by telling a dream. Instead of analyzing the content of the dream, the group members may respond with expressing their feelings about the fact that the patient chose to tell a dream at that particular moment; or they may respond to the manner in which the dream was told, or they may analyze the impact of this event upon the group. For example, one female patient told a dream about sharing the superintendent of the house in which she lived with a roommate for sexual purposes. In response to this, one female group member said: "I feel uneasy about your dream and your way of telling it." Another patient said he perceived a certain demeaning attitude in the manner of presentation of the dream. Another patient remarked: "It seems that you told the dream in order to cover up your embarrassment over the competitive striving which you have for the doctor." At this point, the first patient said: "Now I understand why I felt so uneasy about your dream. I think we are competing for the doctor and I am the roommate of your dream." Another patient summed it up by saying: "You are demeaning the doctor because you are ashamed of your cravings for him and find it humiliating to compete for his attention."

The experiential elements of the situation in which an interaction occurs, illuminate the content in a particularly meaningful way (12). The ontological essence and existential meaning of a dream or communication are to be found primarily in its basic climate (*Gestimmtheit*) and only secondarily in its symbolic content.

Significantly enough, the capacity to be aware of the experiential impact of the others upon oneself and vice versa tends to open up a new dimension of consciousness which leads to a growing understanding of one's own structure of being-in-this-world or failing to be-in-this-world due to various defensive attitudes and strivings. As one patient put it: "I can feel myself standing in my own way."

The experiential awareness of one's own defensiveness converts the meaning of the defense from comfort to obstacle and impediment. The moment one experiences one's own defenses as impediments, one becomes eager to let go of them. The moment one experiences one's own strivings as a source of stress, anxiety, and conflict, one becomes eager to give them up. The moment one becomes aware of one's own temporality and spatiality—that is, one's own relationship to time and space—one becomes sensitive to conflicts which arise in contact with others whose temporality and spatiality may be different from one's own. The group situation provides the opportunity for experiencing the self-defeating nature and burdensomeness of defensive attitudes and strivings.

The change to authenticity of being is characterized above all by truthfulness of expression, mutual regard, respect for the freedom and integrity of all, increased perceptivity and creativity of thinking. The use of language becomes dedicated to communication in its stricter sense rather than to anything else. This is not easily attained. As one patient put it: "One of the most difficult things is to talk in such a way as to really say something rather than seek to get something."

Another patient followed this up by saying: "It is almost as if we had to die before we could really live."

Indeed, the periods of silence are at times so painful that some patients experience dizziness and fleeting reactions of depersonalization and derealization on such occasions. The dread of nothingness appears to be related to the phenomena which occur in man when exposed to perceptual isolation (13).

The problem of loneliness and isolation is overcome through self-transcendence in the sense of the existential meeting, which is a mode of relatedness described by Martin Buber as "mutual spiritual inclusion," or by Gabriel Marcel as "intersubjectivity." In terms of the therapy groups, it means a mode of "being-there" involving the total experiential sphere and communication potential of all participants. The capacity for this kind of presence is rooted in the attainment of authenticity of being.

Group psychotherapy provides the patients with an opportunity to recognize, understand, and liberate themselves from the obstacles and impediments which have hitherto stood in the way of their free, full, and conscious participation in the process of existence as it unfolds in the "coinos cosmos."

REFERENCES

1. Binswanger, L.: Grundformen und Erkenntnis Menschlichen Daseins, Max Niehans Verlag, Zürich, 1942.
2. Hora, Thomas: Ontic Perspectives in Psychoanalysis, Am. J. Psychoan., XIX, 2, 1959.
3. Heidegger, M.: Sein und Zeit, Max Niehans Verlag, Tuebingen, 1953.
4. Hora, Thomas: Ontic Integration. Paper read at the International Congress of Group Psychotherapy, Barcelona, Spain, September, 1958.
5. Hora, Thomas: Group Psychotherapy, Human Values and Mental Health, International Journal of Group Psychotherapy, VIII, 2, April, 1958.
6. Riesman, D.: The Lonely Crowd, Yale University Press, New Haven, 1950.
7. Hora, Thomas: Transcendence and Healing. Paper read at the Annual Conference of Existential Psychology and Psychiatry, Carnegie Endowment Center, New York City, February, 1960.
8. Lilly, J. C.: Some Thought on Brain-Mind and on Restraint and Isolation of Mentally Healthy Subjects, Journal of Philadelphia Psychiatric Hospital, 1957.
9. Hora, Thomas: Beyond Countertransference, American Journal of Psychotherapy, Vol. 10, 1956.
10. Hora, Thomas: Existential Communication and Psychotherapy, Psychoanalysis, Vol. 5, No. 4, Winter, 1957.
11. Krishnamurti, J.: Commentaries on Living, Harper, New York, 1958.

12. Hora, Thomas: Tao, Zen and Existential Psychotherapy, Psychologia, Kyoto, Japan, 1960.
13. Wexler, Mendelson, Leiderman and Solomon: Perceptual Isolation: A Technique of Studying Psychiatric Aspects of Stress, Annual Meeting of APA, Chicago, 1957.

THE PHENOMENOLOGICAL APPROACH TO THE PROBLEM OF FEELINGS AND EMOTIONS

by F. J. J. BUYTENDIJK *

During the many years of my investigations of animal behavior I have become more and more convinced that we ought to understand the observable vital phenomena such as actions and expressions. Behavior can never be reduced to physiological processes and explained as a result of the integration of reflexes. The reflex is a reduced action, stabilized by the constant signification, for example the dangerousness, of the situation in which it occurs. The characteristics and the entire signification of behavior become intelligible in the light of their relation to the essence of the animal being in general and the definite mode of existence of the species.[1] The proper content or signification of the concept of behavior presupposes that being an animal is absolutely different from being a crystal, a drop of water, or a plant.[2] These

* F. J. J. BUYTENDIJK is a professor at the State University of Utrecht, Holland, and is well known for his works on women, pain, play, etc. Although his books have been translated into many languages, virtually nothing is available in English. Some titles of his books are *La femme, ses modes d'être, de paraître, d'exister* (Paris, 1954), *Le football. Une étude psychologique* (Paris, 1952), *Phénoménologie de la rencontre* (Paris, 1952), *Wesen und Sinn des Spiels* (Berlin, 1933), *De la douleur* (Paris, 1951), *Attitudes et mouvements* (Paris, 1957).

1 F. J. J. Buytendijk. *Wege zum Verständnis der Tiere.* Zürich: 1938.

2 Explained in an excellent way by Merleau-Ponty, *La structure du comportement* (Pr. Un Fr.).

ideas and views resulting from concrete experiments and observations have made me appreciate the value of the phenomenological approach and apply the phenomenological method to the problems of psychology.[3] Animals and men are observable subjects,[4] because we understand behavior as a system of intentional acts.

Husserl's phenomenological method [5] is founded on the irreducible fact that consciousness must necessarily be consciousness of something toward which it is intentionally directed and which therefore has a meaning. Consequently consciousness is not considered to be an "interiority," an imaginary space with certain contents and processes, interacting with the physical being and with a sensorially appearing outer world. This conception, implied in various images, has entered psychology as a means of interpreting consciousness (or the self or the ego) as "something" existing (*res cogitans*) that enters into relationship with an existing world (*res extensa*).

Psychology as a positive science has become dogmatic and lacks the radicalism of doubt. The unprejudiced return to the "things themselves," *i.e.,* inspection of knowledge "itself" as given to us *directly,* with nothing mediating or interfering, reveals the intentionality or act-character of all behavior. Feeling, *e.g.,* being pleased, is an

[3] F. J. J. Buytendijk. (1) *Das Spiel von Mensch und Tier*. Berlin: Kurt Wolff, 1933. (2) *Over de Pijn* ("On pain"). Utrecht: 1943. (3) *Algemene Theorie der menselijke Houding en Beweging* ("General theory of human attitude and movement"). Utrecht: 1948.

[4] V. von Weizsäcker. *Angeschaute Subjecktivität*. Leipzig: Der Gestaltkreis, 1943.

[5] A very good survey of Husserl's ideas is to be found in Marvin Farber, *The Foundations of Phenomenology* (Cambridge, Mass.: Harvard Univ. Press, 1943), and Marvin Farber (Ed.), *Philosophical Essays in Memory of Edmund Husserl* (Cambridge, Mass.: Harvard Univ. Press, 1940). A short but very clear explanation of the concept of intentionality has been published by J. P. Sartre in *Situations I* (N.R.F.), Une idée fondamentale de la phénoménologie de Husserl: l'intentionnalité.

act, in which there is reference—not a causal relation—to an object that is intentionally *present*. It may occur without the object existing, for this object is merely *meant* in the act of feeling.

Perhaps, someone might remark, psychology as a pure science has nothing to do with a theoretical conception concerning consciousness, neither the Cartesian nor the phenomenological idea. Science should be limited to establishing *facts*. I can agree with this conception of science, but then, I think, we are obliged to ask what a fact is. Is feeling a fact? Or is it an abstraction? And is it a fact that there exist men who have feeling in certain situations? If we take this question seriously, we should have to know what we *mean* by "exist," "situation," "feeling." This is exactly what it is the aim of phenomenology to reveal.

When we should like, for example, to institute a statistical inquiry into "happy and unhappy marriages," we have to know *what* a marriage is. We can arrange to take it for granted that a marriage can be defined by certain characteristics or properties, just as we identify a substance as oxygen or gold. I will not insist on the dubious value of such an objective determination of a human relationship such as marriage. But what are happiness and unhappiness? Should we calculate in our statistics the subjective opinions of everyone who is asked whether he is happy or unhappy or should we try to know what may be the essential characteristics of the sense of happiness as a pure phenomenon, given to us directly as something that shows itself in itself, with all its immanent characteristics and also its reference to the situation of being married? This analysis of the intentional experience is the phenomenological approach to feelings and emotions.

In phenomenology we should like to know what the

significations of the acts of hating, loving, desiring, rage, joy, etc., are; and we are convinced that these significations or meanings are the real essence of the feelings. Every feeling is feeling of something, and the human attitude in which a feeling is experienced in a positional, not reflective, consciousness results in fuller understanding.

Our feelings are no senseless states of consciousness or psychic facts, but modes to detect the signification of situations, to *know* what is savory, disgusting, alarming, distressing, lovely, etc. Human reality is equivalent to being conscious and this can be defined only as open to the world, as cast upon the world. Being conscious is *s'éclater dans le monde,* to use Sartre's image of this kind of being. A pure description of purified knowledge of the affected and feeling self, of the situation and the concrete mode of existence in this situation, ignores all actual facts, for example, psychogenetic laws and physiological conditions.

In phenomenological psychology man is considered as existing. All mental experiences—perception, remembrance, thinking, dreaming, and also feeling—are relations of an existing human being and his world. They presuppose both the human being and his world, and we ought to know what is meant by these concepts. To discover the definite significance, *i.e.,* the essence of a feeling, we have to start from a conception of human existence. Consciousness exists to the exact extent that it is consciousness to exist. It would be a misunderstanding to think that the a priori concept of existence can be interpreted as a dogmatic a priori, that is, a statement about human existence of irrefutable validity.

Surely all phenomenological analysis of feelings and emotions, such as Scheler's investigations of the modes of sympathy,[6] the research on normal and abnormal feelings by such psychiatrists as Rümke,[7] Binswanger,[8] Minkowski,[9] Kunz,[10] and others, and the analysis of laughing and crying by Plessner,[11] presuppose a certain implicit idea about human reality and man's existence in the world, but this conception becomes explicit in the progress of the phenomenological analysis itself. If the psychologists in their modesty are animated by the laudable hope of realizing later, on the solid ground of their research work, an anthropological synthesis, they are in full contradiction with themselves (Sartre [12]). The traditional theories of feeling and emotion, even all descriptions of these phenomena, are based on the a priori conception of man as a "mundane ego," that is, a constituted object among other objects in the world. We do not agree with this conception.

The phenomenological approach to feelings and emotions starts from the undeniable fact that consciousness is always a being conscious of something else and that we are conscious of our existing, that means our being physically subjected to a given situation. This "being subjected" is not a causal relation, but it means that the situation must be responded to. The reply is the attitude, the feeling, the intentional act and not a reaction in a physiological sense. The fact that we find ourselves as subjects (in our "this-ness") only by standing apart and viewing ourselves in the situations in which we are in-

[6] Max Scheler. *Wesen und Forme der Sympathie*. Bonn.

[7] H. C. Rümke. Zur Phaenomenologie und Klinik des Glücksgefühls. *Monogr. Gesamtgebeit Neurol. Psychiat.*, 1924, 39.

[8] L. Binswanger, *e.g.* Über die manische Lebensform. *Schweiz. Med. Wschr.*, 1945, 75.

[9] E. Minkowski. *Vers une cosmologie*. Paris: Aubier.

[10] H. Kunz, *Aggressivität und Zärtlichkeit*. Bern: 1946.

[11] H. Plessner, *Lachen und Weinen*. Arnhem: 1946.

[12] J.-P. Sartre, *Esquisse d'une théorie des émotions*. Paris: Hermann, 1939. P. 5.

volved is the profoundest basis of the phenomenon of feeling. Feeling and emotion are the affirmations of our attitudes toward situations, and the pure phenomenon of feeling reveals the human being as always projecting it and always projecting the world. The pure description of a feeling is the description of an existing human being in his well-defined attitude toward a situation. The projection is the signification of the act of feeling, a spontaneous movement (*s'éclater vers*—ejecting himself toward), which implies a totality of relations and their development. Feeling is a mode of replying to a situation and transforming it as a projected new world, in which unknown qualities are categorically experienced. There are as many feelings as there are situations, and the situation is created by the mode in which I have accepted it, *i.e.*, by my chosen projection. Of course this projection is not the result of reasoning and my choice is not arbitrary. I choose my emotional attitude in the same unreflective, nonconsidering (thematic, not thetic) mode of consciousness as I choose my words in speaking or writing.

The attitude toward the situation, confirmed by the feeling, is a true reply that is elicited. It is always my own unreflected act. There are, for example, many kinds of being irritated, angry, or furious, in which we choose and project ourselves in the mode of an efficacious revolt, just as I choose the more tasty of two apples. I have no motive in mind for my choice, but still there is in the situation and the backward reference to my existential history an antecedent that works *only* by its signification and hence is no cause.

When the normal impassive contemplative attitude becomes too difficult, so that we cannot meet the exigencies of the situation, we may choose to become angry and to change the situation and our attitude to it by this feeling[13] Every feeling has a signification that makes us find the thing that is signified. Both the dynamic quality of the immediately experienced feeling and the essential characteristics of the expression refer to the signification and the thing signified. Even joy is not an automatic reaction to an impression. Joy may be cheerfulness, high spirits, radiant expansion, dilatation, illumination, elevation.

All these dynamic elements may be the invariant content of a certain kind of joy. They denote the act, by which I affirm my choice of the positive value concealed in the situation and now revealed by my feeling joyous. The phenomenology of feeling has taken only the first step on the way of analyzing the various kinds of joyous feelings. We know—and it is important for psychopathology—that there exists a silent, quiet joy, large, placid, voluminous, embracing as a climate and signifying the mode of possessing and concealing a value which structures our entire existence.

There is also a leaping joy, a being animated, when we shout, jubilate, dance. This joy is allied to and impregnated with impatience (Sartre). It signifies the anticipation, a reaching, longing for some value that is approaching, that is expected.

I will try to give a provisional short sketch of a possible phenomenological genetic analysis of feeling and emotion, starting from the conception of Ruckmick[14] that the affective life begins with consciousness itself. In every concrete existence this "being conscious" is consciousness of existing physically, *i.e.,* being limited. The pure phenomenon of existing is the immediate act of experience of its own limit and this experience includes necessarily

[13] *Ibid.,* p. 22.
[14] C. A. Ruckmick, *Psychology of Feeling and Emotion,* New York and London: McGraw-Hill, 1936. p. 214.

the experience of a possible transcendence of this limit. Conscious existing contains (in its own limitation) the possibility of feeling in its original signification of close relationship to the act of touching.

The sense of touch is the "father" of all senses (Lavelle,[15] Nogué [16]). Touching is the discovery of our real existence in its own limitation. It reveals at the same time the physical self as touched, moved, and something that is touched by our self-movement. Touching is the most original mode of the experience of participation and feeling. In this encounter, for example, feeling the smoothness, slipperiness, stickiness, angularity, roundness, the shape and form of an object, we are intentionally involved in an anticipated developing situation. The act, the answer to the encounter, may be in the direction of the discovery of the qualities felt or of the feeling of something or in the direction of being emotionally stirred up and disturbed. It depends on the situation and our approach to it, whether feeling or emotion will prevail. Every new encounter is at the same time the abolishing of a former mode of being-in-the-world and this former existence is stirred, moved, and emotionalized. Awareness of emotion and also of excitation, I believe, is a nonintentional element of every feeling, just as it may be an element in the act of touching. It depends on the situation and the projection of our mode of relation to it, if feeling, emotion, or excitement prevails. The original signification of the act of feeling and the disturbing function of emotion and irritation, which are included in touching, the most original act of being-for-self in the individual's limited physical existence, inhibit themselves in the manifold situa-

[15] L. Lavelle, *Dialectique du monde sensible*. Strassbourg: 1921.
[16] J. Nogué, *Esquisse d'un systéme de qualités sensibles*. Pr. Un Fr.: 1943. *La signification du sensible*. Aubier: 1936.

tions in which a human being chooses to be engaged. These situations are the affective ones which elicit rage, fright, terror, astonishment, sorrow, joy, shame, jealousy, hate, sympathy, compassion, etc., and unlimited variations of sentiments, passion, and moods. In all these cases the phenomenological analysis will have to detect the full content of the significant formation and the essential history of significance. Many such investigations have appeared in the literature. Typical examples are given by Sartre, who showed the magical transformation of the world by feeling and emotion. He also speaks of the projection of the affective significations on the environment and mentions that consciousness "lives in the new world which it has just constituted. Consciousness is the victim of the trap it has set itself. Consciousness is moved by its own emotion."

Emotion is not an intentional act, but allied to sensation, irritation, and excitation. We may come to understand this fact in the following way: we have only consciousness of ourselves (regaining ourselves in the vision of things). When I admire something or hate someone, I, in *one* intentional act of feeling, project both myself as admiring or hating and the qualitative structure of the object or person. The created situation is not a static pattern, but an animated, vivid, lively unity that appeals to me by the claims of its qualities, provoked by my feeling. As has been demonstrated by V. von Weizsäcker for the act of touching, there is a functional circle of movement and being moved, in which the *Gestalt* is developed. Exactly as in touching, there is in the act of feeling a *closed* reciprocal relation between the subject and its intentional object. Consciousness is shut up with something and isolated from the rest of the world. The *rebound* of my projection of feeling against the created intentional experience has the character of being moved, *i.e.,* of emotion (possibly in the modality of excitation, excitement, or irritation). The result is penetration of feeling with emotion, of emotion with feeling, a stabilization, a continuity of the affected relation, with a certain analogy to the standing vibrations in a closed resonator or the standing waves on a limited surface of water. Thus we conclude that there is no emotion without the act of feeling, but the emotion itself is not an intentional act. It is the specific quality of our own existence, revealed in the regaining of ourselves in the act of feeling.

This may be the reason that I prefer to say: *I am* admiring this picture, *I am* hating that person, and I am moved *by* the beauty of the picture, *by* the untrustworthiness of that person. We must be aware that in every language the verbal expressions are ambiguous. The reason is that the dialectic and reciprocal relation of the involvement of affect makes it possible to describe the experience in a different way. It may happen that the repercussion of the (created) object to my act of feeling is so intense that I am conscious of my existence as a purely-passive-entity-being-moved and that this emotion totally hides the original intentional act that was the creator and also is the maintainer of the emotion. Therefore Sartre could write, "Pain is quite free from intentionality." [17] This is true, but there is no pain without a preceding, original attitude toward our existence as a physical-being-in-the-world. In our well-balanced life this attitude of ours is so "normal" that we forget its intentional character, but the simple fact of being painless in fighting or in hysteria reminds us that the condition of undergoing the sensation of pain is to be *with* ourselves, means to be conscious of our existence. Pain is not a feeling (act) but an emotional sensation only possible in the intentional experience of existence.

[17] *Op. cit.,* p. 398.

Continuing our sketch of a genetic analysis of feeling and emotion, we ought to realize that the encounter of our existence with something that limits it takes place in different intentional experiences. There are, so far as I can see, two extreme possibilities. The intentional object to which we are directed in the act of recognition of our own limitation is presented either as a resistance or as no resistance. The experience of resistance signifies our obstructed existence. The experience of no resistance in the encounter signifies our expanding existence. It seems to me that in grasping the sense of these phenomena we can distinguish four modes of feeling pleasant and four modes of feeling unpleasant, corresponding to the experience of different modes of existence. The four modes of existence that are presented in the feeling of being pleased are (1) being-with-something, that is, being one with something or someone (*e.g.*, in love), (2) flowing-on, flowing-out existence, (3) expansion of the accentuated self, and (4) taking to one's self, assimilating, including as one's own. These four dynamic contents are in outline four kinds of feeling pleasant which are involved in the most different concrete feelings actually experienced in life.

The encounter with a resistance has also a fourfold typical dynamic structure, corresponding to four modes of unpleasantness. They are (1) being thrown back, (2) being subdued, (3) being injured, and (4) losing a part of one's self, abandoning part or all of one's self. Of course the phenomenological analysis of the different types of pleasantness and unpleasantness should be continued. My few remarks will try only to indicate the direction of approach.

Generally we think of feeling and emotion as spontaneous acts. It may be important, especially for applied psychology and psychotherapeutics, to make clear that *what* a feeling, an attitude, an expressive movement or a gesture means can be changed by the situation-creating power of our words. Here I do not think of the intellectualization of feelings, exposed by Dugas.[18] It was Brice Parain [19] who explained that we create a situation by our speaking. When I say (or write), "It is now night," I choose to project an image of a world and at the same time a definite nuance of feeling. It is another feeling and another world from when I say, "It is becoming night." We are able to change, to strengthen, or to weaken our feelings by our language. We may further the genuineness, the truth, and the reality of our feelings or their falseness. Saying "I am hungry" serves to communicate to myself and to others that my trouble is being hungry. By this determination I call forth a situation with many consequences. My words—for example, saying to anyone, "I love you"—throw me into an adventure of affections and a series of situations and also serve to present me in a certain mode of existence. A word is not only a communication concerning a concrete attitude and situation; it also creates new situations, attitudes, and feelings.

It has been my intention to outline the phenomenological approach to the problem of feeling and emotion. I should like to end this short communication by trying to show that the signification of expressions—for example, a smile or a blush—can be understood from the phenomenological discovery of the essential sense of the situations in which they occur.

Dumas [20] concluded from the well-known experiments

[18] Dugas, La logique des sentiments. *Nouveau Traité de Psychologie*, VI fasc. 1. Alcan, 1937.

[19] Brice Parain, *Recherche sur la nature et les fonctions du langage*. N.R.F., 1942.

[20] Dumas, *Nouveau Traité de Psychologie*. III fasc. 2. Alcan, 1937. P. 344.

of Duchenne that "smiling is the easiest response of the facial muscles to moderate excitation." This conclusion is true, but it is not only a physiological moderate excitation that causes a smile. We must ask what is the essential nature and signification of a "moderate excitation" and find out what are the characteristics common to all situations which provoke a smile. Analyzing two situations that typically involve smiling, a friendly encounter and the making of gestures toward a person as if to tickle him, I came to the conclusion that a "moderate excitation" has a special meaning experienced in the intentional act. This meaning is not only that the excitation is small, but also that it will be kept small, kept in check in regard to something else which is anticipated in the encounter. We experience *in* the slight joy, the momentary contentment, a greater joy in the future, without knowing exactly what we are anticipating. For this reason the "moderate excitation" which we reply to by a smile has an ambivalent structure. It is similar to the situation of timidity which elicits a smile so easily.

What does "the easiest response" mean? Dumas writes:

> It is merely choice . . . concerning our cheek and eyelid muscles: we should smile differently if our facial muscles were attached in other relationships or moved differently, and if, by chance, the grimaces which occur in pain had been the easiest facial contractions, those would certainly have constituted the human smile.

When we conceive the body as contingent, the supposition of Dumas is plausible, but when we are sure that human (and animal) being is a psychophysical totality in the sense that there is an essential significant relation between the organization by which the individual exists in the world and the possibilities of the intentional acts which involve being in different situations, then is it inconceivable that the facial expression of pain could be the easiest?

Observation of the young child teaches us that smiling is easy and that crying requires an effort.

The smile wells forth from the unstable tranquil existence that already possesses a background of complacency. This comfort increases in the presence of the other person as a warmth of feeling that fills our existence and comes over us like a tidal wave. This occurs spontaneously, easily, and the irradiating, overwhelming complacency is in us just as a feeling of satisfaction may be in us or the vital cheerfulness after drinking alcoholic beverages. When smiling we do nothing but just smile—"the easiest response" to the moderate excitation of complacency.

The unstable tranquil existence, which is the condition for smiling, is not a sleepy, passive state of consciousness. It is a definite, easy attitude, the attitude of rest, of an active inactivity. We can observe it in every baby that lies awake. We observe it in ourselves in quiet sitting or walking. It is an attitude of confronting environment, which, as a visible world, supposes and composes our existence.

The paradox of smiling is that an activity signifies a relaxation of an active attitude of rest. The smile is in this way the expression of a threshold situation, of an impending outburst of joy, of the opening of a closed being, of a self-sufficient, immanent complacency, combined with a transcendental, anticipated cheerfulness. In the expression of the smile we observe the instability, the twinkling, and the sparking of joy as well as the stability, the durability, and the seclusion of tranquility. It is the ambiguous expression of an ambiguous act.

Already in the first smile of the child we observe the expression of a threshold situation, the first timid, sympathetic encounter. This smile is an answer of the human being in which it constitutes its own transcendental ego, its being-for-self. At the same time the child becomes confused with its own self, leaving the vital immanence and transcending the seclusion of tranquility, finding itself on the threshold of tender communication, called in to this situation by the mother, the matrix of love.[21]

What physiology means by "moderate excitation" and "the easiest response" gets its full significance in the phenomenological approach to human existence, feeling, emotions, attitudes, situations, and expressions.

When feeling and having emotion, man is physically in a definite way involved in the "magic" world he is projecting (Sartre). Always, and this is important to establish, he is *also confronted* with this projected world as with something objective, present, and perceived. This dual relationship is contained in the dynamic structure of feeling and emotion and is to be detected in many human expressions. I think we can find this dual relationship in blushing, the dilatation of the skin vessels in shame, the only *constant* outwardly appearing change. In this case, there *seems* to be no question of any relation to an intentional act and therefore of any signification. Still we are here faced with a phenomenon which is not related to a certain biological situation, but to a specific human mental state, which does not prevent blushing from being quite involuntary, without any reflection.

Blushing for shame, as has been known by scientists as far back as Darwin, takes place among all peoples. Blind persons blush; idiots, however, do not. Children blush more easily than adults; girls more easily than boys.

Shame, as well as shyness or timidity, elicits blushing under certain circumstances, *e.g.*, when blundering, when being praised excessively, when trespassing against the

[21] Amply discussed in F. J. J. Buytendijk, *De eerste glimlach van het kind* ("The first smile of the child"). Nijmegen: 1947.

rules of convention, when being caught in wrongdoing, when accused falsely.

It is not possible to explain blushing physiologically. Even Dumas takes this view. He tries to explain blushing on psychological grounds and points out that it appears in those cases where normal reactions are inhibited, impeded, or falsified. In such cases we can observe the resultant nervous processes, sympathetic effects like sweating and vasodilatation. According to Dumas, the perspiration of a student being examined would be such a resultant phenomenon as well as the blushing of someone who is ashamed. This explanation does not seem to be very satisfactory. Its only advantage is that it draws our attention to the fact that man blushes when he finds himself at an "impasse," when he cannot find a way out and finds himself incapable of doing or saying anything.

In considering the various circumstances which may bring about a feeling of shame, it seems that the general characteristic is the discovery, the unmasking, the exposure of our unworthiness.

A young girl entering a drawing room cannot possibly return every glance thrown in her direction. Such glances do not require any return. They convey a certain opinion, formed independently of her words or actions. The real intentional act on her part is the recognition of the indiscreet glance for what it is. It is therefore the dialectic relationship that is lacking, the interaction between the person entering and those already present. Inasmuch as the girl suffers—or experiences—their glances, she is not alone but in the others' presence. The others are in proximity to her only as her critical observers, and more specifically the observers of her bodily presence. The glances directed at her hands, her feet, her belt, the style of her coiffure, and her back indeed touch these parts of her outward appearance, but through these, they touch herself as she exists physically *for others* in these hands, this way of dressing her hair, etc. All parts of her body and clothes are suddenly felt as her own, but at the same time as insufficient to cover her physical being in the world. Not capable of parrying these glances by returning them, the person experiences them as penetrating, discovering, unmasking. Attitudes, movements, words, and even clothes lack the power to meet, to divert, to hold those glances. One is at a loss as to what to do, loses one's self-confidence and one's self-esteem. Shame is the feeling of existential *unworthiness* and blushing is the expression of this feeling. Sartre has in the chapter entitled "L'Existence d'autrui" in his *Être et le Néant* described the characteristics of shame. He concludes that shame is the apprehension of a unit of three dimensions: "I am ashamed of *myself* before *others*." The essence of pure shame is in his opinion "to be a thing."

But why exactly blushing and not something else? No matter how often a slight feeling of shame occurs, particularly on account of a clumsy remark, an offense against etiquette, etc., most people, even adults, will find it difficult to recall exactly what they experienced while blushing. Most of us are so strongly armed by the certainty of acting aright that we are able to respond in all situations without having the feeling of being virtually undressed. Only in our dreams is this different. When dreaming, the feeling of helplessness and unworthiness may come over us so strongly that we are deeply ashamed. We remember this very well after waking up. We don't know if we have blushed, but we do know that we felt oppressed and hot to the point of suffocation. This feeling is the vital, dynamic component, which necessarily accompanies the realization of existential unworthiness. Being ashamed is indeed not only an acceptance of suffering; it also contains an act of resistance, a revolt. This is explained by the fact that helplessness is the result of failing to do something which one should have been able to do and ought to have done. If we call this the ethical component of shame, the revolt will be its intentional correlate. Now we can also understand why we should feel oppressed to the point of suffocation when ashamed. It is the expression of an "effort," an unsuccessful effort, a superhuman effort to conquer an inadmissible and therefore unreasonable impotence. Once more I refer to dream experiences. The same feeling of oppression we experience when being deeply ashamed we feel during the well-known impotence when we dream that we are trying to run and cannot. So far as our dream consciousness can see, every condition for running is fulfilled in the situation constituted by the consciousness when dreaming. No cause to prevent it is experienced. And nevertheless it is impossible to run. An imperceptible, viscous mass seems to hold us back. We get hot and oppressed and may very well wake up wet with perspiration. In nightmares it is not an emotion that disturbs our inner existence; it is the *existence itself* that is changed. *Shame is a nightmare being lived while wide awake.*

Blushing is an outburst of oppression which finds its source inside us, in an unacceptable unworthiness, and which finds its outlet in our face, because that is where our self-being is really in the world.[22] The emotion from within overflows the cheeks in the form of a blush.

[22] We experience our self-being as present *in* the face. There is another explanation for this besides the social function of the face, besides its being the uncovered part of the body which we turn to our fellow men. Independent of any relation to others, our transcendental "ego" is present in our face, or rather, right behind it, so that the ego "looks out through" the eyes. If we ask a person to indicate the plane separating things in front from those behind him he will indicate a plane going through the ears; the separation between things above and below him will go through the eyes. Feelings con-

Now why is there no perspiration? This does occur occasionally, but as a rule it does not. There are fewer sweat glands in the cheeks than in the upper lip and the skin of the nose. Moreover, reddening is not a real reaction to warmth, but an outburst of effort in the revolutionary action of the individual. A physiological predisposition to blushing exists. We notice it only in people with a highly reactive vascular system whose color also changes for other reasons. That is why women and girls blush more than men and boys. But this is not the only reason. The chief cause of blushing lies in the situation as projected by feeling, and that is, under similar outward circumstances, different in men and women, in the young girl and the adolescent boy. To be discovered, undressed, seen through whether literally or figuratively, has an entirely different meaning for both sexes, as men and women experience their own bodily existence and their being-in-the-world in such different ways. As explained elsewhere, sexual life does not determine the nature of men and women, but their mutual existential relation, and consequently the way they experience sex, results from the essential diffrence between the sexes.

Woman's inclination toward taking care of people and things expresses itself even in the young girl in a form of self-grooming through which she experiences her bodily existence as her own much more strongly than boys do. She is, and feels herself to be, in contact with others through her body, but only through the fact that her clothing is seen *before* her and at the same time *for* her. It is this clothing that gets such full attention dur-

---

nected with human (ethical) relations express themselves exclusively in the face.

"Envy, shame, remorse, desire are limited to the facial expression and make the face the real mirror, the sounding-board of feeling and emotion, specifically through growing pale or red." (Plessner. *Lachen und Weinen*. Arnhem: 1941. Pp. 57–58.)

ing a girl's adolescence. It is during this period that girls discover the dual function of clothes: to cover and to uncover. Both functions require a personal relation to clothes. In the period during which this relation is realized, self-esteem is most vulnerable in the matter of clothing. This is the period when the slightest occasion will bring about blushing and when the sensation of shame on being uncovered is greatest. A very slight stimulus—a word, a question, a glance—suffices to make one feel naked, and therefore helpless, inasmuch as one is stripped of all means of covering and uncovering on which well-balanced social relations and self-esteem are based. Like a flame, *hot* and consuming, the feeling of shame wells up from within into the face, the part of the body through which we are in the world.

The vegetative effects of emotion may certainly often be meaningless, unspecific side phenomena, irradiations of stimuli in the field of the sympathetic nervous system. In animals they may have a certain type, which then may become purposeful characteristics of the emotional reaction. In man, however, they come to a phenomenon expressing the essential nature of the feeling and emotion. The most striking example of this is blushing for shame.

To understand the value of the phenomenological approach to the problem of feelings and emotions, we have to establish the value of description in general and distinguish between the introspective and the phenomenological methods. Introspection is always an inspection of subjective experience. I describe this kind of experience exactly in the same way as any observer gives a report on his sensory simultaneous and successive perceptions. In both cases we observe facts, their positions in time, and in a real or imaginary space. When I should like to describe the mutual relations of these facts, I must have a categorical system of references, for example, the physical concept of causality or the metaphoric and often mythological notions used in physiology and psychology. The phenomenological description, however, is directed immediately toward experienced phenomena, as well as toward the different acts—the acts of perception, remembering, thinking, feeling, etc. All these phenomena are taken exactly as they belong to the phenomenal world. This world is given to us directly and shows itself in itself, in its meaning. The question whether the phenomenon is real or not is disregarded. The only interest of the phenomenologist is directed toward the *essential* structure, the intrinsic connections, and the self-revelation of the significance in the full context of the phenomenal field. So the question, "*What* is happiness or shame?" is the same question as the one put in common life: "What is a chair or a box?" or "What is red?" In both cases we are not satisfied with the indications of the conditions necessary to produce these phenomena, neither with the description of the material of which they are made nor with the result of an investigation into the causal relations to other things. I want to know exactly what kind of thing a chair or a box is, what it signifies in the world, where chairs and boxes are experienced, and what is the inner *essential* structure by which these significations are clarified. Just as in common life, phenomenology wants an evident insight in the sense of experience, for example, in feelings and emotions.

The continued research on feelings and emotions as stimulated by the phenomenological approach will require exact and repeated observation of the phenomenon in the above-mentioned sense of this notion. This observation or contemplation must be performed with the aim of penetrating to the essential sense as it is presented in the intentional act itself. Of course our experience is never complete. Everyone who has read the *Farbenlehre* of Goethe will have learned how "rich" the content of a simple perception of color is. The word "red" or "violet" is neither only a sign to indicate something nor only an abstract notion, but we use these words also to express our direct experience of these colors. In daily life as well as in science a word generally functions like a chain to get hold of a dog, to have the dog near us, and to do with it what we like. The phenomenologist, however, is not interested in the chain but in the dog itself. This is what Valéry meant when he wrote: "Every word is a bottomless pit."

In this way we understand that development of the phenomenologically orientated psychology depends on the dialectic relations between exemplary contemplation and the verbal expressions in living language developed out of unreflected intuitive views, signifying the essential sense. Perhaps one would assume from this that the phenomenology of feelings and emotions may be better furthered by artists than by psychologists. First of all I should like to reply that art has proved its high value for psychology; second, that psychology requires the most thorough description of experience; and third, that applied psychology has proved the importance of the phenomenological method along with the analytic, functional, statistical viewpoints. It is impossible to know what an abnormal feeling is without an insight into the essential significance of normal feeling in the context of human existence. It is impossible to understand or even to describe sex relations when we do not know the essence and meaning of sexuality, bodily existence, femininity, or masculinity. Pedagogics requires understanding the full content of sense of the phenomenon of play as well as of the mode of existence of the adolescent.

We are at the beginning of the phenomenological approach to all these matters and to the feelings and emotions in particular, but it is desirable for us to be aware of the richness of phenomenological analysis gathered in ancient and recent psychological literature, for example, in the publications of *Gestalt* psychologists.

An important starting point for further research is, among other things, the statement of William James: "We ought to say a feeling of *and,* a feeling of *if,* a feeling of *but,* and a feeling of *by,* quite as readily as we say a feeling of blue or a feeling of cold." And he adds: "Yet we do not: so inveterate has our habit become of recognizing the existence of the substantive parts alone, that language almost refuses to lend itself to any other use." [23]

The progress of phenomenological analysis of feeling and emotion depends on the discovery of the invariance which occurs during the continual experience concerning a feeling in various situations in relation to the modes of existence of normal and also of neurotic individuals, of men, women, children, primitive people, and animals.

The implicit conception of human reality and of the characteristics of human existence must become explicit during such a research through the evidence of insight into the signification of every intentional act of a concrete mode of feeling.

Repeatedly the question has been raised as to what is the guarantee that the phenomenological statement is true and not a pure subjective opinion. The answer to this is simple. The evidence of a statement about the essence and sense of a phenomenon can be proved only by the affirmation of everyone who, without prejudice, directs himself to the phenomenon in question. It is possible that some observer will find new, more detailed, more specific essential characteristics. Scheler, who has

[23] W. James. *Principles of Psychology*. Vol. I, pp. 245–246.

enriched us with so many phenomenological analyses—for example, about repentance, resentment, and sympathy—once said that the phenomenological approach offers the advantage of a continuous progress of insight after every return to the "thing-itself in its thisness." Such progress is the aim of science.

DANGERS IN THE RELATION OF EXISTENTIALISM TO PSYCHOTHERAPY

by ROLLO MAY *

There has not yet been time for the existential approach in psychiatry and psychology to find its particular form in this country, nor time yet for the contributions here to become significant. So far, the writings and speeches on existential psychotherapy in America seem to be a "Tower of Babel," a confusion of tongues. There are voices which say that existential psychology is Adlerian, others that it is all in Jung, others that it is encompassed in Freud, still others that it is identical with psychodrama and so on. Existential psychiatry is identified with Zen Buddhism and anti-intellectual trends on one hand; or with a super-intellectual philosophy composed of untranslatable German terms on the other. It is said to be therapy which everyone does when he is doing good therapy, and also to be—especially in its classical phenomenological wing—a philosophical analysis which has nothing to do with the practice of therapy as such. These spokesmen seem blithely unaware of their patent contradictions: if existential psychiatry is one of these things, it cannot be the others.

* ROLLO MAY is a practicing analyst in New York City and is a Fellow and member of the Faculty of the William Alanson Institute of Psychiatry, Psychology and Psychoanalysis. He is the author of *The Meaning of Anxiety* (1950), and *Man's Search for Himself* (1953), and the editor of *Existence: A New Dimension in Psychiatry and Psychology* (1958), *Symbolism in Religion and Literature* (1960) and *Existential Psychology* (1961).

In the Tower of Babel story in the book of Genesis, it will be recalled, the Lord sent the confusion to confound the pride and grandiosity of the builders. I suspect that another purpose, or at least opportunity, which this confusion of voices lays upon us now is to force us to cut through the faddist and band-wagon tendencies which bedevil any new movement of ideas, and to ask ourselves as incisively as possible what are the negative as well as the positive aspects of the present relation of existentialism to psychotherapy.

Since I have elsewhere concentrated on the positive aspects, I shall here cite some of the negative trends in this relationship.[1]

A first trend that, in my judgment, is unconstructive is the anti-scientific tendency in some existential psychiatry. This trend has become linked with the anti-intellectual trend in our country. Certainly one of the abuses to which the existential movement in parts of Europe fell unhappy heir was the anti-intellectual tendency. But one cannot be against science or reason as such. I am reminded of Margaret Fuller's pompous statement, "I accept the universe," and Carlyle's rightfully famous rejoinder, "Gad, she'd better." For science is part of our universe, and it makes no sense not to accept it. The fact that many thoughtful psychiatrists and psychologists and other sensitive intelligent people in our culture recognize the inadequacies of present scientific method for a study of man should lead us not into an anti-scientific trend but into the effort to find *new scientific methods which will be more adequate for revealing the nature of man*. The endeavors of our European colleagues, such as Binswanger, Buytendijk, and Van Den

[1] For a survey of the positive aspects, see Chapters I and II in *Existence: A New Dimension in Psychiatry and Psychology,* New York, 1958.

Berg to develop a phenomenological context for a science of man is in the constructive direction.

The same with anti-intellectualism. The tendency to distrust reason as such in our culture has arisen from the fact that the alternatives that intelligent and sensitive people have presented to them have seemed to be only arid rationalism and positivism on the one hand, in which one saves one's mind by losing one's soul, or vitalistic romanticism on the other, in which there has seemed at least a chance, for the time being, of saving one's soul. The existential approach is not to be rationalistic or anti-rationalistic, but to seek the underlying ground in human experience in which both reason and unreason are based. We must not be "mis-ologists," Socrates cautions us; but the "logos" must be made flesh.

The essay by Paul Tillich in this book is a splendid example of the profound union of reason with the existential inquiry that goes beyond mere rationalism. Tillich is existential without rejecting essences and logical structure. The scholarly work of R. D. Laing also seems to me to show this endeavor

The second negative trend is the tendency to identify existential psychiatry with Zen Buddhism. The widespread interest in Zen these days, especially among intellectuals in this country, is a symptom of the constructive religious questioning of our day. Let me state immediately that I have great respect for Zen Buddhism as represented by those genuinely devoted to it, like Suzuki. I also value greatly the serious interpretations of it, like Alan Watts, despite my disagreement with some of his points. Zen Buddhism certainly has a great importance as a corrective to our Western over-activism; its emphases on immediacy of experience, *being* rather than *doing,* are a great relief and a significant guidance to many sorely beset competitive and driven Westerners.

But the identification of Zen Buddhism with existential psychiatry is a different matter. It oversimplifies both. One of my colleagues, doing research in a mental hospital, holds that he has repeatedly achieved satori by means of the drug lysergic acid. Then "working back from the drug experience," he writes, "I have finally reached satori repeatedly without the drug." Now satori is the result of years of discipline. If we can achieve it so easily by drugs, why do we need Zen Buddhism or any other religion? And if we can overcome the despair, the agony, the *angst* of life that way, we certainly shall not need any psychotherapy. As William Barrett noted in his review of a book by Alan Watts in *The New York Times,* referring to Watts' similar claim of achieving satori by means of the drug, what authorities on which criteria are going to decide who receives the drug and who does not? I cannot believe that the approach to satori and clarification by means of drugs will be taken seriously as the way in the long run.

The existential approach in psychotherapy, as I understand it, is that only in a *heightened consciousness* of the problems of guilt, anxiety and conflict—an awareness that leads to some form of either/or choice—can these problems be met. The alteration of awareness which occurs by means of drugs, pleasurable or ecstatic as it may be, seems to me by definition to involve a greater or lesser surrender of conscious decision.

The liaison between oversimplified Zen Buddhism and existential psychiatry has within it, as I have observed it, the tendency to bypass and evade anxiety, tragedy, guilt, and the reality of evil. But one of the lasting contributions of the psychotherapeutic movement in all its forms is in helping people frankly to admit and confront their *angst,* hostility, and guilt, to face the fact of destructiveness and evil psychologically as well as culturally in the world. The existential approach is the achieving of individuality, not by avoiding the conflictual realities of the world in which we find ourselves (which for us is perforce Western culture), but by confronting these directly, and through the meeting of them, to achieve individuality and meaningful interpersonal relations.

It is important to make these criticisms in order that the positive contribution of Eastern thought to our Western parochialism will not be lost. Zen Buddhism has had and will continue to have (if its adherents do not run it into the ground) radical significance as a corrective to Western over-individualized will and consciousness. Certainly many psychotherapists, such as Horney, Fromm, Hanna Colm, Paul Weisz, and others, have shown the lasting contribution of Zen Buddhism to our orientation in psychotherapy.

A third danger in existential psychiatry arises directly out of the above. It is the tendency to use "transcendence" and similar concepts as a way of bypassing existential reality. My objection to such papers as Thomas Hora's on "Transcendence and Healing" arises at this point. Dr. Hora lists the following eleven forms of transcendence assumedly occurring in the therapeutic process: "Transcendence of the subject-object dichotomy between therapist and patient, transcendence of the body-mind dichotomy, transcendence of dualistic thought, transcendence of the ego, transcendence of disease as expression of the pleasure-pain duality, transcendence of causal and teleological thinking, transcendence of the motivational split of means and ends, transcendence of the temporespatial coordinates of experience, transcendence of the epistemic barrier between mind and world, transcendence of the duality of being and non-being, transcendence of the separation between man and Ultimate Reality (God)." [2]

But what happens in such an approach is that practically all the age-old problems of human existence, with which thinkers have struggled since human consciousness was born, are bypassed by a word. It is argued that in this "transcendence of dualistic thought," for example, the therapist uses a mode of thinking that is "beyond language and symbolic imagery," that he is freed from concepts which hamper "the capacity to see what really is," and that in such "moments of understanding there is no understander." But symbols, language of one form or another, are always the form and content of any thinking. Is it not manifestly impossible to use a mode of thought that goes beyond symbolic imagery? Husserl's phenomenological approach is often mistakenly applied to mean that the psychotherapist observes a patient without any concepts presupposed in the therapist's mind at all. But this too is impossible. Concepts are the orientation by which perception occurs; without some concepts presupposed the therapist would not see the patient who is there or anything about him.

There must be an "understander" if there is to be understanding. The psychotherapist had best realize that he is seeing the patient through his own eyes, understanding the patient in his own way, which will always be limited and biased to some extent. If the therapist does not assume this but absolutizes his own perception and understanding, he will automatically dominate the patient by his own subjectivity, a danger against which Sartre has warned us. Then the therapist is playing God

[2] "Transcendence and Healing," by Thomas Hora, *Journal of Existential Psychiatry,* Vol. 1, No. 4, 1961, p. 501. Though we criticize this viewpoint above, we also wish to remark that Dr. Hora has made a positive contribution in respect to the phenomenological emphasis in some of his papers.

as surely as if he had an absolute technique. The existential therapist can overcome so far as possible his own tendency to straight-jacket the patient by subjectivity by admitting his own bias and limitations to start with. Once these are admitted, the phenomenological approach can be of great help, as many of us have discovered, in seeing and relating to the patient as he really is.

A final danger is making existential psychiatry into a special school. One of the groups in this field proposes to establish a training institute in existential psychiatry based on the concept of "ontoanalysis." There are two errors, in my judgment, in such an approach. One is that there cannot be any special "existential psychiatry," as Leslie Farber has well remarked, any more than there can be Hegelian, Platonic, or Spinozan psychiatry. Existentialism is an *attitude,* an approach to human beings, rather than a special school or group. Like any philosophy, it has to do with the presuppositions underlying psychiatric and psychoanalytic technique.

It is doubtful, for example, whether it makes any sense to speak of an "existential psychotherapist" at this stage of the development of the movement. The existential approach is not a system of therapy—though it makes highly important contributions to therapy. It is not a set of techniques—though it may give birth to them. It is rather a concern with understanding the structure of the human being and his experience which to a greater or lesser extent should underlie *all* technique. Those who call themselves existential psychoanalysts, as for example Boss and his Daseinsanalytic group, already presuppose a long and complex training in psychoanalysis; Boss himself is a member of the International Psychoanalytic Association, and a Director of the Zurich Psychoanalytic Society. My own training, for another example, is in the

William Alanson White Psychoanalytic Institute. I would identify myself as a psychoanalyst of this approach—which does not make me any the less existential in my presuppositions.

I obviously do not imply that the existential approach must be allied with the particular form of psychotherapy called psychoanalysis. Nor do I deny that attitudes and presuppositions about human beings will be more determinant (as Rogers' studies have shown) of the success of psychotherapy than the particular technical school to which the therapist belongs. But we must not fall into the frequently oversimplified sentimental view that implies that in psychotherapy mere benevolence is enough.

There is another error in the term "ontoanalytic," a word which literally means "analysis of being." You cannot analyze being, and if you could do so it would be a harmful thing to do. *Being* must be assumed in psychotherapy, not analyzed: an individual's being is shown, for example, in his right to exist as a person, his possibilities for self-respect and his ultimate freedom to choose his own way of life. All these must be assumed when we work with a patient, and if we cannot assume them about a given person, we should not work with him. To try to analyze these evidences of being is to violate the fundamental being of the person himself. Bringing our technical attitudes to bear on being itself is to repeat the same error for which existentialists criticize not only classical psychoanalysis but our whole culture, i.e., making the person subordinate to techniques. To analyze the "psyche" as in psychoanalysis is difficult enough and can and should be done only within limits. The blockages the person suffers which will not let him gain adequate self-esteem, for example, can be analyzed. But that is a far different thing from analyzing ontology, calling into question the fundamental qualities which constitute him as a human being. To analyze being is parallel to repressing it in the sense that it subordinates being to a technical attitude; except that analyzing is a little more harmful in that it gives the therapist a nice rationalization for his repression and relieves him of guilt for his failure to exhibit the reverence and humility with which being should rightly be regarded.

Having cited these criticisms, let me end by saying that I believe the movement in modern thought called existentialism will make a unique and highly significant contribution to the future of psychotherapy.

AN APPRAISAL OF EXISTENTIAL ANALYSIS

by EUGEN KAHN *

I

If one plans a discussion of *Daseinsanalysis,* it is necessary to go back to Existentialism, from which it springs. Mentioning Existentialism makes it inevitable that one say something of its founder, Soren Kierkegaard.

Soren Kierkegaard's father had been a poor lad who had attained a fortune as a merchant. He died in 1838 in his 80's.[1] Before he died—the writer does not know how long before—he told his son the following story: he had worked as a shepherd in his youth. Once while minding his sheep in complete loneliness, he cursed God. He was never able to get over this sin. He was a sober, maybe even melancholy, man. Throughout his life, he could never enjoy himself. It would be vain to inquire into how far this curse motivated his unhappiness or how much, perhaps, the curse was motivated by an unfortunate personality make-up. It may be taken for granted that Soren Kierkegaard—always a devout man of high sensitivity—was immensely impressed with his father's confession; he was perhaps unable ever to rid himself entirely of its impact.[2]

* EUGEN KAHN is an M.D. and a psychiatrist. He is with the Department of Psychiatry, Baylor University, College of Medicine, Houston, Texas.

[1] He apparently was in his late 50's when Soren Kierkegaard was born.

[2] "Scripture teaches that God visits the sins of the fathers upon the children unto the third and fourth generation; verily, life is telling this in a loud voice" (Kierkegaard).

Soren Kierkegaard was born in 1813. He died in 1855. Because of his father's means, he was never compelled to work for a living. He studied theology and became a minister, though he never had a parish. He studied for the most part in his homeland, Denmark, and for a time in Berlin with his foremost interest in philosophy. He began to write in his early life, emphasizing the role of the individual and the fact of his existence in opposition to the teaching of the Protestant clergy of his time. Of Kierkegaard's person and personal life, it should be added that he was a hunchback and that for some time he was engaged to a young girl whom he probably loved very dearly. Nevertheless, he broke off the engagement in 1834, but appeared disappointed and dismayed, as the young lady did not show any tendency to reapproach him but married somebody else. For all that seems to be known, Kierkegaard did not have any other dealings with women. He lived as an unhappy, lonely creature, reminding one of his father. However, he wrote most amply,[3] mostly under pseudonyms, using a variety of them during his literary career. His writings are very hard to understand. He sometimes gets himself into very long and involved sentences. Often he appears extremely bitter, in spite of apparent humor, or rather biting wit. It is the interjection of ironic and witty remarks which makes the understanding of his productions still more difficult. However, it may well be that the translations are not perfect in all places.

In the original writings of Kierkegaard that the present writer has himself seen and according to various inter-

[3] Kierkegaard wrote about boredom, dread, melancholy and despair. He stated that "in the beginning was boredom." He called melancholy his "intimate, confidential friend"; he said: "The man who is plagued by grief and worry, knows the causes of grief and worry. If, however, you ask a melancholic man what there is that makes him so melancholic, he will reply: 'I do not know. I cannot tell.' "

pretations and reports, one may venture to say that whatever he wrote was the expression of a haunted person, of a profoundly unhappy human being who, devout as he was, never stopped searching God and who seems to have suffered feelings of guilt for his philosophical inquisitiveness. One may refrain from deciding whether his writings are more often a fusion or a confusion of religion and philosophy. He is the first one to write strictly about existence, about individual existence. He is familiar with the fundamental existential experience: dread.[4] Dread is experienced in the face of Nothing. Whatever excursions into philosophy he made; whatever ideas he expounded about existence, about dread, about fear, about Nothing, his experiential center, if one may call it so, was made and remained the Deity. This haunted man was running, and working, himself mercilessly to death. At the age of 42, he broke down on the street; he was taken to a hospital where he died shortly afterward. Nobody had minded him and his work much while he was alive; nobody minded them for years to come after his death. His most eminent literary contemporary compatriot, Heiberg, "blackballed" him. It must be remembered that Kierkegaard stood up in arms against his then all-too-quiet Protestant church, as well as against the leading philosophers of his time.

It was only around the turn of this century that a few people took notice of Kierkegaard's work. Most outstanding among them were Karl Jaspers and Martin Heidegger who are both profoundly influenced by Kierkegaard's, and incidentally by Nietzsche's, thought. Their interpretations of both Kierkegaard and Nietzsche differ considerably. Both Jaspers and Heidegger were professors of philosophy, in Heidelberg and Freiburg (Ger-

[4] Danish: *angest;* German: *Angst.*

many), respectively. Both were dismissed from their universities as will be noted briefly.

"The Kierkegaard-Renaissance is one of the strangest phenomena of our time," Heinemann writes, ". . . he was a proleptic man, who, as a single individual, experienced in the middle of the last century something which has become common experience in our own day, and who had the power of expressing it in a most interesting, paradoxical and challenging manner. The literary representation of his thought is, moreover, so enigmatic, obscure and sometimes mysterious that his writings make the impression of great profundity and offer an occasion for indefinite new interpretations."

II

Karl Jaspers, born in 1883, is a venerable figure of considerable importance in German psychiatry and philosophy. He read law for a year before going into medicine, where he turned to psychiatry immediately after finishing medical school. On the staff of the Psychiatric University Clinic in Heidelberg, he published outstanding and unusually stimulating papers, and in 1913, his *General Psychopathology*. This book, showing the rare erudition of its author, in particular in psychology and philosophy, became a sort of psychopathological *Bible* for psychiatrists of the German language; its fifth edition appeared in 1948. Jaspers soon began to teach and to work in the philosophical faculty in Heidelberg, in which he attained a full professorship in 1921. He wrote a *Psychologie der Weltanschaungen* and a *Philosophie* in three volumes. The second volume of Jaspers' *Philosophie* bears the title *Existenzerhellung*.[5]

Jaspers had married a Jewish girl. Hence, in 1937, he was dismissed from the university and could not publish

[5] Clarification of existence.

anything again before 1945. Since then, he has published a number of papers and republished some of his books. Reinstated as professor in Heidelberg, he soon accepted a call to the University of Basel, Switzerland, where he is still teaching and writing.

Fully aware of the development of the masses and their aspirations, Jaspers seems to appeal to the individual and his existence. He does not give any definition of existence, and in his philosophizing, has a peculiar attitude of *"Schweben,"* [6] assuming that it is not feasible to come to grips with the problems involved in the way one can with less ethereal problems. He says: "A philosophy of existence is a way of thinking which uses and transcends all material knowledge in order that man may again become himself." In 1950, Jaspers declared that his philosophy was not—or rather was no longer—a philosophy of existence, but was a philosophy of reason. There will be no more detailed discussion of Jaspers' work here, as, in spite of the great impact his *Psychopathology* exerted in psychiatry, his philosophy did not influence the psychiatric existential analysts with whom this paper will deal. It might be noted, though, that Jaspers sees in Heidegger's attempt "regardless of the value of his concrete discussions principally a philosophical error." [7] Accordingly, Jaspers considers Ludwig Binswanger's particular existential analytic attitude and aspect "a philosophical and scientific error." [8]

III

An interpolation about Edmund Husserl (1859-1938) appears indicated. Husserl was Heidegger's teacher.

[6] "Floating."

[7] *"Unbeschadet des Wertes seiner konkreten Ausführungen halte ich den Versuch im Prinzip für einen philosophischen Irrweg"* (Jaspers).

[8] *"ein philosophischer und ein wissenschaftlicher Irrtum"* (Jaspers).

Heidegger was Husserl's successor as professor in Freiburg in 1929. A philosopher of high significance in Germany, Husserl lost many of his pupils when he published his *Ideas About a Pure Phenomenology.* Husserl wanted to get directly to "the things themselves."[9] He tried to analyze what was immediately given in consciousness. He tried to deal with the essence of the given material and did not pay any attention, so it appears, to the existence of the world—apart from the actual matter he was investigating. It has been said that existentialists and others found it impossible to follow him because he considered essence to be prior to existence. It is held, however, that there cannot be any essence unless there is some existence and unless there is something and/or someone existent that, due to its existence, is capable of being endowed with essence.

It has been claimed that Husserl's phenomenological method has profoundly influenced contemporary philosophical thought. As it is, the phenomenological methods used by philosophers and psychologists appear to be definitely different from Husserl's. Jaspers, for example, writes that he uses the word phenomenology and the phenomenological method in his *General Psychopathology* in the sense originally used by Husserl, that is, " 'descriptive psychology' of manifestations of consciousness," while for Husserl, it later became "*Wesensschau*" (intuition). It is outside the present writer's competence to participate in these particular discussions of the philosophers. Yet mention of their dissensions seems indicated. The dispute leads some writers to a pretty free use of the word and concept, phenomenology. All manner of verbosities and mental gyrations have been called phenomenological.

Husserl had to leave Germany under the Nazi regime.

[9] "*zu den Sachen selbst*" (Husserl).

IV

Martin Heidegger (1889-), who is considered the godfather of *Daseinsanalyse* (existential analysis) had been professor of philosophy in Marburg an der Lahn before he was called to Freiburg to succeed Husserl in 1929. He had been educated as a Jesuit novice, but obviously became estranged from the Roman Catholic Church. He appeared for a time to be wholeheartedly Nazi, as rector of the University of Freiburg, with the consequence that he was dismissed in 1945. He is now again lecturing at that university.

Heidegger published, in 1927, the book, *Sein und Zeit* [10] that made him famous. Heidegger seems to have admired Kirkegaard greatly; later, it is true, he considered Kierkegaard to have been a religious writer rather than a philosophical thinker.[11] Like Kierkegaard, he approaches existence from, and as, individual existence. *Dasein,* about which more will be said later, always refers to the human individual; it actually means for Heidegger a human mode of individual existence. Hence early in *Sein und Zeit* he writes, "Human existence is a being which does not only exist among other beings. It is rather characterized as a being that in its Being is concerned about this Being itself." [12] And, "The Being itself to which human existence can refer in this or that way and to which it always refers in some way is called existence." [13]

This may sound less strange if one tries to clarify

10 *Being and Time.*

11 *According to Löwith.*

12 *"Das Dasein ist ein Seiendes, das nicht nur unter anderen Seienden vorkommt. Es ist vielmehr dadurch gekennseichnet, dass es diesem Seinenden in seinem Sein um dieses Sein selbst geht"* (Heidegger).

13 *"Das Sein selbst, su dem sich das Dasein so oder so verhalten kann und immer irgendwie verhaelt, nennen wir Existenz"* (Heidegger).

some of Heidegger's terminology. It has already been remarked that by *Dasein* [14] he means the individual mode of human existence; *Dasein* will, in the following discussion be rendered, for brevity's sake, as human existence: the reference to the individual should always be kept in mind. The German words *sein, Sein, seiend* and *Seiendes* mean: "to be," "Being," "being," and "existent," respectively. The word *sein* is the infinitive that corresponds to "to be"; it is spelled with a small "s" unless it begins a sentence, which will be avoided here. The word *Sein,* always spelled with a capital "S," is a noun; it means existence per se, the existence due to which all existing things—living and not living—exist; the sentence just quoted "The Being itself to which human existence can refer in this or that way and to which it always refers in some way is called existence," may be quite understandable now, although at first sight it may have looked odd.

The word *seiend* is the present participle of the verb *sein; seiend* is related to *sein* as "being" with a small "b," is related to "to be." From this present participle, *seiend,* the noun *Seiend* is derived. It can be used for people (male and female) and things (neuter); in order to avoid confusion, *Seiend* will be translated as "the existent." "Existent" will be used only as a noun. If an attribute (adjective) is needed, "being," as well as "existing," is available. One might now slightly change the sentence quoted first: "Human existence is an existent which does not only exist among other existents,

[14] The German word *Dasein,* noun with capital "D," is generally used in the German language to denote existence or life. Heidegger uses *Dasein* with the special meaning mentioned. So do his followers, although, at a closer view, not all of them really mean exactly what Heidegger does. Writers who are not existentially oriented usually take the word in its general meaning. The use of the word *Dasein* is no certificate of existentialism.

it is rather characterized as an existent that in its Being it is concerned about this Being itself." There is no doubt that many a sentence of Heidegger's must be read repeatedly and carefully before it actually "gets home."

Human existence, as he wants to have it understood, is *"geistig,"* [15] Heidegger says. It does not occupy any space like physical things, but has *Spielraum,* in which there is direction and distance. Human existence is thrown into its world or rather into its being-in-the-world. Its being-in-the-world is occasionally equated with human existence. This world is always "world-with"; other existents belong to the world in which I exist. The relation of human existence to its world is care, taking care, which in a broader sense might be interpreted as responsibility. "I myself am the existent that we call human existence; I am human existence as a possibility of existence concerned to be this existent." [16] This very "I" refers to and "means the existent that is concerned about the existence of the existent that it is." [17] "In saying 'I' human existence expresses itself as being-in-the-world." [18]

The "Time" of human existence is not "a one after the other," it is rather temporality [19] and temporalization.[19] Temporality means "the future that has been being and is being present." [20] As human existence, I am still my past, my past belongs to me, is part of me, in my present; yet from my present, I am reaching into the future, anticipating—expecting, planning, hoping—

[15] Spiritual.

[16] *"das Seiende, das wir Dasein nennen, bin ich je selbst und zwar als Seinkönnen, dem es darum geht, dieses Seiende zu sein"* (Heidegger).

[17] *"meint das Seiende, dem es um das Sein des Seienden, das es ist, geht"* (Heidegger).

[18] *"Im Ich-sagen spricht sich das Dasein als In-der-Welt-sein aus"* (Heidegger).

[19] *"Zeitlichkeit und Zeitigung"* (Heidegger).

[20] *"gewesend-gegenwärtigende Zukunft"* (Heidegger).

in a manner that makes my past and my present and my future one—not one time, but one temporality. "Temporality is the Existential sense of care." [21]

The notions of care and time will be more easily comprehended through the "myth of Care" which Wild has translated from *Sein und Zeit:* "Once when Care was crossing a river she saw a sounding piece of earth. Taking it up thoughtfully, she began to form it. As she was wondering what she would make, Jupiter appeared. Care asked him to bestow spirit on it and he readily agreed, but when Care wished to have her name given to the creature, Jupiter forbade this and said his name should be used. While Care and Jupiter were arguing over this, Earth also arose and sought to have her name imposed, since she had given it a piece of her body. They turned to Saturn to judge between them, and he rendered the following judgment in all fairness: 'You, Jupiter, because you have given the spirit, shall take the spirit at death. You, Earth, since you have given the body, shall have the body returned. But Care, since she first formed this being, shall possess him as long as he lives. Now since there is disagreement over the name, let him be called "homo" because he is made out of "earth" (humus).' "

Saturn is Time! In the threefold structure of Time, "All the manifestations of human existence are filled with care. In whatever he does, man is led by a devotion to something. He is a center of care" (Wild). For Heidegger, the myth of Care appears to have the implication that "homo," man, is human existence as well as human being. Thus he can say, as already quoted: "I myself am the existent that we call human existence . . ."

Like Kierkegaard, Heidegger distinguishes between

[21] *"Zeitlichkeit ist der Seinssinn der Sorge"* (Heidegger).

dread[22] and fear.[23] In fear, there is always some threat. In dread, that "springs from human existence itself,"[24] threat is nowhere and everywhere; it signifies facing "nothing" or "nothingness." However, can "nothing" be faced? Can "nothing" be the content of dread? Can "nothing" exist? Can "nothing" whose existence, whose possibility appears questionable, be at the root of dread? One might conjecture that "nothing" is only created by dread. This may well be what Heidegger has in mind. It is characteristic of his dealing with language that he never says, "Nothing" exists, but formulates, "Nothing is nothinging."[25] It is left to the human being to consider that he came from "nothing" and will go to "nothing"; thus when he, or rather human existence, is grasped by dread without any primary threat, he may come to using this "nothing," secondarily elaborated, to give this eerie dread a cause and content. Dread is thought to represent an existential crisis.

Human existence, exposing itself to crises and going through them, is called "authentic existence."[26] Such human existence remains authentic in its communication with other human existences: "Human existence always has the existential mode of being together."[27] There is, in spite of communication and togetherness, always a certain distance between authentic human existences. There is another mode of being, "unauthentic existence,"[28] everyday life in which all and sundry participate. Here "Everyone is the other one and nobody is him-

[22] *Angst.*

[23] *Furcht.*

[24] *"... entspringt aus dem Dasein selbst"* (Heidegger).

[25] *"Das Nichts nichtet"* (Heidegger).

[26] *"eigentliches Dasein"* (Heidegger).

[27] *"Sofern Dasein überhaupt ist, hat es die Seinsart des Miteinanderseins"* (Heidegger).

[28] *"uneigentliches Dasein"* (Heidegger).

self." [29] This is called the existence of *Man,* which in this context might best be translated as Tom, Dick and Harry.[30]

Thrown into its existence in the world, human existence dreads the existence in the world. In a certain way, human existence dreads itself. This makes sense in view of its coming from and going to "nothing," and of Heidegger's remark: "Dread isolates and manifests human existence as '*solus ipse.*' " [31] Furthermore, human existence is "existence to death," [32] or as Bollnow words it, "To exist means to be faced with death." [33] Human existence is unfinished as long as it exists. "The death of human existence is the possibility of being unable to exist further." [34] As all existence is possibility, death belongs to the possibilities of existence; this concerns authentic human existence. In unauthentic existence, in everyday life, death is not "a mode of being" [35] that is faced, but "a certainty that is avoided." [36]

"Time" is, as has been said, not a "one after the other" but, as the present writer would call it, the trinity of past, present and future. In its temporality and temporalization, human existence remains unfinished as long as there are possibilities, that is, as long as there is a future: "Only the existent 'between' birth and death

[29] *"Jeder ist der andere und keiner er selbst"* (Heidegger).

[30] The German *man* might in this context be translated as "the common man." This would, however, lead to confusion between the English "man" (German *Mann, Mensch*) and the German *man,* which is a pronoun.

[31] *"Die Angst vereinzelt und erschliesst so das Dasein als 'solus ipse'* " (Heidegger).

[32] *"Sein zum Tode"* (Heidegger).

[33] *"Existieren bedeutet im Angesicht des Todes stehen"* (Bollnow).

[34] *"Sein (des Daseins) Tod ist die Möglichkeit des Nicht-mehr-seinkönnens"* (Heidegger).

[35] *"eine Seinsweise"* (Heidegger).

[36] *". . . kennt die Gewissheit des Todes und weicht dem Gewissein doch aus"* (Heidegger).

represents the whole that we search." [37] "The attainment of the wholeness of human existence is also loss of the existence of human existence." One might perhaps say: When human existence has run its whole course it is over.

There is public time, "world time" (*Welt-Zeit*). We are dealing with world time when we look at the clock, and if we say "now."

V

In the preceding section there has been an attempt to give a condensed picture of Heidegger's *Sein und Zeit* or rather of a few of the many ideas contained in it. Heidegger coined the term existential analy*tics*. He writes in *Sein und Zeit:* "All efforts of existential analy*tics* aim at one goal, to find a possibility of answering the quest for the sense of Being itself." [38]

Heidegger has, in a number of points, changed his attitudes and/or his interpretation. In the discussion among philosophers, he has been reproached about these changes. He has been blamed in particular for the introduction of the notion of "ek-sistence." One of his critics, Heinemann, states that Heidegger has rejected existentialism and "has risen again as an 'ek-sistentialist.'" Heinemann quotes from a later paper of Heidegger's: "The essence of man consists of ek-sistence. It is this that matters essentially, i.e., from the point of view

[37] *"Erst das Seinde 'zwischen' Geburt und Tod stellt das gesuchte Ganze dar"* (Heidegger).

[38] *"Alle Bemühungen der existentialen Analy*tik *gelten dem einen Ziel, eine Möglichkeit der Beantwortung der Frage nach dem Sinn von Sein überhaupt zu finden"* (Heidegger). Heidegger uses *"existentiale analy*tik" and *"Daseinsanaly*tik" as synonyms. Both terms here are rendered as *"existential analy*tics."

of Being, in so far as Being itself installs man as ek-sistent as guardian of the truth of Being." [39]

There does not seem to be even *one* interpretation of "ek-sistence" among philosophers. In ek-sistence, Heidegger tries to conceive of man's ability to look at himself and at the "truth," which presumably is, or is meant to be, the truth of his existence. Despite a lively, partly outspoken, antagonistic discussion among philosophers, the continuing interest of Heidegger in Being and its sense is denied by nobody. It is not up to this writer to decide against earlier or later concepts and interpretations. After all, even a thinker is, in the writer's belief, entitled to, and justified in discarding former, and presenting new, ideas. Heidegger has let it be known that nobody really understands him.[40] The writer could scarcely claim that he, of all people, might understand him. As it is, there are no limits to any interpretation as, curiously enough, people generally find what they are seeking. In Heidegger's case, everything would be definitely easier if there were not that sore spot which Blackman touched in observing ". . . a greater tenderness with common sense might better serve the cause of a 'guardian of Being.' "

The writer is not going to go into detail about Heidegger's rough handling of the German language. Yet one cannot avoid thinking *"Quod licet Jovi, non licet bovi"*

[39] *"Das Wesen des Menschen beruht in der Ek-sistenz. Auf diese kommt es wesentlich d.h. vom Sein selbst her an, insofern das Hein den Menschen als den ek-sistierenden zur Wächterschaft für die Wahrheit Seins in diese selbst ereignet"* (Heidegger). This sentence is quoted by Heinemann; it is taken from Heidegger's paper, *"Platons Lehre von der Wahrheit," Jahrbuch für geistige Überlieferung,* 1941. The English translation is from Heinemann.

[40] It is of some interest that Heidegger occasionally defended himself against the reproach that his *Sein und Zeit* was atheistic.

when one studies the vast liberties some of his psychiatric pupils permit themselves with the same language.

Heidegger has objected to being classified as an existentialist. He considers, and wants others to consider, his philosophy as fundamental ontology. It appears to be useless, at least here, to argue about this. It is more appropriate to understand with Bollnow: "There is . . . no pure existential philosophy. . . . It is according to its essence a transition, leading into a deepened concept of philosophizing." [41] Bollnow writes: "The thinking of the existing thinker is determined through the definite task and difficulties of his life. Hence the purpose of his thinking is not this very purpose itself; his thinking rather serves his very existing." [42] According to the same author, who does not restrict himself in his book to Heidegger's work ". . . existence in the meaning of existential philosophy has nothing to do with an outer existence. Existence rather refers to a last inner core of man, to a last, unconditional center." [43] With unmistakable reference to Kierkegaard, Bollnow gives the opinion that this philosophy stems "from a definite attitude toward Christianity . . . one may understand the interest in existence from the care for the salvation of the soul." [44]

While Jaspers states: "I am only in communication

[41] *"Es gibt . . . gar keine reine Existenzphilosophie . . . Sie ist ihrem Wesen nach ein Durchgang, der in eine vertiefte Auffassung des Philosophierens hineinführt"* (Bollnow).

[42] *"Der existierende Denker ist ein solcher, dessen Denken durch die bestimmten Aufgaben und Schwierigkeiten seines Lebens bestimmt sind, dessen Denken also nicht Selbstzweck ist, sondern im Dienst seines Existiernes steht"* (Bollnow).

[43] *"Existenz im Sinne der Existenzphilosophie (hat) mit einer solchen äusseren Existenz nichts zu tun. Sie bezeichnet vielmechr im vollen Gegensatz dazu einen letzten inneren Kern des Menschen, ein letztes, unbedingtes Zentrum"* (Bollnow).

[44] *"Aus einer bestimmten Auffassung des Christentums herausgewachsen . . . darf man das Interesse am Existieren von der Sorge ums Seelenheil her verstehen"* (Bollnow). (See footnote 40.)

with the other," [45] Heidegger writes: "Human existence is essentially Being-with."[46] Even Being-alone is Being-with. To this observation, which first does not appear plausible, Bollnow remarks: "Only a creature is able to be alone that is according to its nature living with others." [47] The present writer might express the same thus: Only a creature whose natural life is lived with others is able to experience loneliness.

VI

When Heidegger discusses human existence, he does not seem to think of the body. As already mentioned, he considers human existence to be "spiritual." He expounds about dread and care in their relations to human existence; there is a remarkable passage in *Sein und Zeit:* "Dread is often 'physiologically" conditioned . . . Physiological precipitation of dread is possible only because human existence is dreading in the ground of its Being." [48] There may be several interpretations of this passage. The writer understands it in the sense that human existence, *Dasein,* is considered to have a sort of priority: Only "because" human existence is there, can anything physiological—in this instance precipitation of dread—happen, and this only because dread appears to be an essential mode of human existence. This attitude of Heidegger has allowed some of his pupils to go "back stage" every time they want to interpret anything phenomenologically. This will be seen in the further discussion. It has, indeed, with several of these pupils, gone

45 *"Ich bin nur in Kommunikation mit Anderen"* (Jaspers).

46 *"Dasein ist wesentlich Mitsein"* (Heidegger).

47 *"Allein sein kann nur ein Wesen, das seiner Natur nach in Gemeinschaft lebt"* (Bollnow).

48 *"Oft ist die Angst 'physiologisch' bedingt . . . Physiologische Auslösung der Angst wird nur möglich, weil das Dasein im Grund seines Seins sich ängstet"* (Heidegger).

so far that they propose and pretend to solve or dissolve the body-mind dualism through making *Dasein* into the very ruling aspect of the human individual—a sort of commanding general who disposes of physical properties and psychological attitudes and performances in a manner that permits the adept to interpret, and thus to understand completely, practically every experience of the human individual. The writer, for one, doubts that Heidegger ever meant it this way.

What Heidegger considers the goal of his existential analy*tics*[49] to be has already been discussed. This must be referred to when one now turns to dealing with existential analy*sis*[50] as developed and propagated by Ludwig Binswanger. He defines Heidegger's existential analy*tics* as the "philosophic-phenomenological clarification of the a priori or transcendental structure of human existence as being-in-the-world."[51] Binswanger defines existential analy*sis* as "the empirical-phenomenological, scientific analysis of actual ways and *Gestalten* of human existence."[52] Existential analy*sis* as developed in the hands of Binswanger and his pupils purports to be a method of interpretation, of hermeneutics, based on the presupposition of a certain "a priori structure of human existence as being-in-the-world."[53] This a priori structure is taken over from Heidegger's thoughts and formulations.

[49] Heidegger's *Daseinanaly*tik or *existenziale Analy*tik. (See footnote 38.)

[50] Binswanger *Daseinana*lyse.

[51] *"die philosophisch-phänomenologische Erhellung der apriorischen oder transcendentalen Struktur des Daseins als In-der-Welt-sein."*

[52] *"die empirisch-phänomenologische, wissenschaftliche Analyse faktischer Daseinsweisen und Daseinsgestalten"* (Binswanger). One may remind the reader here that, for Heidegger, *Dasein* always refers to a human mode of individual existence, which for the sake of brevity and readability is rendered as "human existence." See page 194.

[53] *"apriorische Struktur des Daseins als In-der-Welt-sein."*

Binswanger emphasizes that he accepts "Being-in-the-world as existence in which human existence is concerned about myself. But [he understands] this self not only as the actual I-myself of human existence as mine or thine or his, but also as the we-our-selves a priori to that I-myself as ontologic possibility, as 'our' human existence, as primal meeting." [54] Binswanger concedes the "overwhelming impression" which *Sein und Zeit* made on him. But he soon notices "that the loving existence-together, love, stands in the cold outside of the doors of this project of Being." [55] Binswanger sees a contrast between care and love. On the ground of care there is "the nothing—eerie, overwhelming and overpowering," [56] on the ground of love there is "homey security, protecting home . . ." [57] Binswanger considers love the ontological opposite of care. He sees "in the eternity-aspect of *de facto* love a structural moment essentially immanent in love." [58] As already indicated, he declares Being-together as the very ground or foundation of love. He says many things about love, about "human existence as the we-ness of love." [59] "Love conquers 'space' and

[54] *"In-der-Welt-sein als ein Sein, darin es dem Dasein um es selbst geht, dass wir dieses Selbst aber nicht nur in dem faktischen Ich-selbst des Daseins als je meinem, deinem, seinem zu erblicken vermögen, sondern auch in den jenem Selbst vorgelagertem Möglichkeinten des Wir-selbst, des Daseins als 'unserem,' als Urbegegnung"* (Binswanger).

[55] *"dass das liebende Miteinander-sein, die Liebe, frierend ausserhalb dieses* [Heidegger's] *Seinsentwurfes steht"* (Binswanger).

[56] *"das 'unheinliche,' überwältigende und übermächtigende Nichts"* (Binswanger).

[57] *" 'heimliche' Geborgenheit, schützende Heimat."* The play with the words *"heimlich"* and *"unheimlich"* cannot be rendered in English as is regrettably the case with a great number of words and phrases in both *Daseinanaly*tik and *Daseinana*lyse. See page 200.

[58] *"in dem Ewigkeitsaspekt der Liebe tatsächlich ein ihr wesenhaft immanentes Strukturmoment"* (Binswanger).

[59] *"Dasein als Wirheit der Liebe"* (Binswanger).

'time' and 'history,' for it is not 'worlding' but eterning." [60] Binswanger says: "I can die only as an individual, but not as the thou of an I. Even if I die as an individual, I am, in dying, thine, a part of our we-ness." [61] Care does not have the aspect of eternity that love has. Yet, in the Being-in-the-world of the patient with a flight of ideas, Binswanger sees "The best example for the fact that both care and love belong equally to the full phenomenon of human existence . . . and that wherever either emancipates itself from the whole, the other 'gets altered' so that human existence becomes strange (alien) to itself and we talk about alienation, human existence in the form of estrangement, alienation, of insanity. The whole of psychopathology can (and must) be understood and described from the viewpoints of these two constituents of human existence, viz., care and love." [62]

There is another digression from his teacher, Heidegger, which Binswanger stresses: ". . . If we talk of human existence, in fundamental opposition to Heidegger we *never* mean human existence, as mine, thine, or his, but human existence in general, or the human existence of

[60] *"Liebe an und für sich überschwingt wie 'dem Raum' und 'die Zeit' so auch 'die Geschichte'; denn sie 'weltet' nicht, sondern ewigt"* (Binswanger).

[61] *"Sterben kann ich nur als Individuum, aber nicht als Du eines Ich. Wenn ich als Individuum auch sterbe, so* bin *ich doch noch im Sterben, ja jetzt erst recht, der Deine, Glied unserer Wirheit"* (Binswanger).

[62] *"das beste Beispiel dafür, dass zum vollen Phänomen des menschilichen Daseins Sorge und Liebe zusammenghören . . . und dass, wo das eine sich vom Ganzen emanzipiert, das andere sich 'alteriert,' so dass das Dasein sich selber fremd* (aliéné) *wird, und wir von alienation, Dasein in der Gestalt der Entfremdung, des Wahnsinns sprechen. Die ganze Psychopathologie kann* (*und muss*) *von diesen beiden Konstituentien des Dasiens, der Sorge und der Liebe, aus verstanden und beschrieben werden"* (Binswanger).

mankind if one wants to say so . . ." [63] It may help to understand the preceding and some of the following quotations from Binswanger when one of his much-emphasized observations is rendered in a somewhat simplified manner: It is not due to language and consciousness that man is man; it is primarily existence-with which makes man; only on this basis do language and self-consciousness become possible.

"Body and soul," we are told, "are abstractions from the inseparable unity of Being-human, seen from the anthropological viewpoint." [64] Admitting that body and soul are abstractions, one must wonder why the modes of Being as offered by Binswanger should and could be anything else but abstractions from the anthropological or any other viewpoint. Binswanger writes that plurality, duality and singularity are fundamental modes of Being-human: "Only in these modes and their special modifications and interweavings ('complexions'), is human existence really by itself. Where one cannot speak of an I, a thou, a dual we, a he or she nor of a plural we or they, there human existence is no longer 'by itself' but 'beside itself.'" [65] "'Between' Being-by-itself and Not-being-here is Being-beside-itself as we call the 'furor of passion,' of anger, of rage, of jealousy, of despair of any

[63] *". . . wenn wir con Dasein sprechen, meinen wir ja in fundamentalem Gegensatz zu Heidegger, nie nur das Dasein als je meines, deines oder seines, sondern das menschliche Dasein überhaupt, oder, wenn man will, das Dasein der Menschheit"* (Binswanger).

[64] *"Lieb und Seele sind lediglich Abstraktionen aus der untrennbaren Einheit des Menscheins, aus dem Sein als anthropologischem"* (Binswanger).

[65] *"Nur in diesen Modi, ihren speziellen Abwandlungen und Verflechtungen ('Komplexionen') ist das Dasein wirklich bei sich. Wo von keinem Ich, keinem Du, keinem dualen Wir, keinem Er oder Sie und keinem pluralen Wir die Rede sein kann, da ist das Dasein nicht mehr 'bei sich,' sondern 'ausser sich'"* (Binswanger).

kind. There human existence is no longer entirely by itself, here it approaches naked existence, horror." [66]

Binswanger observes that "cognition of human existence can never come to 'an end' " [67] and "that cognition of human existence is based not on logical reflection, but imaginative intuition of *Gestalten* and on the imaginative cognition of the change of *Gestalten*." [68] In other words: We shall never get close to his thinking when we approach it with logical reflection. If we desire to gain any understanding of his elaborations we have to accept his intuition and the products of his intuition.

Binswanger defends himself against the reproach that he has misunderstood and supplemented Heidegger's teachings. He missed the anthropological aspect in Heidegger's thought and tried to add it. He considers Heidegger's existential analy*tics* as fundamental for psychiatry. Binswanger has attempted to plan a "building" [69] of psychiatry in which Heidegger's existential analy*tics*, Heidegger's *Daseinsanaly*tik,[70] is said to be the "foundation." [71] Upon this foundation, in an architectural sense, the first story consisting of Binswanger's existential analy*sis*, *Daseinsana*lyse,[72] is to be erected. In the upper stories, clinical psychiatry and psychopathology, plus all auxiliary sciences, would be assigned their

[66] *"Gleichsam 'zwischen' dem Bei-sich-sein und dem Nicht-da-sein des Daseins steht das Ausser-sich-sein, wie wir die 'Raserei der Leidenschaft' nennen. Hier ist das Dasein nicht mehr ganz bei sich, hier nähert es sich dem nackten Dasein, dem Grauen"* (Binswanger).

[67] *"dass Daseinerkenntnis schon ihrem Wesen nach niemals an ein Ende gelangen kann"* (Binswanger).

[68] *"Dass das Wesen der Daseinserkenntnis keineswegs auf der logischen Reflexion, sondern auf der imaginativen Gestaltenschau und imaginativen Erkenntnis von Gestaltwandel* (*beruht*)" (Binswanger).

[69] *"Gebäude."*

[70] See page 200.

[71] *"Grundriss."*

[72] See pages 203-204.

places. Binswanger apparently sees in his existential analy*sis* a step forward into anthropology. He has reported that existential analy*sis* grew out of the wish to clarify "the conceptual bases of the psychological and psychotherapeutic observations, thought and actions of the psychiatrist at the 'sick bed.' " [73] One wonders how logical reflections, concepts, observations, thoughts and actions were taken care of by intuition. Anyway—slowly—so Binswanger tells us, he came to believe that there were psychotherapeutic possibilities in existential analy*sis,* namely when some patients seemed to show an understanding of the new manner of being understood; "when the experience of insight into their own structure of human existence and the pertinent knottings, bendings and shrinkings" [74] seemed to carry a certain therapeutic effect.

Binswanger, after him, Boss, Kuhn and others, went under full sail into this apparently new understanding and published a number of books and papers, some, if not most, of them based on their interpretations of patients, or on what the authors chose to consider, the human existences of patients. As the understanding of the working of existential analy*sis* may best be won from such publications, some of the published material will be presented in the following, first from Binswanger.

VII

In his study on flight of ideas, Binswanger deals with three patients in three chapters. He first states that flight

[73] *"die begrifflichen Grundlagen dessen, was der Psychiater in psychologischer und psychotherapeutischer Hinsicht 'am Krankenbett" wahrnimmt, überlegt und tut"* (Binswanger).

[74] *Dass "das Erlebnis der Einsicht in die eigene Daseinsstruktur und ihre konstitutionell oder geschichtlich bedingten Verknotunger, Verbiegungen oder Schumpfungen . . . oft schon allein einen psychotherapeutischen Effekt hat"* (Binswanger).

of ideas is a certain way of experiencing, and wonders about the "form of being-human in which something like flight of ideas is at all possible, i.e., which is, clinically speaking, the anthropological structure of 'mania.'"[75] He sees, in or behind the thinking in flight of ideas, a leveling of order in which the individual's or rather the *Dasein's,* world becomes smaller, but in which the manic "sprints"[76] or even jumps when the healthy person moves warily in small steps. The existence of the manic has the "structure of festivity."[77] "In the anthropological structure of the manic-depressive forms of being-human this experience of rising and of its opposite, of falling or sinking, plays a central role, so much so that dreams, in which the experience of one's own rising or the rising of something and then of sinking occurs first can be considered as manic-depressive 'psychoses' *in nuce.*"[78] While the world of the manic appears to be smaller—to the manic—he himself behaves like a powerful man, using big gestures and big words.[79]

Referring to Heidegger's observation concerning physiological precipitation of dread,[80] Binswanger remarks that "the manic excitation does not make the ecstasis of victory and the festive jubilation, but only makes it come

[75] "*. . . diejenige Form des Menschseins, in der so etwas wie Ideenflucht überhaupt möglich ist, klinisch gesprochen die anthropologische Struktur der 'Manie'*" (Binswanger).
[76] "*springt.*"
[77] "*Struktur der Festlichkeit*" (Binswanger).
[78] "*In der anthropologischen Struktur der manisch-depressiven Formen des Menschseins spielt dieses Erlebnis des Steigens und seines Gegenteils, des Fallens oder Sinkens, eine zentrale Rolle, sodass man Träume, in denen zuerst das Erlebnis des eigene Steigens oder des Steigens von etwas und dann des Sinkens vorkommt, als manisch-depressive 'Psychosen'* in nuce *aufassen kann*" (Binswanger).
[79] Binswanger here uses the adjectives "*grossmächtig,*" "*grosszügig,*" and "*grossmäulig.*"
[80] See page 205.

out of man.[81] He adds a footnote, "All 'the brain' or 'the organism' is able to achieve, here too, is only the physiological 'precipitation' of ontological-anthropological moments of structure." [82]

Dealing with two different patients in the second and third chapter, Binswanger is desirous of establishing a world of optimism, that is the world of the optimist where things are light, volatile. The optimist is correlated to this world, the optimist in the sense of an individuality with flight of ideas, i.e., with a "style of thinking" [83] corresponding to, or correlated to, that world of optimism. We are then told about melancholy and mania: In the first "the *Dasein* may stand still under its burden of guilt, grief and dread . . . in mania . . . decisions . . . are reached in springing . . ." [84] The writer cannot go into all details; he must particularly desist from a detailed report on what Binswanger does with the word "big-mouthed" [85] which for him has great importance in the manic person. It is characteristic that, in interpreting his three cases of flight of ideas, Binswanger not only discusses various kinds of flights of ideas as he finds them established in clinical psychopathology, but broadens out into an interpretation of the manic-depressive psychosis and of schizophrenia. In this respect, he writes, for example, "that the 'manic-depressive psychosis' does not teach us anything anthropologically new about 'man' but that it rather answers our question, 'what

[81] *". . . die manische Erregung (macht nicht) den Siegestaumel und Festesjubel, sie lockt ihn nur aus dem Menschen heraus"* (Binswanger.)

[82] *"Was 'das Gehirn' oder 'der Organismus' überhaupt zu leisten vermag, ist auch hier nur die physiologische 'Auslösung' ontologisch-antropologischer Strukturmomente"* (Binswanger).

[83] *"Denkstil."*

[84] *". . . (erfährt) unter dem Lastcharakter des Daseins, unter Schuld, Leid und Angst, einen völligen Stillstand . . .; in mania . . . decisions . . . are reached in springing . . ."* (Binswanger).

[85] *"grossmäulig"* (Binswanger).

is man?' in more conspicuous form and in more outspoken extremes." [86] Binswanger sees "manic-depressive man . . . on the ground of his existential 'insecurity' and 'lack of protection,' the creature that doubts everything." [87] The "manic-depressive" says yes and no to life—"I love to live but life is not important for me." [88] Furthermore, "the manic and the depressive form of existence represent, despite their inner contrariness, only two kinds of one and the same existential attitude, two contrasting attempts, at self-concealment and at self-flights." [89] Apparently, Binswanger wants to say that the manic runs from the problems of existence to the joy of life and is happy in his very existence, while the depressive is defeated by the problems of existence, and wonders whether he belongs to it (to existence) at all.

In the life of the schizophrenic there is no "springing," but "some sort of development in a life history"; [90] this development occurs along a straight, if often broken, line. The manic-depressive goes through his *Dasein* "in rhythmic-concentric motion." [91] "We call the man healthy who is able to go his way 'between' the two extremes.

[86] "*. . . das das 'manisch-depressive Irresein' anthropologisch uns über 'den Menschen' nichts Neues lehrt, dass es uns vielmehr nur in auffälligerer Form und in deutlicheren Extremen eine Antwort gibe auf die Frage, 'was der Mensch ist'* " (Binswanger).

[87] "*Vielmehr ist der manisch-depressive Mensch . . . das auf Grund seiner existentiellen 'Unsicherheit' und 'Ungesicherheit' an allem zweifelnde Wesen*" (Binswanger).

[88] "*Ich lebe zwar gerne, das Leben ist aber für mich nichts wichtiges*" (Binswanger).

[89] "*Die manische und die depressive Form der Existez stellen also bei aller inneren Gegensätzlichkeit doch nur zwei Arten ein und derselben inneren Haltung dar, zwei zu einander gegensätzliche Versuche der Selbstverdeckung und der Selbstflucht . . .*" (Binswanger).

[90] "*er entwickelt sich irgendwie lebensgeschichtlich*" (Binswanger).

[91] "*in rhythmisch-konzentrischer Bewegung*" (Binswanger).

The way of life of the healthy does not resemble either the circle or the 'straight line' but the spiral." [92]

Binswanger has published several cases of schizophrenic patients. In those that the writer has had the opportunity to read, there was no existential analytic therapy done or even planned. These patients were analyzed phenomenologically in Binswanger's manner under viewpoints which might be called existential-analytical or ontological or anthropological, according to the thought or intuition the author followed or wanted to convey in each particular instance. He attempts to show the profound change in the human existence of the pertinent patients. One of them, Lola Voss,[93] a Latin-American girl in her 20's, behaved oddly from the age of 12 or before. She felt insecure, hated to be alone, and developed obsessive-compulsive notions and actions early in her teens. She was extremely superstitious. In her early 20's there was a paranoid development. She suffered indescribable fears; she mistrusted people; people wanted to kill her. She was extremely unhappy. A feeling of eeriness overcame her that she was unable to describe. Later the eeriness made way for a feeling of secrecy [94] in which everything was evil and threatening her. Binswanger's interpretation is condensed here: Lola's ideal was to have peace.

[92] " *'Gesund' nennen wir, wer seinen Weg 'swischen' beiden Extremem hindurch zu nehmen vermag. Der Lebensweg des Gesunden gleicht weder dem Kreis noch der 'Geraden,' sondern der Spirale*" (Binswanger).

[93] The case of Lola Voss has been critically analyzed in an excellent lecture by Theodor Spörri. This analysis, the script of which the writer was permitted to read, has, regrettably, not been published so far. It should be noted that this patient was fluent only in Spanish. One may have some doubts whether the phenomena Binswanger undertook to interpret in his manner could be satisfactorily understood, because of mutual language difficulties.

[94] There Binswanger plays a little with the German words *umheimlich* (eerie) and *heimlich* (secret). See footnote 56.

She was unable to attain this ideal; instead, behind the picture of obsessions and delusions, she underwent a complete "voiding" of her human existence; she lived in the present, perhaps somewhat ailing from the past, but not really seeing any future for herself. The patient became increasingly "less human": finally she sank down into animal-like voraciousness.

In a short paper, Binswanger reported the case of a middle-aged American woman, Mary, who described herself as living in two worlds and at two speeds. One of these worlds was her marriage and her home in which the role of an understanding husband appeared to be paramount. The other world was the world of sensuality, in which she gave in to any desire and went through some "romance" at least once annually.

In the first world of relative stability there was, according to Binswanger's interpretation, "the mode of temporalization of the authentic present that temporalizes itself equally from the future and from the past." [95] Here the patient thinks, acts and experiences with deliberation at a relatively low speed. The patient calls the other world "the world of sensuality, of heightened speed, . . . the world of rapid burning, comparing it with a big flame which burns a candle faster than a small flame does." [96] Binswanger makes the interpretation that the "spiritual" [97] (Binswanger's quotation marks) world of lower speed is spatially characterized by rising vertically, while the sensual world of higher speed is char-

[95] *"den Zeitigungsmodus der eigentlichen Gegenwart, die sich gleicherweise aus der Zukunft wie aus der Gewesenheit zeitigt"* (Binswanger). The present writer here translates *Gewesenheit* literally "been-ness" as "past."

[96] *"Die Welt des 'Sensualismus' der erhöhten Geschwindigkeit . . . die Welt der raschen Verbrennung, derart wie eine grosse Flamme eine Kerze rascher aufbrauche als eine kleine"* (Binswanger).

[97] *"geistig."* See footnote 15.

acterized by running or riding horizontally. He conjectures that human existence of this kind "must be called disproportioned from the 'humanistic,' dissociated from the psychopathological, viewpoint." [98] Binswanger writes that this patient, Mary, "shows, like most polymorphous schizophrenics, cyclothymic features," but he finds and interprets her utterances differently from those of manic-depressive patients. He discovers the "symptom of queerness" [99] in this patient, and believes, "that we are able to understand the symptom of queerness, i.e., that we can refer it to an alteration in the basic structure of human existence." [100] It can scarcely be denied that one can refer everything to anything if one has made one's mind up to do so.

It should be mentioned that in his case presentations, Binswanger usually gives an extensive case history, a psychopathological discussion and analysis which are followed by his existential-analytical discussions and elaborations. As it seems very difficult, if at all possible, to keep them apart, it happens that existential-analytical and psychopathological terms get somewhat mixed. It is always obvious that the existential-analytical pattern or mode is seen—presumably in many instances intuited—by the author first and that the pertinent considerations are shaped according to this pattern.

In another schizophrenic patient, Ellen West, Binswanger is anxious to show how a human existence, formerly flexible, is sinking and drowning while time is crawling and ultimately getting rigid. Here Binswanger observes: " 'Pressing' upon human existence, the past

[98] " *'humanistisch' als unproportioniert, psychopathologisch al dissoziiert bezeichnet werden muss*" (Binswanger).
[99] "*das Symptom der Verschrobenheit*" (Binswanger).
[100] "*das wir auch das Symptom der Verschrobenheit daseinsanalytisch verstehen, d. h. auf eine Veränderung der Grundstruktur des Daseins zurückführen können*" (Binswanger).

robs it of every view into the future . . . Where the past of lived life has become overpowering, and where the life still to be lived is dominated by the past, we talk about old age." [101] In Ellen West, Binswanger says human existence has become emptied in her youth, "existential aging had preceded biological aging, and existential death, 'to be among people like a corpse' [patient's remarks], had preceded the biological end of life." [102] Binswanger's interpretation continues: "Ellen West's world underwent an obvious change from the liveliness, width, brightness and colorfulness of the ether over the dimness, mistiness, rotting, decomposition and putrefaction to the narrowness, darkness and grayness of dead earth. The existential analytical precondition of the possibility of this change is an obvious unitary phenomenon. This phenomenon is the phenomenon of temporalization." [103] The schizophrenic process is seen as "a process of existential voiding and impoverishment in the sense of an increasing rigidity ('congealment') of the free self into a less and less free ('more dependent') object that is strange to itself." [104]

[101] *"Indem die Vergangenheit auf das Dasien 'drückt,' benimmt sie ihm jede Aussicht auf die Zukunft. Wo aber die Vergangenheit, das gelebte Leben, übermächtig geworden ist, das noch zu lebende Leben von der Vergangenheit beherrscht wird, sprechen wir von Alter"* (Binswanger).

[102] *"Das existentielle Altern war dem biologischen Altern vorausgeeilt, wie auch der existentielle Tod, das 'wie eine Leiche unter Menschen sein,' dem biologischen Lebensende vorausgeeilt war"* (Binswanger).

[103] *"die existential-analytische Voraussetzung dafür, dass die Welt Ellen West's eine so eindeutige Wandlung con der Libendigkeit, Weite, Helle und Farbigkeit des Äthers über die Verdüsterung, Vernebelung, Verdorrung, Moderung und Faulung zur Enge, Dunkelheit und Grauheit der Verschalung und Vererdung der toten Erde durchzumachen vermag, ist, dass dieser Wandlung ein eindeutiges, einheitliches Phänomen zugrundeliegt. Dieses Phänomen aber ist das Phänomen der Zeitigung"* (Binswanger).

[104] *"ein existentieller Entleerungs-oder Verarmungsprozess, und zwar*

These are only a few examples of Binswanger's very copious writings. When his writings are called copious, it is meant that he wrote many papers and several books. The books, as well as the papers, are, as a rule, rather long. That this author gives all those who want to believe a profusion of material is clear. It is to be wondered at that he has not been criticized more. Binswanger starts from "a certain way of experiencing," [105] the flight of ideas. In this discussion, as in others, there is much talk about experiencing–normal or pathological –although it is emphasized that existential analy*sis* is neither psychology nor psychopathology. In the work on flight of ideas, the following terms occur: human existence, life, form of life, way of life [106] without clear definition of any of them. There is the *ad hoc* production "big-mouthed form of existence," [107] there are the manic, the depressive and the manic-depressive man.[108] There is also the manic form of being-human [109] and the manic being-in-the-world.[110] Also, the *"ideenflüchtige Individualität"* is to be found. There is, last but not least, the joy of existence, the *Daseinsfreude;* in respect to conditions of confusion with flight of ideas,[111] one reads: "Language as a tool of thinking is turned into verbosity or rather bombast as a toy of the joy of existence." [112]

---

im Sinne einer zunchmenden Erstarrung ('Gerinnung') des freien Selbst zu einem immer unfreieren ('unselbständigern') selbstfremden Gegenstand" (Binswanger).

105 *"eine bestimmte Erlebensweise"* (Binswanger).

106 *Dasein, Leben, Lebensform, Lebensweg* (Binswanger).

107 *"grossmäulige Existenzform"* (Binswanger).

108 *"der manische, der depressive un der der manisch-depressive Mensch"* (Binswanger).

109 *"manische Form des Menschseins"* (Binswanger).

110 *"das manische In-der-Welt-sein"* (Binswanger).

111 *"verworrene Ideenflucht"* (*ideenflüchtige Verwirrtheit, Kraepelin*).

112 *"Anstelle der Sprache als eines Werkzeugs des Denkens tritt dann der Wort—oder richtiger Lautschwall als eis Spielzeug der Daseinsfreude"* (Binswanger).

One may wonder whether something like this did not happen to the author—who rejoiced after finding a tool or toy that, in his conviction, made it possible and permissible to give free rein to his intuitive phenomenology or phenomenological intuition. The observer or critic who has been informed that phenomenology is dealing with reality, with the data as given immediately, wonders about the cheerful subjectivity with which allegedly phenomenologically immediate data appear, are followed and juggled around *ad libitum auctoris.*

VIII

Medard Boss is a writer of a fertility equal to Binswanger's. Of all the practicing psychiatrists who have accepted Heidegger's teaching, he appears to be closest to the teacher. Boss writes with a tremendous élan, with an admirable vocabulary and, like Binswanger, with the obviously unswerving conviction of being a prophet of a new, unshakable truth.

Boss explains that he considers the "psychotherapeutic practice and technique" [113] of psychoanalysis according to the " 'basic rules' of Freud" [114] valid. He writes "that Freud could intuitively invent all his 'basic rules' of psychoanalytic practice, but was able to support them only with astonishingly superficial and unsafe arguments." An analytical cure is not decisive for: "If a psychotherapist experiences the essence of man as existence in the sense of Martin Heidegger, he will speak of complete cure only when a formerly sick man becomes able to comprehend himself, as it were, as a light out of concealment of Being, a light in whose shining all things

[113] "*psychotherapeutische Praxis und Technik* (Boss).

[114] " '*Grundergeln' Freuds*" (Boss).

and fellowmen may unfold according to their own essence." [115]

Existential analy*tics, Daseinsanaly*tik, "has nothing at all to do with therapeutic practice, with practical intentions and purposes. As the fundamental ontology of Martin Heidegger, it asks 'only' for the Being of all being, . . . for the mode of existence of man and his belonging to Being. Even there where existential analy*tics* is modified and restricted to Ludwig Binswanger's existential analy*sis* as a merely anthropological method of research, it is nothing else but phenomenological examination and elucidation of essence of the healthy and sick human existence." [116] Boss discusses the necessity "of a definite *Weltanschauung* or metaphysics without which he (the physician) would not want to help at all." [117] He calls this the doctor's "Faith" [118] "based on the desire to open to our patients the way to their being fully human." [119] Boss does not leave us in any doubt

[115] *"Erfährt jedoch ein Psychotherapeut das Wesen des Menschen als Existenz im Sinne Martin Heideggers dann wird er von einer vollen Heilung erst reden, wenn sich ein bisher kranker Mensch gleichsam als ein Licht aus der Verborgenheit des Seins zu begreifen vermag, in dessen Schein sich alle Dinge und Mitmenschen ihrem eigenen Wesen nach entfalten dürfen"* (Boss).

[116] *"Denn Daseinsanaly*tik *an sich hat . . . mit praktischen Absichten und Zwecken nicht das geringste zu tun. Als Fundamentalontologie Martin Heideggers frägt sie 'nur' nach dem Sein alles Seienden . . . nach der Seinsart des Menschen und dessen Zugehörigkeit zum Sein. Auch dort noch, wo sich die Daseinsanaly*tik *zur Daseinanaly*se *Ludwig Binswangers als einer rein anthropolgischen Forschungs methode modifiziert und einschränkt, will sie nicht anderes als phänomenologische Untersuchung und Wesenserhellung des gesunden und kranken menschilchen Daseins betreiben"* (Boss).

[117] *"einer ganz bestimmten Weltanschauung oder Metaphysik, ohne die er (der Arzt) würde gar nicht helfen wollen"* (Boss).

[118] *"Glaubenshaltung"* (Boss).

[119] *"Das gesamte ärztliche Denken und Handeln . . . (sollte) von dem Bestreben getragen sein, unseren Kranken den Weg zu ihrem vollen Menschsein zu bahnen"* (Boss).

about his *Weltanschauung* or metaphysics, or if one wants to call it so: his faith. It is grounded in Heidegger's teaching. It is as though he were backing up Freud's psychoanalytic technique with the theory offered in Heidegger's ontology.

Boss seems to have oriented his thinking according to Heidegger's ideas. Using and admiring psychoanalytic technique, Boss writes: "The marvelous unity and conciseness of the psychoanalytical theory of perversions had to be gained through a very far-reaching loss of reality and an enormous rape of reality . . . the dynamisms and mechanisms are 'assumed' . . . nothing but products of thinking attributed to the given reality." [120] The implication is that existential analy*tics* is dealing with reality, that the findings arrived at on its background *are* reality. We are not informed exactly what reality Boss has in mind. However, Heidegger's existential analy*tics* is interpretation. Why this particular manner of interpretation should get hold of reality is never expounded. One must submit that at best it is a manner of interpretation by which its psychiatric adherents believe they get closer to what they mean by reality.

Boss berates the physicians for their biologistic-mechanistic attitude and thinking, and does not tire of telling them that human existence, *Dasein* in the sense of Heidegger, comes first. He deems necessary "a thinking which does not simply transfer the former objective notions about the human body onto the psychic realm, but which tries to see both in a basically new manner according to the unobjective essence of human existence to which all

[120] *"Die grossartige Einheitlichkeit und Geschlossenheidt der psychoanalytischen Perversionstheorie hatte . . . mit einem sehr weitgehenden Wirklichkeitsverlust und einer enormen Wirklichkeitsvergewaltigung erkauft werden müssen . . . die bloss 'angenommenen' Dynamismen und Mechanismen . . . lediglich der gegebenen Wirklichkeit zugeordnete Denkprodukte sind"* (Boss).

bodily and psychic phenomena belong." [121] Objectivity appears to be replaced by belief in the reality of the material gained by the phenomenological method. Even forgetting the observations submitted in the foregoing, one cannot but remain skeptical in regard to the reality and immediacy of the phenomena the existential-analytically oriented psychiatrist deals with: Do these phenomena *de facto* originate in the patient? One could formulate more succinctly: The patient is steered toward or helped into a world of alleged reality where the meanings provided by the analyst play a predominant role.

Boss wants to get rid of the body-soul dualism and proposes to accomplish this with existential analy*tics.* Human existence is "spiritual"; [122] it is "carried out" [123] in the body, its organs and its functions: "the body is bodying." [124] This is a point of particular interest. In his great enthusiasm, Boss does not seem to see that he is doing what many psychotherapists do; but he does it with the ample use of resounding words and with all the convert's fervor.

In his book *Sinn und Gehalt sexueller Perversionen,*[125] Boss emphatically agrees with Freud's statement:

[121] *"ein Denken, das nicht einfach die früheren gegenständlichen Vorstellungen über den menschlichen Körper auf den seelischen Bereich überträgt, sondern sowohl jenen wie dissen von Grund auf neu, entsprechend dem ungegenständlichen Wesen des menschlichen Daseins, dem alle lieblichen und seelischen Erscheinungen angehören, zu verstehen versucht"* (Boss).

[122] *"geistig,"* see footnotes 15 and 95.

[123] *"ausgetragen"* (Boss).

[124] *"Der Leib leibt"* (Boss). The German words *Körper* and *Leib* must both be translated as "body." In the psychological and psychopathological literature there is a tendency to use the noun *Leib* whenever there is a reference to or an implication of the psyche or the spirit. This holds true also of Boss' use of the words. *"Der Leib leibt"* is a formulation quite obviously shaped after Heidegger's *"Das Nichts nichtet."* See footnote 25.

[125] "Sense and Content of Sexual Perversions."

"The omnipotence of love is perhaps nowhere more clearly demonstrated than in its aberrations." [126] Boss writes that the fetishists and coprophiles are content "to see their mode of human existence and their world projects covered by the worldly barriers of dread, shame and disgust. Thus they become aware only of parts of the heterosexual *Gestalt* of human existence; love seems to shine only through rifts, and to become more or less transparent to them." [127] The disturbance that is begun with fetishists and coprophiles is continued by the kleptomaniacs, the exhibitionists, voyeurs and sado-masochists; in them "the narrowness, rigidity and resistivity of their worlds widen and strengthen increasingly, with the consequence that they can come to a loving communication only through an ever more violent breaking through of those worldly barriers." [128]

Of homosexual types, Boss distinguishes a variety of groups, each of which is "characterized by specific modes of existence and corresponding world projects." [129] Boss presents, among others, a homosexual woman who, because of a psychoneurotically-conditioned standstill of her maturation, fell into "this mode of human exist-

[126] *"Die Allgewalt der Liebe zeigt sich vielleicht nirgends stärker als in diesen ihren Verirrungen"* (Freud).

[127] *"ihre Daseinsverfassung und ihre Weltentwürfe durch die weltlichen Schranken der Angst, der Scham und des Ekels derart verdeckt zu sehen, dass ihnen nur noch durch gewisse Ausschnitte der gegengeschlechtlichen Daseinsgestalt hindurch die Liebe mehr oder weniger transparent werden konnte"* (Boss).

[128] *"die Enge, Starrheit und Widerständigkeit ihrer Welten* (*hatte sich*) *zunchmend ausgedehnt und verstärkt, sodass sie nicht mehr anders zu einer Liebeskommunikation zu gelangen vermochten, als dass sie diese Schranken auf immer gewaltsamere Art und Weise durchbrechen"* (Boss).

[129] *"zeichnet sich durch ganz spezifische Seinsverfassungen und entsprechende Weltentwürfe aus"* (Boss).

ence"; a schizophrenic man whose homosexuality was due "to a later psychotic re-disappearance of the world, to a secondary schizophrenic loss of his own self" [131] which brought about the " perversion' of his love" [132] as a manifestation "of the same schizophrenic shrinking and destruction of human existence." [133] In contrast to Freud, Boss sees this kind of homosexuality and the formation of delusions in the schizophrenic as parallel manifestations.

Boss notes that "an existential narrowness of personality," [134] analogous to the narrowing assumed in the two instances just mentioned, may stem from "a genuine psychopathic *Anlage* and then result in a so-called constitutional homosexuality." [135] He describes such a case, a woman, Claudine (with two homosexual relatives on the paternal side) who resembled her father almost completely except for the sexual organs. She had a uterus bicornis like her mother. There was no possibility of changing her love life by means of psychoanalysis. Falling in love, Claudine loved her girl friend "as only a man can love a woman." [136] The world grew open to her in an unheard-of width and fullness. She felt herself reborn in a deeper sense than at her physical birth. Even death meant to this love not ending and nothinging . . . (but) . . . a door, an entrance, a signpost to eternal

[130] *"diese Seinsverfassung"* (Boss).
[131] *"einem nachträglichen psychotischen Wiederversinken von Welt, einem sekundären schizophrenen Selbstverlust"* (Boss).
[132] *" 'Pervertierung' seiner Liebe"* (Boss).
[133] *"derselben schizophrenen Schrumpfung und Zerstörung einer menschlichen Daseinsgestalt . . ."* (Boss).
[134] *"existentielle Persönlichkeitsenge"* (Boss).
[135] *"einer genuinen psychopathischen Anlage . . . und dann resultieren in einer sogenannten konstitutionellen Homosexualität . . ."* (Boss).
[136] *"wie nur ein Mann einen Frau lieben kann"* (Boss).

union." [137] Claudine, in fact, committed suicide when her brother intervened in her love. Concerning Claudine's father identification and her refusal to accept the female role, Boss observes: "It is grounded in the fact that Claudine's existence was in respect to body, impulse and spirit and their manifestations as a *Gestalt,* far-reachingly molded through the same 'constitutional' barriers, through the same 'hereditary *Anlagen*' as her father's . . ." [138]

One will admit that the mention of constitution and hereditary *Anlagen,* though put cautiously between quotation marks, betrays a considerable liberality in this author who so gravely condemns the medieval thinking of his biologistically-mechanistically oriented colleagues. His liberality is no less pronounced in his free use of psychoanalysis, although its background must appear mechanistic to him. He wants to do full justice to psychoanalysis, as is witnessed, for example, in the following observation: "We know that the world project is narrowed in a specific manner in the various pervert human beings. This knowledge permits us to comprehend how it happens that the Oedipus and castration complexes, which psychoanalysis has recognized as ubiquitous, can, as important concretizations and points of break-through

[137] *"Die Welt eröffnete sich ihr in einer unerhörten Weite und Fülle, sodass sie sich noch einmal 'und in einem tieferen Sinne als bei ihrer leiblichen Geburt' geboren fühlte. Selbst der Tod bedeutete dieser Liebe nicht Ende und Nichtigung . . . (sondern) wurde verwandelt in ein Tor, einen Eingang, in einen Wegweiser zu ewiger Verbundenheit"* (Boss).

[138] *"Sie gründet vielmehr darin, die Existenz Claudines eben leiblich, triebhaft und geistig sehr weitgehend durch die gleichen 'konstitutionellen' Grenzen, durch die nämlichen 'Erbanlagen' in ihrer Erscheinungsgestalt geprägt wurde, wie es beim Vater der Fall war"* (Boss).

of existential dread, motivate once a 'normal,' another time a hysterical or a perverse personality . . ." [139] Despite Boss' desire to keep existential analy*tics* out of therapeutic practice, the practical and theoretical sides of his procedure are so close to each other that one is tempted to ask: What is explaining what to whom?

Boss' exposition and presentation are just as brilliant and entertaining in his two other books. One may turn to his dream book. Boss holds that dreamers "perceive the dream phenomena . . . not either as pictures or as symbols . . . they experience them as real, physical data: a thing as a real thing, an animal as a real animal, a man as a real man, a ghost as a real ghost. In our dreams we are in a world just as genuine and graspable as in our waking; there and here we carry out our human existence in our relations with, and in our behavior to, the things and to our fellowmen." [140]

A 34-year-old woman, in psychoanalysis for three years, dreamed: She was jailed in a cell; there were many clocks; a burglar came and destroyed them, but they continued ticking. "The ticking warned me that second after

139 *"Und das Wissen um den in je besonderer Weise verengten Weltentwurf der verschiedenen perversen Menschen erlaubt uns, zu verstehen, wieso die von der Psychoanalyse als ubiquitär erkannten Oedipus und Kastrations komplexe als wichtige Konkretisierungen und Einbruchsstellen der Daseins-Angst die Entwicklung bald einer hysterischen, bald einer 'normalen' Persönlichkeit, bald einer perversen motivieren können . . ."* (Boss).

140 *"die Traumerscheinungen . . . weder als Bilder noch als Sinnbilder wahrnehmen. Sie erfahren sie vielmehr träumend als uirkliche, physische Gegebenheiten: ein Ding als ein wirkliches Ding, ein Tier als ein wirkliches Tier, einen Menschen als einen wirklichen Menschen, ein Gespenst als ein wirkliches Gespenst. Wir sind in unseren Träumen in einer ebenso echten, handgreiflichen Welt wie in unserem Wachen und tragen dort wie hier unser Dasein in unseren Beziehungen und in unserem Verhalten zu den Dingen und Mitmenschen aus"* (Boss).

second passed, but real time stood still."[141] She noticed that outside time went on because she became wrinkled. An attendant brought a big green bottle which had the shape of a man and smelled wonderfully. Then the bottle became a man who led her to the wedding. "Now I was really living again, and the hands of the clock no longer stood still."[142] As a young girl of strong sensuality, this woman had been abused by a man. She had run back to her parents to stay under their protection: For her, time no longer progressed. The discrepancy between the unmoving temporalization of her existence and the continuing world time made her feel eerie. Boss interprets this discrepancy as the one "between her childish being-in-the-world and the superficial relations in which she is posing in the world of the grown-ups."[143] In psychoanalysis, she learned to let her erotic relations ripen. She found the way to the other sex, could marry in dream and in waking. The temporalization of her own existence had begun again.

Another of Boss' dreamers was a woman who was a successful physician. She had "hidden her female possibilities . . . behind the façade of masculine-aggressive behavior."[144] She went through psychoanalytic treatment. She dreamed of a great journey, living through half a life within half an hour, finding the man whom she could love and with whom she lived happily for years

[141] " '*Das Ticken mahnte mich daran, dass doch noch Sekunde nach Sekunde verrann, aber die wirkliche Zeit stand still*' " (The patient's remark).

[142] " '*Ich lebte jetzt auch wirkliche wieder. Und die Zeiger der Uhren standen nicht mehr still*' " (The patient's remark).

[143] "*zwischen ihrem eigentlichen in der Kindlichkeit verharrenden In-der-Welt-Sein und den oberflächlichen Beziehungen, in denen sie noch notdürftig in der Welt der Erwachsenen mitmacht*" (Boss).

[144] *Sie hatte "ihre weiblichen Moeglichkeiten . . . hinter einer Fassade des rein männlich-aggressiven Verhaltens . . . verborgen gehalten"* (Boss).

in her dream. "This dream was possible only because now the horizon of expectation reached so far into her future. Her inner temporalization, her history, her existential openness, which she lives and is authentically, unfolded in this dream in such far-reaching a manner." [145]

"Regardless as to whether he is waking or dreaming (the human individual) . . . is concerned in his relations to things and men, he authentically is, exists, as being related to them. This relation to his world we saw comparable to the relation of a light to those who stand in its shining . . . dreaming or waking the human individual can carry out his existence in very different kinds of behavior and relations." [146] Boss is of the opinion that we become aware of the historical continuity of our waking life through the discontinuity of our dreams.

A few examples may be added from Boss' *Psychosomatic Medicine.* These patients, like those already reported on, were in psychoanalytic therapy with him, mostly for years. A "perfect lady of the world, an irreproachable housewife, wife and mother" [147] had grown up in a conventional, rigid family, where she had been tutored by governesses. She was a lively person, but all around her was spiritual narrowness. She became perfec-

145 *"Darum war dieser Traum nur möglich, weil jetzt der Erwartungshorizont so weit in die Zukunft hineinreichte. Ihre innere Zeitlichkeit, ihre Geschichte, ihre existentielle Offenheit, die sie eigentlich lebt und ist, war es, die sich in diesem Traum in so weitreichendem Sinn erschlossen hatte"* (Boss).

146 *". . . träumend nicht minder, als wenn er wacht* (der Mensch) *. . . im Bezughaben zu den Dingen und Menschen aufgeht, als Bezogensein auf sie eigentlich ist. Diese seine Weltbzogenheit aber sahen wir dem Verhältnis eines Lichtes zu dem in seinem Scheinen Stehenden gleichen . . . dass der Mensch träumend ebenso wie wachend in sehr verschiedenen Arten von Verhaltungsweisen und Weltbezügen seine Existenz austragen kann"* (Boss). See page 218.

147 *"eine perfecte Dame con Welt, eine untadelige Hausfrau, Gattin und Mutter"* (Boss).

tionistic and compulsive; finally she played the great lady while she was actually still the helpless little girl. At the age of 43, "grave neuritides . . . [with] almost untolerable pains . . . [and] a high degree of muscle weakness" [148] developed; for weeks and months she was bedridden. She reported dreams in which she underwent heavy and painful accidents, and another dream in which, as a little girl, she comprehended "her own life-long captivity within the narrow and meager mentality of her ascetic and conventionally rigid family and of her thin governesses." [149] Although she soon became more active than before, "the pains and the weakness in her extremities disappeared after existential widening and unburdening. The severely pathological changes in tendon reflexes and the electrical excitabilities of the nerves returned to normal as soon as she had renounced enough of her attitude as a conventional lady, which was not in harmony with her real nature." [150] The former complaints recurred "with the certainty of an experiment . . . as soon as she fell back into her old mentality, a little, even if there had not yet been the slightest change in her behavior." [151] Boss deems it possible "that occasionally even such polyneuritides which can be recognized neurologically as 'organic' with

[148] *"schwere Nervenentzündungen . . . [mit] fast unerträglichen Schmerzen . . . [und] eine hochgradige Muskelschwäche"* (Boss).

[149] *"ihre eigene lebenslängliche Gefangeschaft innerhalb der engen und kargen Mentalität ihrer asketischen und konventionell erstarrten Familie und ihrer dürren Erzieherinnen"* (Boss).

[150] *"verschwanden nach der existentiellen Weitung und Entlastung. Auch die zuvor schwer pathologisch veränderten Schnenreflexe und elektrischen Erregbarkeiten der Nerven kehrten zur Norm zurück, sobald sie sich von der ihrem eigentlichen Wesen so ungemässen Lebenshaltung einer konventionellen Dame genügemd losgesagt hatte"* (Boss).

[151] *"mit der Sicherheit Experiments . . . , sobald sie geistig auch nur ein wenig in die alte Mentalität zurückfiel, selbst wenn sich dabei in ihrem äusseren Verhalten noch nicht das geringste geändert hatte"* (Boss).

all their manifestations of weakness and pains are nothing else but the somatizing of an inadequate relation to life which can be influenced psychotherapeutically." [152]

Boss has a good deal to say about accident-prone people, who "always have accidents whenever they get into serious conflict situations that they do not see any way to settle through impulsive breaking of tense interhuman relationships or through running away from too tense social situations." [153] Boss conjectures that "people often break their inner bodily relationships, their own connecting and supporting tissues, instead of breaking relationships in the world in which they live." [154]

A patient, R.U., was highly intelligent, although "as a whole human being she had remained a very infantile creature." [155] She was attached to her mother and flirted around, "just in the manner a young cat deals with other young cats." [156] One day "a young man broke into her world as a male and shook her world." [157] She made a date with him in a winter spa where she became exceed-

[152] "*unter Umständen selbst derartige mit neurologischer Sicherheit als 'organisch' zu erkennende Polyneuriden samt all ihren Schwäche und Schmerzerscheinungengelegentlich nichts anderes als die Lieblichung eines inadäquaten, psychotherapeutisch beeinflussbaren Lebensbezuges sein* [*könnten*]" (Boss).

[153] "[*sie*] *verunglücken immer dann, wenn sie wieder einmal in eine schwere Konfliktsituation hineingeraten sind, aber keinen Weg schen, sie durch impulsives Brechen der konflikthaft gespannten Situation oder durch ein Ausreissen aus einer allzu gaspannten Lage erledigen zu können*" (Boss).

[154] "[*Dabei*] *zerbrechen diese Menschen oft genug an Stelle ihrer mitweltichen ihre innerleiblichen Verbindungen, ihre eigenleiblichen Binde und Stützgewebe*" (Boss).

[155] "*Als ganzer Mensch jedoch war sie ein hochgradig infantiles Wesen geblieben*" (Boss).

[156] "*so, wie eine ganz Katze mit ihresgleichen umzugehem pflegt*" (Boss).

[157] "*ein junger Mann als Mann in ihre Welt einbrach und diese Welt erschütterte*" (Boss).

ingly tense, "almost exploding." [158] She passed some of her time on her skis. Her friend found her in the hospital with a complicated fracture of a leg. Later she married and had a child. She still was dependent on her mother in whose home she lived. She went into psychoanalysis. She made up her mind to move with her husband and child into quarters of her own. After a dream that showed her dependence, she decided to do something about it and "immediately squeezed her right forearm into the door so badly that the torn muscles and tendons frustrated her good intentions for quite some time." [159]

Boss reflects that there are people who exist in situations no less tense than those of accident-prone individuals; however, they do not try to break out of the conflict-situations nor do they break tendons and bones, but proceed cautiously. Some of them remain in tension throughout their lives; they have to pull themselves together without any respite and cannot but develop high blood pressure. "Ultimately they wall themselves in secretively while they are still alive, as though they wanted to make certain that their particular world relations would remain fixed in the media of their bodies. If this process has developed far enough, we are faced with people petrified through the calcification of their arterioles, *i.e.*, the petrified sequela of preceding essential or idiopathic hypertension." [160] The association of calcifi-

[158] *"zum Zerreissen gespannt"* (Boss quotes the patient here).

[159] *"Da klemmte sie aber auch schon ihren rechten Unterarm so schwer in die Türe ein, dass die Muskel-und Schnenzerreissungen die Ausführung aller ihrer guten Abischten (für geraume Zeit vereitelten"* (Boss).

[160] *"Schlisslich mauern sie sich insgeheim lebendigen Leibes ein, gleichsam um das Steckenbleiben ihres so gestimmten Weltverhävltnisses im Medium der Lebiblichkeit zu sichern. Ist dieser Prozess einmal weit geung gedichen, dann haben wir den an Arteriolenverkalkung versteinerten Menschen vor uns, den petrifizierten Folgezustand einer vorgängigen essentiellen oder idiopathischen Hypertonie"* (Boss).

cation and walling in is unmistakable; so is the verve of the discourse.

It is apparent that Boss, like the rest of us, is using a variety of nouns when he speaks about patients. In the case just mentioned, there are *"diese Menschen," "als ganzer Mensch," "ein infantiles Wessen."* With whatever interpretation one wishes to clarify and to understand what these people are doing, one is faced with them as *"ganze Menschen"*; not merely as *"Dasein,"* a word which Boss, like Heidegger, uses synonymously with existence. It impresses one, not rarely, as an ingenious performance when interpretations which are obviously shaped in the writer's mind according to the pattern of Heidegger's thought seem to be taken as reality and as originating with the patient. Although once in a while Boss' writing not only sounds—but is—fantastic, there is something appealing in it which is missed in Binswanger's, and still more in Kuhn's, publications. The writer cannot help assuming that this is due to several factors, among which Boss' sense of humor and his undeniable, if often hidden, common sense are as relevant as his style and his convert's fervor.

IX

Roland Kuhn is the third and last representative of existential analysis about whom the writer wishes to report here. Although, so far, his productions do not approach those of Binswanger and Boss—he is considerably younger—he has already written a goodly number of papers. One may best consider him as a devoted son-pupil of Binswanger and an adoring grandson-pupil of Heidegger. His writings do not seem to be easily produced; they are not entertaining to read. Despite all his courtesy, once in a while he seems to be unable—or unwilling?—to suppress a certain hostility against non-adherents to his creed. The "it is so" of the psychiatric existential analysts is very outspoken in Kuhn. He knows as well as anyone that his existential-analytical excursions, discourses and discussions are interpretations; yet he is so sure of them that he cannot but consider them as certain—at least more certain than anything that may be deemed to be facts or interpretations by any other school of thought.

In a paper in which Kuhn discusses transference from the existential analytical point of view, particular attention is paid to the interruption of communications, in order to show that new relations will follow the interruptions. These interruptions are said to give the therapist a particular chance "to an encounter with himself." [161] Kuhn emphasizes that the existential-analytical therapist must be sure of himself. Like Binswanger and Boss, he realizes that not every individual is accessible to, and apt to go through, a deeper reaching psychotherapy; he writes: "In psychotherapy, the attempt is made to extricate the patient from the bane of his past. To the degree to which this attempt succeeds, the patient becomes free, open to the new, and able to unfold his creative faculties . . ." [162] This is, one conjectures, likely to reduce the number of candidates for such therapy to a rather modest figure.

Among other papers on patients, Kuhn published a rather extensive one on a man who, at the age of 20, shot a prostitute. Rudolf, born in 1918, had some schizophrenic, depressive and epileptic heredity. He early lost his mother (1922) whose shining eyes he never forgot, and whose dead body he saw, as he later saw the dead body of his father (1939). He seemed to go through a violent affect of mourning when his father's body was

[161] *"zu einer Begegnung mit sich selbst"* (Kuhn).

[162] *"In dem Masse, als es der Psychotherapie gelingt, dem Kranken dazu zu verhelfen, sich von dem Bann seiner Vergangenheit zu lösen, wird er frei, dem Neuen offen und er kann seine schöpferischen Fähigkeiten entfalten"* (Kuhn).

taken away. The father died (January 17 or 18, 1939), several weeks after Rudolf had had an argument with him (Christmas 1938). On March 23, 1939, Rudolf had unsatisfactory intercourse with a prostitute whom he shot after she had put on her clothes. The wound was slight. He went to the police soon afterward. As a schizoid-hysterical psychopath who had acted in a neurotic state, he was committed to a mental hospital where he remained until 1948. During these nine years, he "had to undergo a very thorough psychoanalytic examination, observation and treatment." [163]

Rudolf was always a daydreamer. Working as a butcher's apprentice, he had occasionally had intercourse with hogs that he afterward killed; he also had intercourse with his master's wife whereupon he was discharged. He continued his apprenticeship with another butcher. He had a variety of heterosexual relations. Kuhn found that Rudolf was sexually perverted (fetishistic, sodomistic, sadistic, with passive homosexual trends); that he was compulsive; and that he had shot the prostitute in a psychotic depression with schizoid trends.

Half of this paper consists of Kuhn's "attempt to understand Rudolf's act existential-analytically." [164] Some of his statements and explanations are reported. He writes, "The act was committed in cold blood during the depression that followed the sexual discharge; it was not performed in order to gain highest sexual or other excitation." [165] Kuhn conjectures that the act "originated from genuine compulsive experiencing" [166] but was "not

[163] This quotation is taken literally from the English summary of Kuhn's paper.
[164] *"Versuch, Rudolfs Tat daseinsanalytisch zu verstehen"* (Kuhn).
[165] *"Die Tat wurde nicht zur Gewinnung höchster sexueller oder auch sonstiger Erregung ausgeführt sondern kaltblütig in der sexuellen Entladung nachfolgenden Verstimmung"* (Kuhn).
[166] *"aus echtem Zwangserleben . . . entstanden"* (Kuhn).

a compulsive action."[167] He explains that Rudolf's *Dasein* rolled off horizontally on the street which is full of thrills. "The life in thrills is basic for this world project of Rudolf's . . . Where there is no thrill, there is for him no world, there is nothing at all, emptiness, coldness, senselessness, and boredom."[168] Kuhn tells us: "The thrilling form of human existence has its own laws; they are, as far as we see, insufficiently investigated in psychology and psychiatry. However, the science of literature has recognized the thrilling style of life in dealing with the dramatic problem in art and life."[169]

In Rudolf's dreams and reveries, Kuhn found ample material to make out that there was a "vertical axis in Rudolf's existence,[170] too." Kuhn goes into many details about the "subterranean nature of the cellar,"[171] of "this rotting world," as contrasted by the "shining world of the street."[172] To the subterranean also belongs the interior of the body. Kuhn reasons that necrophobic and necrophilic features must be assumed in Rudolf's attitude toward dead bodies; that the "necrophilic features belong to the world of active life."[173] "The necrophobia must be related to a nocturnal existence, as we know that

167 *"keine Zwangshandlung"* (Kuhn).

168 *"Das Leben in der Spannung liegt diesem Weltentwurf Rudolf's zugrunde . . . Wo keine Spannung ist, da ist für ihn auch keine Welt, da ist überhaupt nichts, Leere, Kälte, Sinnlosigkeit und Langweile"* (Kuhn).

169 *"Die spannende Daseinsform hat ihre eigenen Gesetze; diese sind in Psychologie und Psychiatrie, soweit wir sehen, nur ungenügend untersucht; dagegen hat sich die Literaturwissenschaft seit langem durch die Beschäftigung mit dem Problem des Dramatischen in Kunst und Leben mit dem spannenden Lebensstil auseinandergesetzt"* (Kuhn).

170 *"vertikale Daseinsachse"* (Kuhn).

171 *"die verwesende Welt des Kellers"* (Kuhn).

172 *"die glänzende Welt der Strasse"* (Kuhn).

173 *"die nekrophilen Züge gehören zur Welt des tätigen Lebens"* (Kuhn).

Rudolf is afraid of corpses only at nighttime." [174] Among the depositions Rudolf made soon after the shooting were remarks on his wish "to avenge himself on prostitutes . . . to appear a hero in the war against prostitution . . . to avoid the temptations of the world and continue his life in the isolation of a penitentiary cell . . ." [175] Kuhn points to the "tremendous influence which Shakespeare's dramas had on Rudolf during the therapy . . . In the dramas, he sees something that reaches beyond the mere human being, namely, the action of men, the decisive deed with which they take their destiny into their own hands. . . ." [176] One wonders whether in Kuhn's view the hero is seen as part of the shining world, reaching "beyond . . . ," presumably in Kuhn's, or rather Rudolf's, vertical axis of existence. At any rate, Kuhn appears to draw two lines: the necrophobic-features-and-nocturnal existence-world of the cellar, of fantasies and dreams—versus the necrophilia-shining-existence-world of active life, of everyday life. He adds warily: "With certain reservations, we may designate the two worlds as Rudolf's past and future." [177] Kuhn believes that the two world-projects interact very dynamically, and that, hence, there are connections between Rudolf's mourning after his father's death and the shooting: "In Rudolf's

[174] *"Die Nekrophobie . . . muss mit einen nächtlichen Dasein in Zusammenhand stehen, da wir von Rudolf wissen, dass er die Leichen nur nachts fürchtete"* (Kuhn).

[175] *". . . sich an den Dirnen rächen . . . als ein Held erscheinen, der den Kampf gegen die Prostitution wagt . . . den Versuchungen der Welt aus dem Wege gehen und in der Abgeschiedenheit der Zuchtauszelle weiterleben"* (Kuhn).

[176] *"des gewaltigen Einflusses . . . , den Shakespeares Dramen auf Rudolf während der Behandlung ausübten . . . In den Dramen sicht er etwas, über den blossen Menschen hinausgeht, und zwar die Handlung der Menschen, die entscheidende Tat, mit der sie ihr Schicksal selbst in die Hand nehmen . . ."* (Kuhn).

[177] *"Mit gewissen Vorbehalten dürfen wir wohl die beiden Welten als Rudolfs Vergangenheit und Zukunft bezeichnen"* (Kuhn).

affect of mourning, there are the living women who have sexual needs and are seductive; they become a burden to Rudolf, and he gets rid of them in his act. Afterward he is free and hungry like the normally-mourning person is if, after the burial, he can again get hold of reality." [178]

Kuhn contrasts Rudolf with Binswanger's Ellen West [179] and writes referring to Binswanger's considerations: [180] "In one case action, in the other rigidity. Are we perhaps standing here at the point where the problems of the manic-depressive psychosis with its antinomic structure and the problems of schizophrenia as a destructive process are facing, touching and crossing each other with the result that the existential-analytical examination flows back into the clinical field?" [181] From the clinical viewpoint, it is quite improbable that Rudolf ever had a manic-depressive psychosis and/or belonged to the cyclothymic group in the narrower, or even broader, sense.

Kuhn's case has been presented at some length, as the writer presumes that his method and its shortcomings become visible step by step. One is often impressed with the tendency to complicate matters which in all likelihood are not so complicated at all, and with the tendency to use a flood of words where a few words would be

[178] *"Im Traueraffekt Rudolfs sind es die lebenden, geschlechtlichen Anspruch stellenden verführeden Frauen, die Rudolf zur Last werden und deren er sich in seiner Tat entledigt. Er ist nachher befreit und empfindet Hunger, wie der normal Trauernde nach der Beerdigung, wenn er sich der Wirklichkeit wieder bemächtigen kann"* (Kuhn).

[179] See pages 215-216.

[180] See pages 211-212.

[181] *"Im einen Fall Handlung, im andern Erstarrung. Stehen wir hier viellecht an jener Stelle, wo die Problematik des manisch-depressiven Irreseins mit seiner antinomischen Struktur und diejenige der Schizophrenie mit ihrer prozesshaften Destruktion sich gegenüberstehen, berühren und überschneiden, so dass daseinsanalytische Untersuchung wieder in die klinischen Bereiche mündet?"* (Kuhn).

more telling. Who thought and who experienced this or that—the intuiting doctor or the patient under treatment—is often not discernible. One cannot be sure where the doctor's influence ends and where Shakespeare's influence begins, the less so as the reader does not know who discusses what in the conversations between Dr. Kuhn and his patient about Shakespeare. Even the author's erudition and his exploitation of other fields of knowledge which serve his purpose, cannot conceal the fact that this is not so much an existential analysis of the case of Rudolf as a free-wheeling interpretation of it by Dr. Kuhn who, like his colleagues, follows his *"Einfällen,"* his intuition.

Kuhn believes that his case could not be clarified so far as he went with any other method. Kuhn emphasizes that the therapist finds starting points from the "knowledge of the structure of human existence," [182] he then can lead the conversation and awaken the patient's interest. With all or despite all the emphasis on human existence and its structure, it is always inevitably the patient, a human being in his particular situation, with whom the physician, existential analyst or not, conducts the conversation. Could one expect that a therapist working with a certain method of interpretation, for which he has prepared himself enthusiastically, and which has become a Faith, a *"Glaubenshaltung,"* [183] for him, would not pay tribute to this very method in awakening the interest of the patient and in conducting the conversation? Why should it be so extremely difficult to appreciate and to admit that in such and similar situations one is likely to find what one is seeking? Kuhn makes an appropriate observation: "Let us not underestimate habit." [184]

182 *"Kenntnis der Daseinsstruktur"* (Kuhn).
183 See page 219.
184 *"Hüten wir uns, die Gewohnheit zu achten"* (Kuhn).

X

Whatever contemporary and future philosophers will think about Heidegger's work, there is little doubt about his ability to say what he has to say in powerful language. While his dealings with the German language are at times outright painful, one should not forget that he strove to express his ideas in a vocabulary never used before. Löwith observed: "Often one cannot determine whether Heidegger composes poems as a thinker or whether he thinks as a poet, since he condenses an associatively loosened thinking very considerably." [185] Heidegger complained that no one understood him. Occasionally a most receptive philosopher seems to wonder about the "sphinx Heidegger." [186]

The present writer hardly needs to say that he is no philosopher. He has worked hard to come to some understanding of Heidegger. He is not "overwhelmed," as Binswanger confessed to being.[187] The writer did not fall prey to the magic of Heidegger's language. However, he is captivated by several of his ideas, for example the trinity of time, the being-thrown-into-the-world. These and several other ideas of Heidegger can be useful in psychopathology, without necessarily reconstructing psychopathology and clinical psychiatry on the basis of Heidegger's system.

Binswanger discovered Heidegger for psychiatry. He ought to have full credit in this respect. The present writer realizes and acknowledges the great stimulation

[185] *"Es ist oft nicht zu entscheiden, ob Heidegger denkerisch dichtet oder dichterisch denkt, so sehr verdichtet er ein assoziativ gelockertes Denkin"* (Löwith).

[186] From a letter written by Peter Wust and printed in Heinemann's *"Existenzphilosophie—lebendig oder tot?"*

[187] *"unter dem überwältigenden Eindruck von 'Sein und Zeit' . . ."* (Binswanger).

psychopathology has received from Binswanger's effort. Binswanger accepted the new teaching and immediately set to work to communicate his fascination to other psychiatrists. However, he felt chilly when he was faced with Heidegger's existential experience, with the cold nothingness and what not; hence he added love to the picture total. The writer conjectures that he persuaded himself this would provide the human warmth he missed in *Sein und Zeit*.

Binswanger stressed the difference between Heidegger's existential analy*tics* and its purpose and existential analy*sis* and its purpose, as he, Binswanger, proceeded to describe, to circumscribe and, in a sense, to create it. He stressed the difference as he saw it. He realized that Heidegger's teaching concerned ontology while he, Binswanger, wanted to move toward anthropology. With all his use of the phenomenological method, as he adapted it to his needs, Binswanger remained under the shadow of his teacher Heidegger. Unafraid of writing and expounding most volubly, he did not come to any particular clarification of Heidegger's thought, nor was he much happier in respect to his own derivations, in which he often followed his intuition in an enviably arbitrary manner.

On the one side, Binswanger was anxious to show that his existential-analytical writings were no psychopathology, but aimed in the direction of Heidegger's analyses of human existence, which he, Binswanger, considered basic to biological, psychological and psychopathological data and interpretations. On the other side—old psychopathologist and psychoanalyst that he was—he could not abandon Freudian teachings. Again and again, he pointed out that his existential-analytic expositions and explanations as well as his existential understanding, were entirely different from explanations and understanding as practiced in psychology and psychopathology. Nevertheless, even when he applied existential analy*sis* he frequently dealt with and interpreted experiences in a psychological or psychopathological manner. It seems to me that Szilasi, a philosopher and one of Heidegger's students, strikingly and briefly expressed what I have been trying to present in so many words; Szilasi says that Binswanger dwells "in his own intermediate territory between psychoanalysis and existential analysis." [188]

Heidegger, the philosopher, has no psychological ambitions. Binswanger, the psychiatrist, psychopathologist and psychoanalyst, has definite philosophical ambitions. It has been known for quite some time that psychiatry cannot do all that it will have to do ultimately, without some philosophical understanding and without the insight that not everything can be dissolved in biological formulae. Jaspers' work is not forgotten. Natural scientists, physicists and others are rather philosophically minded nowadays. This does, however, not legitimatize the attempt to build up psychiatry on a philosophical credo—on a philosophical credo from which Binswanger derived an "empirical" tool which *is not,* but is said to be existential-analy*tics* and which *is,* but is said *not* to be psychopathology.

It is appropriate to observe here that the phenomenological material was only partly derived from phenomena the patients allowed to appear; much of it was not originally found in the consciousness of the patients but owed its appearance to the intuition of the existential analyst regardless of what Binswanger considered the "fundamental principle of the phenomenological method: the restriction of the analysis to what can really be

[188] *"dass sich Binswanger in einem eigenen Zwischenterritorium zwischen der Psychoanalyse und der Existentialanalyse befindet"* (Szilasi, quoted from Spörri).

found in consciousness . . ." [189] Does the existential analyst after all analyze his own experiences in his dialogue with his patient? [190]

Heidegger formulated clearly: "Phenomenology of human existence is hermeneutics in the original meaning of the word in which it designates the business of interpretation." [191] Although Binswanger wishes to comprehend mankind,[192] he is dealing with human individuals, and his analyses of these individuals are, despite his use of Heidegger's terms, psychopathology. Binswanger is searching sense, meaning in everything, but he wrote himself: " 'Sense and significance' have sense and significance only for the individuality, *i.e.*, for this definite I and his world. Everything else is abstract theory." [193] "Sense and significance" can be squeezed into and out of human behavior and experiencing. The fact that this can be done in such a variety of ways ought to warn every interpreter not to consider his method and his interpretations the sole truth. Scholars who have learned about possibilities in Heidegger's school ought to think of their interpretations as possibilities.

Binswanger first made the attempt to derive from Heidegger's existential analy*tics* a method of interpretation on the presupposition of a "certain a priori struc-

[189] "*. . . Grundprinzip der phänomenologischen Methode: die Berschränkung der Analyse auf das im Bewusstsein wirklich Vorfindbare . . .*" (Binswanger).

[190] Kuhn has made remarks on this dialogue in his paper "Man in the Dialogue of the Patient with His Physician, and the Problem of Transference" (*Der Mensch in der Zwiesprache des Kranken mit seinem Arzt und das Problem der Übertragung*). See page 232.

[191] *Phänomenologie des Daseins ist Hermeneutik in der ursprünglichen Bedeutung des Wortes, wonach es das Geshäft das Auslegens bezeichnet* (Heidegger).

[192] See page 206.

[193] "*'Sinn und Bedeutung' haben Sinn und Bedeutung überhaupt nur für die Individualität, d.h. für dieses bestimmte Ich und seine Welt. Alles weitere ist abstrakte Theorie*" (Binswanger).

ture of existence."[194] Later he came to see in this method, his existential analy*sis,* therapeutic potentialities which he and Kuhn tried to make practically usable. The cases they published were, as far as they were accessible to the present writer, psychoanalyzed, and afterward interpreted existential-analytically. Kuhn's Rudolf is a particularly impressive example. Kuhn writes about him: "He felt as if newly born, declared that he had discovered the beauties of the world little by little and had just learned to know human beings."[195] It would be easy to ask a number of questions about this sentence, especially about the world, *i.e.,* about the meaning the word "world" has in it. This question might be the more justified as the sentence is found twenty printed pages before Kuhn begins to report the attempt to understand Rudolf's act existential-analytically. In this, as may be read in the foregoing, Rudolf's world is looked at horizontally and vertically and interpreted accordingly.[196]

Boss declines to make any practical application of existential analy*tics;* he accepted Heidegger's philosophy as his metaphysics of *Weltanschauung.*[197] It is unmistakable that here, in Heidegger's work, he found and founded his Faith, his *Glaubenshaltung.* In his writings, it is obvious that he is not a one-sided psychoanalyst but knows how to adjust his therapeutic procedure to the individual patient and his problems. To the present writer, Boss appears to be a genuine psychotherapist. His familiarity with Heidegger's work is complete, and his devotion to it is perfect. Boss tries to convey an "existen-

[194] *"eine gewisse apriorische Struktur des Daseins"* (Binswanger).
[195] *"Er fühlte sich wie neu geboren, behauptete, nun erst nach und nach die Schönheiten der Welt zu entdecken und die Menschen kennen zu lernen"* (Kuhn).
[196] See pages 233-235.
[197] See page 220.

tial-analytical understanding of human being-sick." [198] It is impossible to argue with him as to whether and how far he keeps existential analy*tics* out of therapeutic practice. There is no doubt, though, that his thinking has been shaped thoroughly in the school of Heidegger, whose ideas he has assimilated and whose vocabulary he masters to perfection.

If one has once become used to Boss' style, it is relatively easy to understand what he means, but also to see where he forgets something important: the circumstances that his method of elucidation and understanding does not produce "facts," but is bound to move within the realm of interpretation. If one—like the present writer—has never adhered to psychoanalysis, it is particularly interesting to read that for Boss, who is still practicing psychoanalysis, "the psychoanalytical dynamisms and mechanisms are 'assumed' . . . nothing but products of thinking attributed to the given reality." [199] He seems to overlook that what he is doing and finding now is just as much based on assumptions and that what he now attributes to the "given reality" represents "products of thinking," too.

From his *Glaubenshaltung,* Boss admonishes physicians to remember that they are "descendants of ancient priest-physicians." [200] He asks the rhetorical question, "Did not a division of the healers of mankind into priests and physicians then occur, the priests wanting to bring

[198] *"existential-analytisches Verstehen menschlichen Krankseins"* (Boss). The present writer realizes that "human being-sick" sounds rather clumsy. However, in this being-sick, the notion of *Dasein* is obviously implied. It is not sickness, *Krankheit,* that the existential-analytical psychiatrists seek to deal with, but the change of human existence, *Dasein,* through sickness.

[199] See page 220.

[200] *"Nachfahren wralter Priester-Arzte"* (Boss).

many only salvation, the physicians wanting to bring him nothing but healing?" [201] One cannot but admire such eloquence, but one will wonder whether a physician, a psychotherapist of the experience and perspicacity of Boss, would forget that there is here made an implication as regards the miracle being the dearest child of Faith. Soberly expressed in its application to medicine: If the physician is devoted to his faith and is practicing this faith in his work, his patients will fall in line and share his faith. This is the secret of the genuine psychotherapist. He is able to transfer his faith to his patient. It does not matter what this faith is. What matters is the doctor.

Many great physicians have taught us that we are always faced with the patient as a whole human being. One of Boss' pertinent remarks reads: "From the simplest technical-surgical procedures and operations to the technique of psychoanalysis, the whole thinking and acting of the physician ought to be concerned with the desire to open to our patients the way to their being fully human." [202] This sounds as admirable and rhetorical as the question just quoted. Boss knows that there is more than one way of "healing" and more than one way of becoming "fully human."

Heidegger taught, "If there is no human existence, there is no world either." [203] He later taught about human

[201] *"Spalteten sich dann jedoch nicht die Heiler der Menschheit in Priester, die dem Menschen nur noch das Heil, und in Ärzte, die ihnen lediglich Heilung bringen wollten?"* (Boss). In the German original, there is some play with the words *Heiler* (healer), *Heil* (salvation) and *Heilung* (healing).

[202] *"Immer bewusster sollte vielmehr das gesamte arztliche Denken und Handeln, von den einfachsten technisch-chirurgischen Handgriffen und Eingriffen bis zur Technik der Psychoanalyse, von dem Bestreben getragen sein, unseren Kranken den Wig zu ihrem vollen Mensohsein zu bahnen"* (Boss).

[203] *"Wenn kein Dasein existiert, ist auch keine Welt da"* (Heidegger).

ek-sistence concerning which Boss formulated: "Man ek-sists in the most literal meaning of this word. He is always outside, meeting with the things, animals and human beings of the world." [204] As far as I understand, man is the only existent capable of ek-sistence. This ek-sistence is said to open the world for him and to keep it open. Even without going into details, it may be permissible to say that the use of both these notions—existence and ek-sistence—facilitates interpretations for the existential-analytically minded psychiatrist; but it is not clear, for instance, in which relation the "human existence that is no longer by itself" stands to ek-sistence. It may not always have been easy for the psychiatrists to keep step with Heidegger's thought. Needless to state that his and theirs is the right to change theories. The doctors have discarded Freudian theory, but remained faithful to psychoanalytical technique. What will happen to their adherence to Heideggerian theory and its use in their interpretations remains to be seen.

What worries the writer is the notion of these colleagues that, with the introduction of the concept of *Dasein,* everything becomes or can be made meaningful —everything that happens to or is experienced by patients; and that every interpretation is looked at as valid which expounds this in pertinent vocabulary and shows how *Dasein* sets body and soul to work. The body-soul dualism is artificial, another theory produced by thinking. This dualism serves in psychiatry and psychopathology as an "empirical dualism," as it was called by Kurt Schneider, who emphasized: "This does not imply an attitude toward a metaphysical interpretation of the

[204] *"Der Mensch ek-sistiert in dieses Wortes wörtlichstem Sinne. Er ist schon immer 'draussen,' bei den ihm begegnenden Dingen, Tieren und Menschen der Welt"* (Boss). See pages 200-201.

body-soul relation." [205] Schneider's caution does not seem to interest our existential-analytical minded colleagues. They settle the problem by pre-ordaining *Dasein* to whatever may be considered physical or psychological, that is, to whatever may concern the human being's body or experiencing. With words like *"Leiblichung," "Der Leib leibt,"* [206] and so on, problems are not solved, but are only verbalized differently. Boss' understanding is through psychology or psychopathology, despite the existential-analytical *Weltanschuung*. If one is certain that everything has a meaning, one cannot fail to dig it out or to implant it wherever he needs it. However, this is no longer knowledge, but faith—for which there should be no less respect than for knowledge when it is recognized for what it is.

XI

It may seem odd that the writer is so critical of a "method," to use a short word, which. under the banner of a contemporary philosophical system, has made inroads into psychiatry. One should acknowledge gratefully that it is at least a contemporary philosophical system. The writer wants to express personal gratitude to the three colleagues from whom he has learned much. But the certainty with which they write—"no doubt," "because it is so," "of course," "naturally"—cannot conceal the fact that concepts, or even mere words, are often gaily tossed around. The ponderousness of the older, the alacrity of the younger, priest and the assiduity of the deacon, though occasionally irritating, show the manner in which each of them goes after his business.

[205] *"empirischen Dualismus. Zu einer metaphysischen Auslegung des Leib-Seele-Verhältnisses ist damit nicht Stellung genommen"* (Kurt Schneider).

[206] See pages 221 and 231.

It is the writer's impression that our existential-analytic friends have overdone it philosophically: Binswanger, in particular, appears, in a sense, to "out-Heidegger" Heidegger. Did they try to be revolutionists? If they had such intentions they were handicapped by their own conservatism, expressed in their sticking to Freudian technique and in their praising phenomenology no end. Karl Jaspers has the undeniable merit of introducing phenomenology into psychopathology; notwithstanding all the efforts of our three existential-analyst colleagues, Jaspers' insight seems to be broader than theirs. While our friends assume that they prepared the ground upon, and the way along, which psychiatry and psychopathology will have to develop, the writer deems it likely that some of their pertinent concepts will be integrated into psychiatry and psychopathology. This will not be the first time that psychiatry and psychopathology have integrated valuable ideas and discarded certain "theories."

Heinemann has told us that Kierkegaard "was a proleptic man, who, as a single individual, experienced in the middle of the last century something which has become common experience in our own day . . .[207] The writer sees no proof that Kierkegaard's existential experience has become common nowadays. It seems to the writer that people feel themselves threatened—perhaps essentially because of information from government and press on bombs and missiles—and so suffer from fear. But even as regards fear, it would be difficult to find out whether there is relatively or absolutely more fear suffered now than during other eras. Man has always had a great ability to provide threats as sources of fear. It might be doubted whether we would have this insight clearly without Kierkegaard.

For Kierkegaard, an unhappy, gloomy man, dread and

[207] See page 191.

fear had particular attraction; he was living in them, he was again and again experiencing them. They belonged to the pessimistic picture of existence and world as he built it up. Heidegger's existence, ek-sistence and world are not joyous, but they are not consistently beclouded. It is noteworthy that Binswanger brings brighter colors into the picture which becomes ever brighter the more that existential analy*sis* (Binswanger, Kuhn) and existential analy*tics* (Boss) are brought into closer contact with people—particularly if this contact is a therapeutic one. Here, it is Boss, above all, whose optimism is unmistakable. At any rate, what began in Kierkegaard's self-analyzing torment shines through in our colleagues' happy willingness to understand and help their patients. Looking at it in this manner, one might find the matter of which name is applied to their procedures to be irrelevant.

Nevertheless, the writer is looking forward to the day when our friends will say in a modification of Bollnow's observation:[208] "There is no pure existential analy*sis* or existential analy*tics;* what is called so is essentially a transition that will lead into a deepened understanding of human experiencing." No one will begrudge it to our friends that it fell to their lot to do some pioneering into a broader and profounder psychopathology.

POSTSCRIPT

Since this "appraisal" was submitted for publication, Binswanger and Boss have continued to publish their works. Their most recent books appeared in 1956 and 1957 respectively. They are briefly reviewed here, in order to round out the picture.

[208] See page 202.

Binswanger's *Three Patterns of Existential Failure* [209] carries the sub-title *"Verstiegenheit Verschrobenheit Manierierheit."* It seems to the writer that "eccentricity, queerness, and stiltedness" come closest to these German words. Binswanger's "eccentric existence" gets stuck in its vertical motion with forgetfulness or insufficient awareness of there being horizontal motion, too. In the world of "queer existence," everything is queer and oblique; among other examples Binswanger describes a father who gives a coffin as a Christmas present to his carcinomatous daughter. In "stilted existence," inability to be one's (natural) self prevails; there is a "sought after, played at, and wanted" height of existence which makes existence appear unauthentic; moving behind a mask.

Binswanger emphasizes that his existential-analytic considerations are entirely different from thinking in clinical and psychopathological terms.

He sees the three existential-failure patterns as facets of one comprehensive rigidity of existence—rigid in the existential sense. Hence, he can dogmatically say that the "vicinity" of schizophrenia and these patterns is demonstrated by existential-analytical understanding. He can also claim that schizophrenic splitting, explained by Eugen Bleuler with a "theoretic-constructive hypothesis," is now understood in an existential-analytical manner. He assumes that he has succeeded "in resolving the rigid concept of autism, as a cardinal schizophrenic symptom through its redirection into the stream of human existence and through the evidence of existential forms and

[209] Binswanger, Ludwig: *Drei Formen missglückten Daseins. Verstiegenheit Verschrobenheit Manieriertheit.* Niemeyer. Tübingen. 1956.

changes . . . which the psychiatric clinic diagnoses as schizophrenia." [210]

What Binswanger has performed here is a tour de force from schizophrenia to schizophrenia, using his particular vocabulary against the background of Heidegger's *Being and Time.*

Boss,[211] regardless of the courtesy he shows toward Binswanger and toward Binswanger's existential-analytical pioneering, emphasizes that Binswanger has not gone beyond Heidegger's *Being and Time.* Hence Boss cannot but adjudge his colleague to be somewhat antiquated. Boss had always tried to keep pace with Heidegger's ideas and publications. Boss finds himself now in a position in which he seems to contend for the papacy in psychiatric existentialism.

Boss stands, in his most recent dissertation,[211] without reservation on the ground of Heidegger's existential analytic and later philosophical concepts, which he accepts and propagates with all the enthusiasm of the fanatically devoted pupil.

Boss is very critical of Freud's theories but finds Freud's practical method of psychoanalysis as acceptable and useful as ever. He tries to show that "Freud's psychoanalytic practice was always existential-analytical understanding . . ." [212] The "harmony of psychoanalytic practice and existential-analytic understanding" [213] is the leitmotiv of Boss' discussion.

[210] *"in der Auflösung . . . des starren Begriffs des Autismus als des schizophrenen Kardinalsymptoms durch seine Rückverwandlung in den Fluss des Geschehens menschlichen Daseins und durch den Aufweis der Daseinsformen und Daseinswandlungen . . . , den die psychiatrische Klinik als Schizophrenie diagnostiziert."*

[211] Boss, Medard: *Psychoanalyse und Daseinsanalytik.* Huber, Bern and Stuttgart, 1957.

[212] *". . . dass die psychoanalytische Praxis Freuds schon immer daseinsanalytisches Verstehen selbst war . . ."*

Boss does not see, or does not want to see, that his explication is thoroughly arbitrary, according to the deplorable fact that one can read anything into and out of anything that one cares to read anything into or out of. Boss seems to ignore the fact that he is constantly interpreting. He appears to be imbued with the conviction that, where one talks about existence, there are facts.

It is promising that quite a few originally hardheaded psychoanalysts are changing their attitude in respect to psychoanalytic theory and practice. There will be more such changes, and there will be—as the parting of the ways of Binswanger and Boss demonstrates—change over change in psychiatric existential analytics. One may hope that the exaggerated feeling of importance, the uncritical fanaticism, the dogmatic pomposity of the discussion will give way to the common sense which is indispensable for the understanding of people and people's experiencing. In this book of Boss, much more is said about the patients—about human beings—than in his previous publications. The writer dares suppose that Boss always treats people, never "existences." And Boss is able to forgive Freud "his unwitting philosophical impedimenta." [214]

But, even so, Boss appears to feel that whatever Heidegger says is the last word concerning existence and related and unrelated problems. One may be glad to leave the pertinent discussion to the philosophers.

REFERENCES

Binswanger, Ludwig: Über Ideenflucht. Orrell-Füssli. Zürich. 1933.

---

213 *"Der Einklang von psychoanalytischer Praxis und daseinsanalytischem Menschenverständnis."*

214 *"seine unwissentlichen philosophischen Behinderungen."*

Binswanger, Ludwig: Grundformen und Erkenntnis menschlichen Daseins. Neihaus, Zürich. 1942.

———: Studien zum Schizophrenieproblem.

Erste Studie: Der Fall Ellen West. Schweiz. Arch. Neur. u. Psychiat., 53, 54, 55, 1945.

Zweite Studie: Der Fall Jürg Zünd, Ibid., 56, 58, 59, 1947.

Dritte Studie: Der Fall Lola Voss, Ibid., 63, 1949.

———: Symptom und Zeit. Schweiz. Med Wochenschr., 81, 1951.

———: Daseinsanalytik und Psychiatrie. Nervenarzt, January 1951.

Blackwell, H. J.: Six Existentialist Thinkers. Macmillan. New York. 1952.

Bollnow, O. F.: Existentialismus. Kohlhammer-Stuttgart. 1950.

Boss, Medard: Sinn und Gehalt Sexueller Perversionen. Huber. Bern. 1947.

———: Der Traum und seine Auslegung. Huber. Bern-Stuttgart. 1953.

———: Einführung in die Psychosomatische Medizin. Huber. Bern-Stuttgart. 1954.

Heidegger, Martin: Sein und Zeit. Niemeyer-Halle. 1. Auflage. 1927.

———: Was Heisst Denken? Niemeyer-Tübingen, 1954.

Heinemann, F. H.: Existentialism and the Modern Predicament. Harper. New York. 1953.

Jaspers, Karl: Allgemeine Psychopathologie. 5. Ed. Springer. Berlin. 1948.

Kierkegaard, Soren: Der Begriff der Angst (1. dänische Auflage. 1844.) Deutsche Übersetzung von Em. Hirsch. Diederichs. Düsseldorf. 1952.

Kuhn, Roland: Mordversuch eines depressiven Fetischisten und Sodomisten an einer Dirne. Monatsschr. Psychiat. u. Neurol., 116, 1948.

———: Daseinsanalyse im psychotherapeutischen Gespräch. Schweiz. Arch. Neurol. u. Psychiat., 67, 1951.

———: Zur Daseinsanalyse der Anorexia nervosa. Nervenarzt., January 1951, March 1953.

Kuhn, Roland: Zur Daseinsstruktur einer Neurose. Jahrb. Psychol. u. Psychother., 1954.

———: Der Mensch in der Zwiesprache des Kranken mit seinem Ärzte und das Problem der Übertragung. Monatsschr. Psychiat. u. Neurol., 129, 1955.

Löwith, Karl: Heidegger–Denker in dürftiger Zeit. Fischer. Frankfurt am Main. 1953.

Schneider, Kurt: Klinische Psychopathologie. 3 ed. Thieme. Stuttgart. 1950.

Spörri, Theodor: Kritik der Daseinsanalyse vom strukturanalystischen Standpunkt aus. Vortrag, 1955.

Wild, John: The Challenge of Existentialism. Indiana University Press. 1955.

BIBLIOGRAPHY

Binswanger, Ludwig, *Grundformen und Erkenntnis menschlichen Daseins,* Zürich, Neihaus, 1942.

——, *Ausgewählte Vorträge und Aufsätze zur phänomenologischen Anthropologie,* Vols. I, II, Bern, Francke, 1947, 1955.

——, *Schizophrenie,* Pfullingen, Neske, 1957.

——, *Sigmund Freud: Reminiscences of a Friendship,* New York, Grune & Stratton, 1957.

——, "The Existential Analysis School of Thought," in *Existence,* ed. Rollo May *et al.,* New York, Basic Books, 1958.

——, "Insanity as Life-Historical Phenomenon and as Mental Disease: the Case of Ilse," in *Existence,* ed. Rollo May *et al.,* New York, Basic Books, 1958.

——, "The Case of Ellen West," in *Existence,* ed. Rollo May *et al.,* New York, Basic Books, 1958.

——, "Symptoms and Time: A Casuistic Contribution," in *Existential Inquiries,* 1960, 1 (2), pp. 14–18.

——, *Über Ideenflucht,* Zürich, Fussil, 1933.

——, "Der Fall Jurg Zünd," in *Schweizer Archiv für Neurologie und Psychiatrie,* 1946–47, pp. 56, 57, 58.

——, "Der Fall Lola Voss," *Ibid.,* 1949, p. 63.

——, "Wahnsinn als lebensgeschichtliches Phänomen und als Geisteskrankheit," in *Monatschrift für Psychiatrie und Neurologie,* 1945, *110.*

——, "Symptom und Zeit," in *Med. Wochenschrift,* 81, 1951.

——, "Daseinsanalytik und Psychiatrie," in *Nervenarzt,* January 1951.

Blauner, J., "Existential Analysis: L. Binswanger's Daseinsanalyse," in *Psychoanalytic Review,* 1957, 44, 51–64.

Blumenfeld, W., "Observations Concerning the Phenomenon and Origin of Play," in *Philosophy and Phenomenological Research,* 1940–41, 1, 470–478.

Bollnow, Otto F., *Neue Geborgenheit. Das Problem einer Uberwindung des Existentialismus,* Stuttgart, Kohlhammer, 1955.

Bollnow, Otto F., *Existentialismus,* Stuttgart, Kohlhammer, 1950.

Boss, Medard, *Psychoanalyse und Daseinsanalytik,* Bern, Huber, 1957.

———, *Einführung in die psychosomatische Medizin,* Bern, Huber, 1957.

———, *Meaning and Content of Sexual Perversions: A daseinanalytic approach to the psychopathology of the phenomenon of love,* New York, Grune & Stratton, 1949.

———, *The Analysis of Dreams,* New York, Philosophical Library, 1958.

———, "Mechanistic and Holistic Thinking in Modern Medicine," in *American Journal of Psychoanalysis,* 1954, 14, 48–54.

Buber, Martin, *I and Thou,* New York, Charles Scribner's Sons, 1958.

Buytendijk, F. J. J., *Phénoménologie de la rencontre,* 1952.

———, *Attitudes et mouvements,* Paris, Desclée de Brouwer, 1957.

———, "The Meaning of Pain," in *Philosophy Today,* 1959, 3 and 4.

———, *The Mind of the Dog,* Boston, Houghton Miffln Company, 1936.

———, *Between Man and Man,* Boston, Beacon Press, 1955.

Cairns, D., "Phenomenology," in *A History of Philosophical Systems,* ed. V. Ferm, London, Rider & Co., 1958.

Collins, James D., *The Existentialists,* Chicago, Henry Regnery Co., 1952.

Colm, H., "Healing as Participation: Comments Based on Paul Tillich's Existential Philosophy," in *Psychiatry,* 16, 99–111.

Combs, A. W., "Phenomenological Concepts in Non-directive Therapy," in *Journal Consult. Psychology,* 1948, 12, 197–208.

———, A Phenomenological Approach to Adjustment Theory, in *Journal Abnorm. Soc. Psychology,* 1949, 44, 29–39.

Creegan, R. F., "A Phenomenological Critique of Psychology," in *Philosophy and Phenomenological Research,* 1948–49, 9, 309–315.

Ellenberger, H. F., "Current Trends in European Psychotherapy, in the *American Journal of Psychotherapy,* 1953, 7, 733–753.

Ellenberger, H. F., "Phenomenology and Existential Analysis," in *Canadian Psychiatric Association Journal,* 1957, 2, 137–146.

Frankl, Victor E., *The Doctor and the Soul: An Introduction to Logotherapy,* New York, Alfred C. Knopf, 1957.

———, *From Death-camp to Existentialism,* Boston, Beacon Press, 1959.

———, "Logos and Existence in Psychotherapy," in the *American Journal of Psychotherapy,* 1953, 7, 8–15.

———, "On Logotherapy and Existential Analysis," in *American Journal of Psychoanalysis,* 1958, 18, 28–37.

———, "Logotherapy and the Challenge of Suffering," in *Review of Exist. Psych. and Psychiat.,*" Vol. I, 1, 3–6.

Gebsattel, V. E. von, *Prolegomena einer medizinischen Anthropologie,* Berlin, Springer, 1954.

———, "The World of the Compulsive," in *Existence,* ed. Rollo May *et al.,* New York, Basic Books, 1958.

Graumann, C. F., *Grundlagen einer Phänomenologie der Perspektivität,* Berlin, De Gruyter, 1960.

Gurwitsch, A., "The Phenomenological and the Psychological Approach to Consciousness," in *Philosophy and Phenomenological Research,* 1954–1955, 15, 303–319.

Heidegger, Martin, *Sein und Zeit,* Tübingen, Neomarius, 1949.

———, *Holzwege,* Frankfurt, Klostermann, 1950.

———, *Erläuterungen* zu Hölderlins Dichtung, Frankfurt, Klostermann, 1951.

———, *What Is Philosophy?,* New York, Twayne, 1958.

———, *The Question of Being,* New York, Twayne, 1958.

———, *Introduction to Metaphysics,* New Haven, Yale, 1959, New York, Doubleday Anchor, 1961.

———, *Existence and Being,* Chicago, Regnery, 1949, Chicago, Gateway Books, 1961.

———, *Essays in Metaphysics,* New York, Wisdom, 1960.

Heinemann, Frederick H., *Existentialism and the Modern Predicament,* New York, Harper Torchbooks, 1958.

Hora, Thomas, Existential Communication and Psychotherapy," in *Psychoanalysis,* 1957, 5, 38–45.

Husserl, Edmund, *Vorlesungen zur Phänomenologie des inneren Zeitbewusstseins,* Halle, Niemeyer, 1928.

———, *Die Krisis der europaischen Wissenschaften und die transzendentale Phänomenologie,* Den Haag (The Hague), 1954.

Husserl, Edmund, *"Phenomenology,"* in *Encyclopedia Brit.*, 1929, 17, 699–702.

Jaspers, Karl, *Allgemeine Psychopathologie,* Berlin, Springer, 1946.

———, *Psychologie der Weltanschauungen,* Berlin, Springer, 1954.

———, *Philosophie,* Berlin, Springer, 1932.

———, *Existentialphilosophie,* Berlin, De Gruyter, 1938.

———, *Von der Wahrheit,* München, Piper, 1947.

———, *Von Ursprung und Ziel der Geschichte,* Zürich, 1950.

———, *The Perennial Scope of Philosophy,* New York, Philosophical Library, 1949.

———, *Existentialism and Humanism,* ed. Hans E. Fischer, New York, Moore, 1952.

———, *Reason and Existence,* New York, Noonday Press, 1957.

———, *Way to Wisdom,* New Haven, Yale University Press, 1960.

Kierkegaard, Sören, *Concluding Unscientific Postscript,* Princeton University Press, 1941.

———, *Fear and Trembling,* Princeton University Press, 1941, New York, Doubleday Anchor Books, 1953.

———, *The Sickness unto Death,* Princeton University Press, 1941, New York, Doubleday Anchor Books, 1953.

———, *Either/Or,* Princeton University Press, 1944, New York Doubleday Anchor Books, two volumes, 1959.

———, *The Concept of Dread,* Princeton University Press, 1944.

Knittermeyer, Heinrich, *Die Philosophie der Existenz von der Renaissance bis zur Gegenwart,* Zürich, Atlantis, 1952.

Kuenzli, A. (ed.), *The Phenomenological Problem,* New York, Harper & Brothers, 1959.

Kuhn, Helmut, *Encounter with Nothingness,* Chicago, Regnery, 1949.

Kuhn, Roland, "Daseinsanalyse im psychotherapeutischen Gespräch," in *Schweiz, Arch. Neurol. und Psychiat.*, 67, 1951.

———, "Zur Daseinsanalyse der Anorexia nervosa," in *Nervenarzt,* January 1951, March 1953.

———, "Zur Daseinsstruktur einer Neurose," in *Jahrbuch der Psychol. und Psychother.*, 1954.

———, "Daseinsanalyse eines Falles von Schizophrenia," in *Zeitschrift f. d. ges. Neur. und Psych.*, 1947, 58, 387.

Kuhn, Roland, "Der Mensch in der Zweispräche des Kranken mit seinem Ärzte und das Problem der Übertragung," in *Monatsschr. Psychiat. und Neurol.,* 129, 1955.

———, "The Attempted Murder of a Prostitute," in *Existence,* ed. Rollo May *et at.,* New York, Basic Books, 1958.

Laing, R. D., *The Divided Self,* London, Tavistock, 1960.

Landsman, T., "Four Phenomenologies," in *Journal Indiv. Psychol.,* 1958, 14, 29–37.

Langeveld, M. J. (ed.), *Rencontre-Encounter-Begegnung,* Utrecht, Spectrum, 1958.

Lauer, Q., "Four Phenomenologies," in *Thought,* 1958, 33, 183–204.

Linschoten, J., Op weg naar een fenomenologische Psychologie, Utrecht, Bijleveld, 1959.

Loewenberg, R. D., "Karl Jaspers on Psychotherapy," in *American Journal of Psychotherapy,* 1951, 5, 502–513.

Marcel, Gabriel, *The Philosophy of Existence,* London, Harvill, 1948.

———, *Being and Having,* London, Dacre, 1949.

May Rollo (ed.), *et al., Existence—a New Dimension in Psychiatry and Psychology,* New York, Basic Books, 1958.

May Rollo, *The Meaning of Anxiety,* New York, Ronald Press, 1950.

———, *Man's Search for Himself,* New York, W. W. Norton & Co., 1953.

———, "The Nature of Creativity," in *Creativity and Its Cultivation,* Anderson (ed.), New York, Harper & Brothers, 1959.

———, "The Context of Psychotherapy, in *Contemporary Psychotherapies,* ed. Morris I. Stein, Glencoe, The Free Press, 1961.

———, "The Meaning of the Oedipus Myth," in *Review of Existential Psychology and Psychiatry,* Vol. I, 1, 44–52.

———, (ed.) *Symbols in Religion and Literature,* New York, George Braziller, 1960.

———, (ed.), *Existential Psychology,* New York, Random House, 1961.

Merleau-Ponty, Maurice, *Phénoménologie de la perception,* Paris, Gallimard, 1945.

———, "What Is Phenomenology," in *Cross Currents,* 1956, 6, 59–70.

Minkowski, Eugene, *Le temps vécu,* Paris, Artrey, 1933.

Minkowski, Eugene, "Phénoménologie et analyse existentielle en psychiatrie," in *Evol., Psychiat.*, 4, 137, 1948.

———, "Bergson's Conceptions as Applied to Psychopathology," in *Journal Nerv. Ment. Dis.*, 1926, 63, 553–568.

———, "Findings in a Case of Schizophrenic Depression," in *Existence,* ed. Rollo May *et al.*, New York, Basic Books, 1958.

Mullan, H., and I. Sangiluliano, "Interpretation as Existence in Analysis," in *Psychoanalysis and Psychoanalytic Review,* 1958, 45, 52–73.

Muus, R., "Existentialism and Psychology," in *Educ. Theory,* 1956, 6, 135–153.

Pervin, L. A., "Existentialism, Psychology, and Psychotherapy," in *Americ. Psychol.*, 1960, 15, 305–309.

Sartre, Jean-Paul, *The Emotions: Outline of a Theory,* New York, Philosophical Library, 1948.

———, *Existential Psychoanalysis,* New York, Philosophical Library, 1953.

Scheler, Max, *The Nature of Sympathy,* London, Routledge and Kegan Paul, 1954.

Schmidl, F., "Sigmund Freud and Ludwig Binswanger," *Psychoanalytic Quarterly,* 1959, 28, 40–58.

Silverman, H. L., "The Philosophy and Psychology of Existentialism," in *Psychiat. Quarterly Suppl.*, 1947, 21, 10–16.

Sonneman, Ulrich, *Existence and Therapy,* New York, Grune & Stratton, 1954.

———, "Existential Analysis: An Introduction to Its Theory and Methods," in *Cross Currents,* 1955, no. 3.

———, "The Human Sciences and Spontaneity: Outline of a Revolution," in *American Journal of Psychoanalysis,* 1958, 18, 138–148.

Spiegelberg, H., "French Existentialism: Its Social Philosophies," in *Kenyon Review,* 1954, 16, 446–462.

Stern, Alfred, *Sartre, His Philosophy and Psychoanalysis,* New York, Liberal Arts Press, 1953.

———, "Existential Psychoanalysais and Individual Psychology." in *Journal Indiv. Psychol.*, 1958, 14, 38–50.

Stern, Karl, *The Third Revolution,* New York, Harcourt, Brace & Co., 1954.

Strasser, S., "Phenomenological Trends in European Psychology," in *Philosophy and Phenomenological Research,* 1956–57, 18, 18–34.

Strauss, Erwin W., *Vom Sinn der Sinne,* Berlin, Springer, 1956.

———, *Geschehnis und Erlebnis,* Berlin, Springer, 1930.

———, *On Obsession: A Clinical and Methodological Study,* New York, Nerv. and Ment. Dis. Monogr., 1948, no. 73.

———, "The Upright Posture," in *Psychiatric Quarterly,* 1952, 26, 529–561.

———, "Aesthesiology and Hallucinations," in *Existence,* ed. Rollo May, New York, Basic Books, 1958.

Teilhard de Chardin, P., *The Phenomenon of Man,* New York, Harper & Brothers, 1959.

Tiebout, H. M., Jr., "Freud and Existentialism," in *Journal Nerv. Ment. Dis.,* 1958, 126, 341–352.

Tillich, Paul, *The Courage to Be,* New Haven, Yale University Press, 1959.

———, *Theology of Culture,* New York, Oxford University Press, 1959.

———, "Existential Philosophy," in *Journal of the History of Ideas,* 1944, 5, 44–70.

———, "Anxiety, Religion, and Medicine," in *Pastoral Psychology,* 1952, 3, 11–17.

———, "Being and Love," in *Pastoral Psychology,* 1954, 5 (43), 43–48.

———, "Psychoanalysis, Existentialism and Theology," in *Pastoral Psychology,* 1958, 9, 9–17.

Trüb, Hans, *Heilung aus der Begegnung,* Stuttgart, Klett, 1951.

Van Den Berg, J. H., *The Phenomenological Approach to Psychiatry,* Springfield, Ill., Thomas, 1955, London, Routledge and Kegan Paul, 1955.

———, *Psychologie en Theologische Anthropologie,* Nijkerk, Holland, Callenbach, 1956.

———, *Metabletica of leer der veranderingen,* Nijkerk, Holland, Callenbach, 1956.

———, *Het Menselijk Lichaam,* Nijkerk, Holland, 1959.

———, "The Handshake," in *Philosophy Today,* 1959, 3 and 4, 28–34.

Van Dusen, W., "Adler and Existence Analysis," in *Journal Indiv. Psychology,* 1959, 15, 100–111.

Van Kaam, Adrian, "The Impact of Existential Phenomenology on the Psychological Literature of Western Europe," in *Rev. Existential Psychology and Psychiatry,* Vol. 1, no. 1, January 1961, 63–83.

Van Kaam, Adrian, "Phenomenal Analysis: Exemplified by a Study of the Experience of 'really feeling understood,' " in *Journal Indiv. Psychology,* 1959, 15, 66–72.

Waehlens, Alphonse de, *Une philosophie de l'ambiguité: l'existentialisme de Maurice Merleau-Ponty,* Louvain, Publications universitaires, 1951.

Weigert, Edith, "Existentialism and Its Relations to Psychotherapy," *Psychiatry,* 1949, 12, 399–412.

———, "The Psychotherapy of Affective Psychoses," in *Psychotherapy of the Psychoses,* ed. Arthur Burton, New York, Basic Books, 1961, 349–376.

Weiss, Edward and English, O. Sp., *Psychosomatic Medicine,* Phil., London, Saunders, 1943.

Weisskopf-Joelson, E., "Logotherapy and Existential Analysis," *Acta Psychotherapeut.,* 1958, 6, 193–204.

Weizsäcker, Victor von, *Der Gestaltkreis,* Leipzig, Thieme, 1940.

———, *Ärzte und Kranker,* Leipzig, Koehier, 1950.

Wolff, Werner, *Values and Personality: An Existential Psychology of Crisis,* New York, Grune & Stratton, 1950.